Alexander Keith

Eminent Aberdonians

Eminent

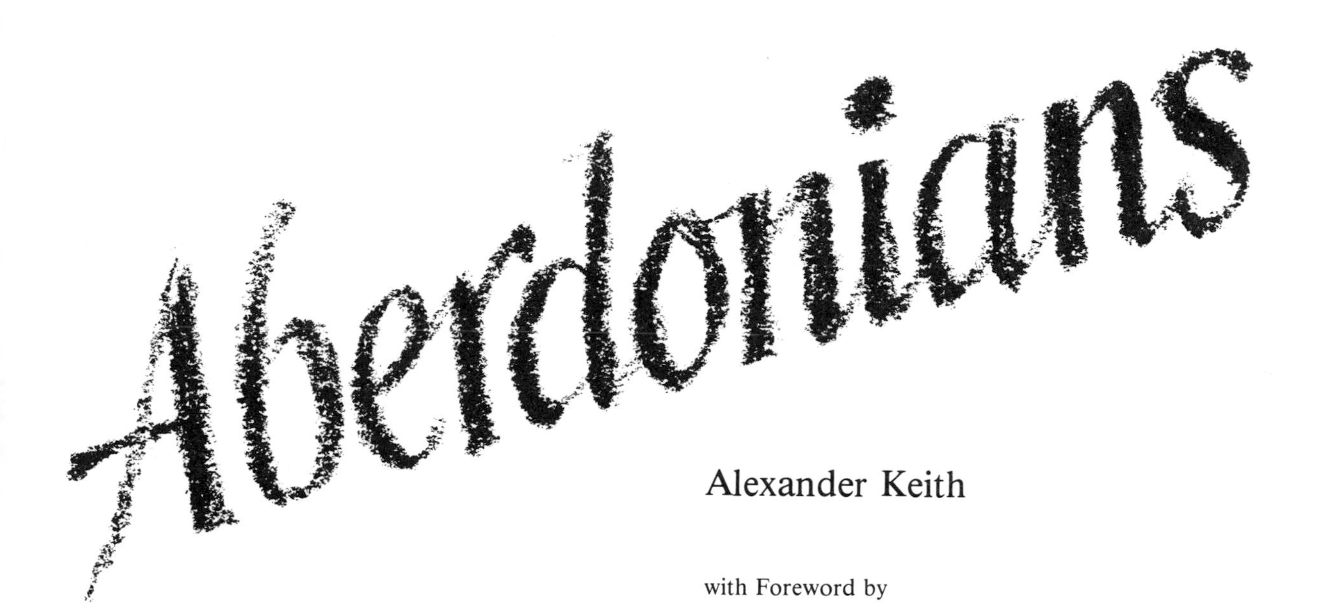

Alexander Keith

with Foreword by

SIR MAITLAND MACKIE

Aberdeen Chamber of Commerce

First published in
Aberdeen Chamber of Commerce Journal
1956–1967
First published in book form 1984
Aberdeen Chamber of Commerce
15 Union Terrace, Aberdeen

British Library Cataloguing in Publication Data
Keith, Alexander
Eminent Aberdonians.
1. Scotland—Biography
I. Title
920′.0411 DA758

ISBN 0-9509842-0-5

Printed in Great Britain
The University Press
Aberdeen

Eisenstaedt

Foreword

Sir Maitland Mackie LL D
Lord Lieutenant Aberdeenshire

And still the wonder grew that one small head could carry all he knew.

May I thank whoever thought of reprinting these 40 brilliant and erudite essays as a book and the Chamber of Commerce and Aberdeen University Press for doing so. Perhaps the book should have had one more chapter, on Alex Keith himself. Certainly he deserves a place among the personalities of his time but in fact it's unnecessary, as for those who knew him his essays make plain the man he was.

'A.K.' was a man who loved all Scotland and in particular his own Aberdeenshire. He was a man with the intimate knowledge of history needed to fit the portraits of his heroes into the bigger picture of the time and, writing with his own wit and wisdom, his own brand of humorous cynicism, make them live again as you read. I have always been proud of my Aberdeenshire forebears but 'A.K.' makes me feel even more proud. This book is not only for Aberdonians, it is a record of people who did great things for their town and country, a record that could and should be told of other people and places in Scotland. That would be a history of Scotland and this book would be part of it, told by a writer who took enormous care to check his own encyclopaedic knowledge of history and literature, which is so evident in every chapter.

I suspect that like me when you finish this book you will have a compelling wish for more and a great regret that 'A.K.' is no longer here to grant that wish.

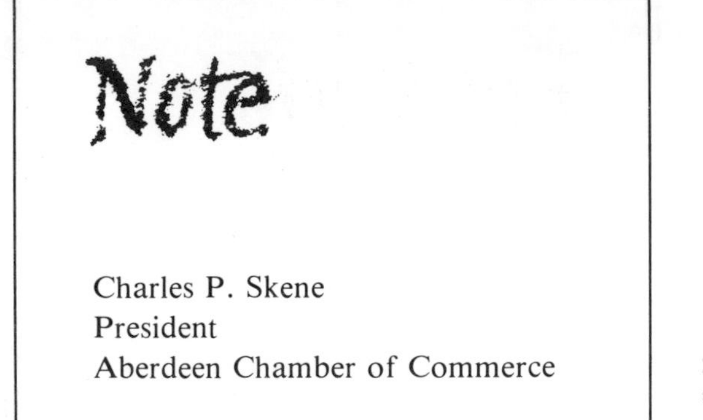

Note

Charles P. Skene
President
Aberdeen Chamber of Commerce

Studio Morgan

To write a series of articles, albeit quarterly, over a ten year period is a daunting task. To write for a business journal and confine your subject to eminent Aberdonians constitutes a *magnum opus.*

Restricting circulation to Chamber of Commerce members was an honour for the organisation in which the author played a prominent part and at the same time a disservice to the community.

Today, some twenty years on, with very few complete sets in existence and increasing interest in Aberdeen, re-publication of Alex Keith's articles is both opportune and overdue.

Eminent Aberdonians gives an insight into the character of those early citizens, born or adopted, whose impact on the local, national or international scene of their day foreshadowed the ability of the current generation to take advantage of today's opportunities.

We are fortunate that in 'A.K.' we had a historian with the literary powers to capture this indefinable mixture of entrepreneurial spirit and artistic flair which pervades the Northeast.

It is our privilege and pleasure to introduce this major work to a wider readership.

Index

Contents

Sir Alexander Anderson

THERE is only one figure in Aberdeen's history that is dominant enough to be the inescapable first subject of a series such as this. When Sir Alexander Anderson died on 11 April 1887, the *Aberdeen Daily Journal,* which had manifested no great liking for him in his lifetime, was constrained to admit that he was the "man to whom Aberdeen is indebted, above all others, for what of the amenities of public life it now enjoys". That testimony still is true. Alexander Anderson made the modern Aberdeen: on the foundations broad and strong that he planned and in large part executed, the modern city administratively, socially, and commercially, has developed.

Born in 1802, a native of Strichen, and son of the Manse, Anderson came of a family on his mother's side that was remarkable for the achievement of several of its members, as will be related in due course. He began his education at the parish school of Strichen, which had not then attained to the eminence it reached later when (perhaps through Anderson's influence) a pupil of the great Grammar School rector, James Melvin, became its dominie. Thence he migrated to the Grammar School of Aberdeen and to Marischal College, where he took his Arts degree, almost immediately entering into a law partnership with William Adam to form the firm of Adam and Anderson. It was later dissolved but its modern representative in Aberdeen legal circles is the firm of Adam, Thomson & Ross, in whose office remain some of the relics of the earlier association. Anderson was admitted a member of the Society of Advocates in 1827.

Even in that heyday of the great Hadden provosts in Aberdeen it became apparent to those who had eyes to see that a new prophet was arising in Israel. Appointed treasurer of the Aberdeen Dispensary, Anderson at once set about reorganising an institution that was rapidly falling into inanition, and under his energetic guidance for the next thirty years it resumed its earlier vigour. But it was in the 'thirties that he blossomed forth into the "back-room boy". An uncle, Dr. George Watt, who had succeeded in amassing a fortune as a medical practitioner in his native parish of Deer, left legacies, the administration of which was entrusted to Anderson, for the founding of a House of Refuge for poor people and a reformatory for difficult youths; and the results were Oldmill and Oakbank.

Inspired by these vicarious exploits, Anderson in 1837 projected and launched two great commercial designs—the North of Scotland

Insurance Company, now the Northern Assurance Company, and the North of Scotland Bank. The following year, 1838, saw the promotion of the Aberdeen Market Company, which by 1842 had effected the building of the New Market and the making of Market Street. In 1844, he started a gas company in opposition to a monopoly concern whose high charges were creating public discontent, and after a fierce commercial battle in which he displayed his ruthless methods for the first time to the full extent, he drove the older company to accept amalgamation in 1847, the united undertaking being eventually taken over by the Corporation.

Anderson's "parentage" of the Great North of Scotland Railway Company is well-known, but what is not well-known is that he was the sponsor of the North British Railway, or at least of the northernmost section of it from Friockheim to Aberdeen, a Bill for the construction of which he carried in 1845 in the teeth of bitter opposition, adding to the main-line project branches to Brechin and Montrose. Next year he promoted Bills for the building of the Great North of Scotland Railway to Keith and of the Deeside Railway, and some years thereafter for the construction of the Buchan Railway very much as we know it. Other branch lines of the G.N.S.R., including the Alford Line, were due to Anderson's initiative, but his methods of financing his ventures in the late 'forties when the railway mania had exhausted itself and capital was less easily acquired, were sometimes questionable and led indeed to one celebrated libel action. Already some years before, about the time when railway finance became difficult he had been involved in troubles arising out of the Illinois Investment Company adventure whereby douce Aberdeen citizens were bereft of the best part of £100,000. This episode, practically unknown to the general public, deserves a word or two.

The Illinois Investment Company was promoted by Adam and Anderson in 1837 at the suggestion of Anderson's cousin, George Smith, later known as Chicago Smith. This gentleman, the first of the great American millionaires, was born in Old Deer (where the Smith Prize to school children is a perpetual reminder of his success), and after three years of medical study at Marischal College and an attempt at farming at Raecloch, Turriff, had emigrated to U.S.A. about 1833, been the first white man to sleep in Milwaukee (now America's greatest brewery city) and apprenticed himself, with his own wits as mentor, to the trade of real estate pedlar in Chicago. The Illinois Investment Company theoretically was intended to bring fortunes into the pockets of the Aberdonians whom Anderson persuaded to take up its stock, but practically it succeeded only in confirming the steadily mounting fortune of Chicago Smith. The entertaining history of this remarkable enterprise is set forth in a little known publication by Alexander Johnston, writer to the Signet, of the Johnston family that lived until fairly recently at Newton Dee, who was one of the directors of the company. A copy of this informative brochure, which came into the possession of the writer of this article on the sale of the effects of William Johnston, was lent to a member of the Aberdeen legal profession who was reputed to have a more profound knowledge of the byways of human endeavour than most of his kindred, and who admitted that he had rarely partaken of a better example of a "dreepin' roast" so far as the commercial frailties of eminent men are concerned.

Chicago Smith died in 1899 at the age of 91, in the Reform Club in London, leaving a fortune which, at a conservative estimate, was five million pounds sterling, and upon which the modest death duties of those civilised days collected a sufficient sum to build a British battleship and so to warm the congealed heart of the contemporary Chancellor of the Exchequer that he permitted himself the epigram that George Smith may not have lived like a lord but he died like a gentleman. As his cousin, Alexander Anderson used sapiently to say, "we maun bigg oor dykes wi' the fell we hae".

Alexander Anderson's morality, whether commercial or personal, was not of the conventional variety. To realise the worldly hopes he set his heart upon he was prepared to go to all lengths. Time and again he was both cause and centre of flaming rows, even scandals, the fires of which would have tarnished the fame of a lesser personality. Alexander Anderson, however, even in the heat of momentary conflict, never forfeited the esteem and respect of his contemporary Aberdonians. He became a legend and a Titan to those who knew him, even while still alive, and he remains on the titanic scale in the minds of those who have knowledge of Aberdeen's history. "An ill shearer", he used to say in his brusque, downright fashion, "never got a gweed heuk", but he was the perfect workman who could make the best of any tools.

For twenty-five years, Anderson was the business man, whose schemes, while they furthered the interests of the community, did so as a result of their success in furthering the interests of himself and his associates. But in 1859 a new era in his life opened. In November of that year he was elected to the Town Council, and at the first meeting after the election he was called to the chair. Four months later, as a result of an outburst of passion (not all on one side) in the Council Chamber, he left the chair and resigned from the Council, but the following month was returned again by his ward with an emphatic majority, and resumed the chair almost as if nothing had happened.

Then he began to work, and when in November 1866 he finally demitted office, he had brought in and put through the scheme for providing the city with an up-to-date water supply, yielding five million gallons daily, the works for which at Cairnton were opened by Queen Victoria a month before his retirement. The scheme cost £150,000—which was a considerable sum in those days. He also had the whole sewage system of the burgh brought into conformity with the requirements of an expanding city and an increasing population. He planned new roads and civic lay-out, being a bit of a surveyor himself in his spare time; there is a story of his having crept out at night to alter the pins marking the line of the western end of Union Street. The present Grammar School, built in 1865—it is of course larger now—was constructed mainly because he was determined upon it, and the present Town House, sanctioned by an Act of 1866, owes its existence to him.

In 1863 he was knighted by Queen Victoria before she unveiled the statue of the Prince Consort, which was originally sited where the King Edward VII statue now is. Her Majesty performed the ceremony from the Royal Northern Club, in the corner block which is now the Northern Assurance building. Three years later the Prince of Wales unveiled his mother's statue at the corner of St. Nicholas Street. That Sir Alexander was in the good graces of the Royal Family is abundantly testified by his having secured the presence of the Queen (who never did like that sort of thing, and particularly so soon after the Prince Consort's death) twice within three years and the Prince's favour once. But Sir Alexander had a way with him when he liked.

In the last twenty years of his life he engaged in a blend of personal and public activities. He was for a time the laird of Blelack. During his provostship his town residence was 198 Union Street, and that the building should now house the Y.M.C.A. must give his ghost a certain amount of sardonic amusement. Latterly he lived in Union Terrace, at 14, next door to the house now occupied by the Chamber of Commerce. In the city he promoted in 1875 the City of Aberdeen Land Association, for acquiring feuing ground in Rubislaw and Torry—he had bought the lands of Rubislaw from the Skenes of Rubislaw in 1860. That flourishing Association is still administered by some of the best business brains in the city.

On the public side he did for Fraserburgh what he had done for Aberdeen. As every good "Brocher" still gratefully acknowledges, without Sir Alexander's magic will Fraserburgh would not be the fishing centre it is. As factor and baron baillie for the superior, Lord Saltoun, he greatly enlarged and improved its harbour and laid down the example that formed the tradition of progressive endeavour which characterises the modern Faithlie. Also, amongst other activities, we find him encouraging experiments with steam ploughing, and that too in his very old age, when most men would have refused to be bothered with such innovations.

Aberdeen Town House has his portrait by Sir

George Reid, Fraserburgh Town House has a copy, and Strichen Public Library (bestowed by his son Andrew, both house and nucleus of the library many years ago) has a second copy. The pen-and-ink sketch from which the portrait overleaf is taken was also by Sir George Reid, done in Sir Alexander's last years, and is in Witchhill House, Fraserburgh.

This plain tale must fail to convey an adequate picture of the great provost, except perhaps that it gives some conception of what he did. His character was not very complex, but it was not simple. Though a son of the manse he was not conspicuously godly. Though so prominent a public figure he was no orator; but in the cut-and-thrust of civic debate he had few equals. His wit was broad, and garnished with apposite proverbial expressions. To one droughty clerk of his who adopted various expedients to "change his breath", he exclaimed—"I'll stan' peppermints, an' I'll stan' cloves, but I'm damned if I'll pit up wi' ingins". The power of him in the land in the forties and fifties of last century is illustrated in the story of the little girl who, unable to answer a question as to the identity of the two first inhabitants of the Garden of Eden, reacted to the prompting "Adam and . . ." with the immediate response "Adam and Anderson". Of that firm he was the heart and driving force, and if every public man in Aberdeen were but to vow that he would endeavour to emulate the great Provost by doing what in him lies for the good of his fellows, the heritage he handed down would be safe for the future.

Provost George Fordyce
and his family

Two families in the history of Aberdeen have been singled out as representing most picturesquely the characteristic versatility and ambition of the Aberdonian. One, which extended its influence over nearly two centuries, was that of the Gregories, of whom much has been written; the other was that of the Fordyces, whose principal distinctions were confined to two generations, but of which an off-shoot is still numbered amongst the county families of Aberdeenshire.

This is one of them—Sir William Fordyce

[From a portrait belonging to the University of Aberdeen.]

The Fordyces emerge into the light of history about the period of the Restoration, there having been born in Haughs of Ashogle, near Turriff, in 1663 to the farmer there, George Fordyce, a son who bore the paternal christian name and who carried on the farm from the father's death in 1681 until his mother's death in 1695. In 1689 this George Fordyce was admitted a burgess of Aberdeen. In 1696 he apparently moved from Ashogle to Mill of Bruxie, Old Deer, where in the Poll-Book of that year, he is described as "merchant ther, his stock is 5,000 merks *inde* with general poll". He had then five children by his first wife, who died in 1705, by which time he was resident in Aberdeen and beginning to interest himself in the affairs of the city. In 1707 he married for a second time, his wife being Elizabeth Brown, a niece of one of Scotland's greatest Grecian scholars, Principal Thomas Blackwell of Marischal College. By his second wife George Fordyce had sixteen of a family, and his wife contrived, despite this recurrent burden, to survive her spouse by twenty-seven years, dying in 1780.

George Fordyce was three times Provost of Aberdeen, on each occasion for the two years it was customary for the chief magistrate to occupy the civic chair. He became proprietor of Broadford, which when he first moved in was a swamp, known through his occupancy as the Provost's Mire, and which, as befitted a good Buchan countryman, he drained and cultivated and turned into a productive holding. He was perhaps lucky in that his first period of office, 1718-19, occurred after the tumults of the first Jacobite Rebellion; his second spell, 1722-23, coincided with a period of bad harvests, and he appears to have been responsible for the decision of the magistrates to purchase large quantities of meal to sell at a reasonable price to the poorer inhabitants. His last provostship was 1726-27, and he died in 1733 having, "by his integrity in publick and goodness in private life, left a better monument in the memory of the good and wise than can be raised to him by posterity".

This Aberdeenshire family of Fordyces

appears to have been related to the Fordyces in Berwickshire who became proprietors of the estate of Ayton in that county. Thomas Fordyce of Ayton was factor to the York Buildings Company which purchased many of the estates expropriated from the Jacobites after the 1715 Rebellion. The Provost's relationship to the factor no doubt explains how the former came to be the proprietor of the lands of Eigie, in Belhelvie Parish, which had belonged to Lord Panmure and of which the Panmure family were deprived on account of their part in the Rebellion. Eigie did not remain longer in possession of the Fordyces than the short lifetime of George Fordyce's eldest son George, who died in 1736 at the young age of 27 years. A brother of the Provost, however, who married into the prominent Aberdeen merchant family of Dingwall, became the progenitor of the Dingwall Fordyces of Brucklay, and of Culsh and Fedderate, who for long took a leading part in the political and agricultural life of Aberdeenshire.

While we know little of the Provost's actual public work there is ample evidence of the great success of his family, of the renown which many of them brought to their native city, and of the good offices by which at least one of them left a permanent mark on the development of the north-east of Scotland. The eldest son George died young as has been stated, but his posthumous son, George Fordyce, M.D., F.R.S., 1736-1802, became physician to St. Thomas's Hospital, London, and a fashionable physician there. Perhaps it should be added that his reputation in the Metropolis and his practice might have been better "if his manners had been more refined and his dress more studied", and if he had curbed his "fondness for society and indulgence in good living and late hours". He was, however, good enough both socially and intellectually to become a member in 1774 of the celebrated Literary Club in which Dr. Samuel Johnson was wont to ventilate his disapproval of Scotsmen, although there were as many Scots in the Club as Englishmen. If the truth were told the intellectual standard of this London club, of which we read so much in our school textbooks, was much lower than that of the Edinburgh Philosophical Society or indeed of the similar and contemporary Aberdeen coterie of which our school children never hear at all.

One of this George's uncles, James, fourth surviving son of the Provost, was also a member of the famous Literary Society and on close terms of friendship with Dr. Johnson, on whose death he wrote an "Address to the Deity" on the passing of the Great Cham. This James, 1720-96 was a Church of Scotland minister who in 1760 was called to the second charge in the collegiate ministry of the Presbyterian congregation in Monkwell Street, London. In this age of Marshall Aid, Lease-Lend, and U.N.O., London goes across the Atlantic to seek the spellbinding revivalists whom she was wont to find across her own northern border. James Fordyce was apparently the first of these for "he soon attracted hearers of all ranks, classes and persuasions. . . . To a cultured understanding were added a warm heart and a great liberality of sentiment; indeed it has been said that from his printed works it would be easier to prove that he belonged to no sect, than that he had the principles of any."

Perhaps today the strongest claim he has on our remembrance is that in 1771 he married the charming and eccentric Henrietta Cumming, governess to the family of the Countess of Balcarres, one of whose daughters was Lady Anne Lindsay, authoress of *Auld Robin Gray,* who left a vivacious description of Henrietta. "Her countenance was pretty and her shape neat; but in that casket lodged powers of every kind, good as well as bad, powers of attaching, powers of injuring, powers of generous magnanimity, obstinacy, prejudice, romance and occasionally of enthusiastic devotion." One need hardly add that the marriage proved a perfectly happy one.

The Provost's second son, David, 1711-51, appointed Professor of Philosophy in Marischal College in 1742, was drowned while returning from a Continental tour, and so did not leave much evidence (apart from three moral treatises) upon which to judge his worth, although his friends regarded him as full of promise. The

Provost's fifth son, John, 1717-60, was a surgeon in the Guards and eventually in practice in London, where he married one Pleasant Lawford, surviving the matrimonial yoke but six months and ten days. He left a posthumous daughter Mary, who married Samuel Birch, later Lord Mayor of London. He was a pastry cook, a vocation which gave the Fordyce family great offence. However, one never knows where one is with a cook; the illustrious Samuel, if he died childless, was the author of *The Abbey of Ambresbury, a Poem* and *Consilia, or Thoughts on Several Subjects.*

William, 1724-92, M.D., F.R.S., was Aberdeen's benefactor, if not the most brilliant member of the family. He was appointed surgeon to the 3rd Regiment of Guards in 1751, served in the Seven Years War, and later set up in practice in London, commanding larger fees than any physician of his time. Much of his income he spent in charity to such an extent that "his expenditure for benevolent objects was the means of very much good and some harm". Cambridge conferred on him an honorary degree; he acquired much praise by a treatise on the importance and proper method of growing and curing rhubarb for medical purposes; he was knighted in 1782; he became Lord Rector of Marischal College in 1790; and when he died, a bachelor, he willed, subject to a life-rent, the sum of £1,000 to Marischal College to found a lectureship in agricultural chemistry. This was the nucleus of the agricultural faculty in Aberdeen University today, and the first stone in the edifice now known as the North of Scotland College of Agriculture.

Most flamboyant of the Provost's family was its Benjamin, Alexander Fordyce, born at Eigie 1729 and bred, like his next elder brother Robert, who spent his whole life in Aberdeen, to the hosiery business. This proved too narrow a stage for Alexander's ambition and he went to London where he became first a banker's clerk, then partner in a great banking house. William, the physician, supplying him with ample funds, he by speculation amassed a huge fortune, but his luck turned, to cover his losses he used the capital of his company, and eventually when the crash came in 1772, "his fall was like the fall of a towering structure, which overwhelms numbers with its ruins". One historian declares that the bankruptcy of the Fordyce concern "may be termed one of the most important domestic events in Britain during the latter part of the eighteenth century", and as evidence of that fondness for good living and high flying which was also manifest in his nephew George, one of his contemporaries declared "the revenue of a kingdom could hardly have sufficed to execute his schemes". He died in 1789.

Alexander purchased the lands of North Colpna, now Orrock, in his native parish of Belhelvie, and he had been Lord Rector of Marischal College. A couple of years before he broke he married Lady Margaret Lindsay, whose governess his brother James was to espouse a year later. One thing must be said about these Fordyces: they knew how to pick their wives. The funeral tribute to the widow of the Provost is one of the most moving epitaphs in Aberdeen's records, while Lady Margaret's letter of comfort to her husband when disaster overtook him was a model of all that a wife's sentiments should be. It may serve to end this essay. "I have sometimes told you I was a philosopher, and if necessary could be an economist. I come now to the test, and I am too proud to be caught shrinking back like a coward, when I have affirmed I could face the foe. Yet we all have a vulnerable part, my dear husband; mine is the thought of your unhappiness. Let me find you composed and comforted. Let me, if possible, see you that I may pour the balm of consolation into your wounded mind; and I shall then hope the time may not be far distant when I may sign myself your happy, as well as your affectionate, wife."

The Haddens
and the extension of the Burgh of Aberdeen

ABERDEEN burgh in its seven or eight hundred years of recorded municipal history has had two dominant families. That of the Menzies ruled the community for close on two hundred of these years up to the outbreak of the Great Civil War (the first shots in which, by the way, were fired in Aberdeenshire); that of Hadden had "the guidin' o't" for nearly a generation before the passing of the Reform Act in 1832. While the Menzies family were territorial magnates, the Haddens were commercial.

Strachan

PROVOST JAMES HADDEN

[From a portrait in the Town House, Aberdeen]

Whatever we may think of the methods of repression employed by the Duke of Cumberland and his minions after the rout of the Young Pretender's forces on Drummossie Moor, no one studying the history of Scotland can fail to catch the echo of a long-drawn sigh of national relief in the years following 1745. In every department of human activity—social, cultural, musical, financial, commercial—there was throughout Scotland an instantaneous outburst of energy and the spirit of adventure. In this renaissance—for it was nothing less—Aberdeen participated to the full. A newspaper, a bank, a musical society, a philosophical society, industrial concerns that were to be very significant in the country's economic development, were founded and prospered. The old family names that had been familiar in Aberdeen's affairs began to give place to new ones, and of these incomers that of Hadden was one.

Haddens had been engaged in the stocking trade, which for long had been one of Aberdeen's staple industries, before the Forty-five. But by then they had become socially important, so much so that Baillie Alexander Hadden had married a sister of Provost William Young, one of the elite of the town. By her he had the then customary large family, two of the sons being destined to fill the civic chair. Of these James Hadden of Persley, born 1758, and Provost 1801-2, 1809-10, 1813-14, 1830-31, was the stronger personality, but Gavin Hadden of Union Grove, born 1770, and Provost 1820-21, 1824-25, 1828-29, and 1832, was not far behind his eldest brother in public service or in the important civic events which took place under his auspices.

Supported by numerous relatives, dependants and business associates, they controlled municipal affairs for the first thirty years of the century. It was the state of affairs in Aberdeen, the system of self-election that obtained within the restricted circle of burgesses legally capable of returning the successive councils, that more than any other single factor was responsible for the passing of the Burgh Reform Act of 1833 which introduced the present principle of election. Whether the contemporary apathy which is responsible for the return of municipal candidates on a minority vote results in a situation any more representative than that of the old "sett" of the burgh is a nice question for the political moralist, if there are morals in politics.

In 1798 there was built in the Green the factory of Alexander Hadden & Sons, which by 1811 had more than twenty machines worked by two steam engines, and produced stockings, mitts, frocks and worsteds. Just as the works celebrated their half century, the company was very seriously shaken by the economic crisis of 1848, the impact of that widespread disaster being probably all the more serious for Hadden & Sons because the firm was very closely linked up with the much greater and more ambitious undertaking of Leys, Masson & Co., linen manufacturers, at Grandholm, which in fact never recovered, and had to be wound up a few years later. Both firms failed and their works closed down. Both reopened, but the Grandholm mill collapsed again in 1854, whereas the factory on the Green contrived to see the century out. Leys, Masson & Co., of which James Hadden was a director, was the biggest business of its kind in the country, the mill housing 131 spinning frames, 15,000 spindles, and 100 power looms. Amongst the more notable features of its economy were the three-halfpenny meals served to its employees in the works canteen in the forties of last century.

The great age of the Haddens was in one respect Aberdeen's most dangerous age, in another its most successful commercially. In 1840 three native banks ministered to a wide variety of industries. The tonnage registered at the port rose between 1836 and 1845 from 27,000 to 55,000. In 1845 no fewer than 81,000 bales of textiles left the city, a tremendous quantity for those days. This halcyon period had succeeded a decade of doubts and fears. It was at the turn of the century that the old burgh became too big, not so much for its boots as for its coat. The harbour, then under municipal management, had to be greatly enlarged, Union Street and King Street had been planned, Union Bridge had to be built. Union Street, so named to commemorate the Legislative Union of Great Britain and Ireland in 1800, was so costly, and the actual figures of construction so vastly exceeded the estimates—not an uncommon feature in the public works of today—that the town eventually went bankrupt.

It is only seemly that Aberdonians should be reticent about this unfortunate episode in their city's history. The Whigs, of course, the majority of the municipal managers being Tories, made the most of the bankruptcy and of the undemocratic ongoings of the Council; and their story, first in the field, has naturally held the field. And it is true that there were deviations even from what was regarded as civic virtue in the degenerate decades after the Age of Reason. The Council's wine bill and travelling expenses from 1799 to 1818 came to £6,123 16s., and to reduce that to present day values it might not be far out to mutiply the total by twelve. The burgh accounts were never presented to the Council. Full of the joy of the economic spring that Watt and Stephenson and Hargreaves and the rest of the inventors had ushered in, the Corporation went blithely forward with a scheme of civic expansion which soon took on, though the Council did not for years recognise the change, the character of a spending spree. It was an earlier and cruder version of the Welfare State: very difficult to prove that the thing was wrong, in fact practically impossible to deny that something of the kind was inevitable; but when the chickens, in the shape of the bills, came home to roost, how like a cloud of vultures they appeared!

But there was much to be said in the Council's favour. They weren't altogether fools. The Haddens were sound business men who knew there is a tide in the affairs of men that taken at tho flood leads on to fortune. The terrific engineering problems involved in the construction of Union Street were perhaps scarcely understood, and then there was old Henry Dundas, Viscount Melville, the dictator of Scotland, down in London, who insisted that Union Street should be ten feet wider than the Corporation's advisers had planned. There was St. Catherine's Hill to be levelled down near the east end of the street, there was the declivity of Putachie-side, where Market Street is, to be levelled up—Carnegie's Brae on the old level indicates what the problem looked like 150 years ago; and from there to Union Bridge, a costly proposition in itself, the whole line of thoroughfare had to take the form of a viaduct, the depth and complexity of whose foundations can still be gauged by a glance at the bridge over Correction Wynd and another from the Green up the steps that take the place of what once was a long slope from Hadden's Mill to Back Wynd.

Not only was the whole character of the western approaches to the city altered, but the cost of the alterations were in the long run borne by the burgesses themselves, the men who formed the close corporation, and not, as in public spending sprees today by the simple expedient of making a comparatively small percentage of the community pay for the benefits which the remainder, who pay little, enjoy. And the Council were acting quite legally. They were fully empowered to spend the Corporation's funds as they thought best.

In February 1817, the City Treasurer found he couldn't meet the city's financial obligations, the annual deficiency since 1810 having been in the region of £5,000. So he suspended payment, and after much parleying between the Council and burgesses, the Council handed over the burgh's property to twenty-one trustees to be administered for behoof of the burgh's creditors. But in eight years—and this is the greatest vindication of the Council's original action, if not of its lack of care in superintending the consequences of that action—the trustees were able to hand back the town's property, the tremendous increase in the town's prosperity and the eagerness with which feus on the two new streets were taken up having made this possible.

Those were the days of squibs and pasquils, when public opinion made its influence felt in rhyming skits upon personalities and institutions. The attitude of the managers was satirically represented thus:

What business has the vulgar rabble
To ken what's done at Council table?
Or whether they keep books ava?
Or books be free from stain or flaw?
What signifies the debt's increasing?
It's no on individuals pressing,
The wheels are aye kept tight and greasy,
And councillors ride soft and easy.

The Haddens had much to do during the city's trials and troubles. James had pressed on the building of Union Bridge. A lord of Session who used to visit Aberdeen on circuit said that Aberdeen had been a town without an entrance, and now when it was completed there was an entrance without a town, for the bridge was up before the eastern stretch of the street was made. Gavin Hadden was Provost when an Act for building the new Bridge of Don was passed, and he was also Provost when another Act was obtained which brought to Aberdeen, hitherto dependent upon various temperamental wells and springs, a filtered supply of water from the Dee, as well as for the improvement of the surface and lighting of the streets and of the sewage disposal. Aberdonians today have much to thank the memory of the Haddens for. It may be added that it was while Gavin was provost in 1828-29 that control of the harbour was taken out of the hands of the Town Council and consigned to the body, partly Council nominated, partly democratically elected, that still functions. The citizens then had never heard of ground nuts, but they were quite able to discern that what is essentially an administrative body cannot by its very nature cope with a great and expanding business.

Hardly had the echoes of the bankruptcy rumpus died away than the Council was confronted with a new and more pressing demand for constitutional reform. Joseph Hume, the most celebrated Radical of his day, had contrived to be elected M.P. for the constituency that numbered Aberdeen as one of its component burghs. And to his invincible pugnacity there was added the infinitely versatile and volatile genius of Alexander Bannerman, son of an Aberdeen wine merchant and of a very old family of the North and North-east. Bannerman in his early twenties had got into the Council as a Haddenite and a Tory, but, just as his greater contemporaries Disraeli and Gladstone both changed sides, so did he. Entering the Council in 1811, in a few years he had become the complete rebel, the ally of Joseph Hume, having the Council's intromissions discussed in Parliament, councillors and officials arraigned, and every public figure in Aberdeen, from the great James Hadden downwards, pilloried and lampooned if they refused to dance to the Bannerman tune. A collection of these squibs is in the Council's possession now. Bannerman was a crack hand at writing them, but his efforts drew forth some equally effective replies.

When the magistrates for some obscure reason purchased twenty copies of *Peacock on Dancing*, Peacock being the Aberdeen dancing-master who gave his name to Peacock's Close, off the Castlegate, there was a magnificent outburst of satirical songs and strouds:

> Now bob for bob, an' loup for loup,
> Forenent the Chamber door ;
> Grave Magistrates will rax their legs
> Fan their sederunt's o'er.

When the pier was breached by a storm, Bannerman, who was mainly responsible for the transfer of the harbour control from the Town Council, had a skit with the verse:

> Our pier can never firmly stand
> Nor sober habits learn ;
> For why? the stones that it compose
> Are all from Dancing Cairn.

The proposals of the Whigs to reform the Council evoked many a lyric effort, the best of which was probably "The Lament of John Home, the Town House keeper", purporting to be addressed to his friend and colleague Symon Grant, the town's sole policeman and thief-catcher. The subject, of course, was the threatened loss of their comfortable jobs, and Bannerman, whose journalistic henchman was John Booth, owner of the short-lived *Aberdeen Chronicle*, was thus portrayed:

> There's yon teem. hungry-looking brat,
> That clashed and sclaved, an' a' that,
> Fan he wis here the ither year,
> A councillor, an' a' that—
> An' a' that, an' a' that,
> O' our bits an' sups an' a' that,
> He raised a sough, wi' Johnny Booth ;
> They'll baith get hell, an' a' that.

At the first General Election after the Reform Act, the candidates for the Aberdeen seat were Alexander Bannerman and James Hadden, but on the eve of the poll Hadden prudently withdrew his name. Bannerman went on to a knighthood and to the governorship of various Crown colonies, including Newfoundland. He married Margaret Gordon, the first sweetheart of Thomas Carlyle, who put her into "Sartor Resartus" as Blumine, with Bannerman as Herr Towgood. By the time Bannerman was Sir Alexander, James Hadden had been dead six years. He had been much maligned in his day, but the solid merit of his public services had survived the allegations of the critics, and he died universally esteemed. Hadden Street was named after him and Lindsay Street, off Golden Square, after a daughter who married a Colonel Lindsay. Gavin Hadden died in 1857.

One other personal item deserves mention for it may perhaps illustrate that inward strength that made the Haddens the power they were. One of their descendants, Todd by name, in a book of reminiscences of his life in India, relates how, being clutched by a Bengal tiger, he so hypnotised his savage antagonist by staring him in the eye, that the beast relinquished its grip and slunk away!

The Menzies family
and the freedom lands

So many and so great have been the changes in our way of life that there is not much of a link, apart from the physical one of situation, between the Aberdeen of pre-Reformation days and of today. But there is one other connection, and although unfortunately it is not altogether of a kind that hard-headed Aberdonians may care to dwell on, we cannot very well ignore its important implications on that account.

It is now just on 550 years since there slipped out of the wings onto the Aberdeen stage the first member of a family that in the next two centuries and more came to dominate the fortunes of the burgh, for good sometimes and at times for the opposite, but always with a glamour about its fortunes that is very fascinating to the historical eye. After it vanished from the scene nothing appeared again at all resembling it. When it disappeared there also disappeared an age in history. It was indeed the end of an auld sang.

Sir Paul Menzies
of Kinmundy

The first Menzies appears to have arrived in Aberdeen about 1408, one Gilbert, son (it is thought) of Sir Robert Menzies of Wemyss in Perthshire. What his business was has never been very clear. He dealt in land, which then as now was a commodity considered desirable to possess, and as a real estate agent he no doubt prospered. Certain it is that within four years of his arrival in the burgh, he was a baillie, and after serving for a decade in the Council he was in 1423 elected Provost. At the same time another Menzies, named David, of unspecified relationship to him, was a burgess and wealthy enough to be one of the hostages selected from amongst the most substantial men in Edinburgh, Perth, Dundee and Aberdeen to serve as hostages for the payment of King James I's ransom money.

The last of the Menzies provosts held office in 1635, so that for a dozen years more than the two centuries the Menzies family was high in the society of the burgh. During these 212 years, the civic chair was filled for 114 years by members of the family, while several of them combined with the provostship the office of town clerk. In the sixteenth century six Menzies, with a descent usually of father to son, were provosts for eighty-three of the hundred years, one of them for forty years altogether, twenty-nine of them right off the reel.

Aberdeen at that time, then as now the most remote of the principal Scottish burghs, partook more than any other town in the kingdom of the character of a city state. In Italy and in Flanders during the late medieval period of the Renaissance and the Reformation, certain cities contrived to become, in Italy, little republics ruled by a hereditary succession, and in Flanders powers within the State governed by burghers in some kind of association. Aberdeen during the long years of the Menzies ascendancy was not quite a Florence and not quite a Ghent, but something between the two, with a more or less single ruling family whose autocracy was sometimes tempered by the asserted rights of the burgesses. There was a certain amount of dictation from the Court and Parliament in Edinburgh, an occasional show of authority by king or sheriff, now and then an attempt by neighbouring landowners like the Forbeses, the Gordons or the Setons to take over the administration of the burgh or to seize some of its perquisites. But to all intents and purposes, within very wide limits, Aberdeen was independent and autonomous.

In 1457 Gilbert's son Andrew Menzies became owner of part of the Badfothalis or Pitfodels property, and in the next generation or two the lands of Cowie, of Findon, and of Gilcomston amongst other properties, while in 1521 Thomas Menzies who had married Marion or Mariote Reid, only daughter and heiress of Alexander Reid (Provost 1492-93), became full proprietor of Pitfodels, which henceforward was to be the main territorial appanage of the family. The family dwelling in the Castlegate, next door to Marischal's Hall, was known as Pitfodels' Lodging. It stood where the Bank of Scotland office now is. Marischal's Hall, whose Castlegate frontage was of two storeys, the whole subjects consisting of a group of buildings surrounding a courtyard with a large garden attached, was purchased and demolished by the Town Council 200 years ago when Marischal Street was being built. Pitfodels' Lodging was a three-storeyed turreted building in its second condition; it was reputed to have been the first private residence in Aberdeen to be built of stone when it was re-erected after being destroyed by fire in 1529.

Pitfodels' Lodging had a troublous history. In the winter of 1526 within its portals, Alexander Seton of Meldrum was killed by the Master of Forbes. It was to the stone house during the troubles of Charles I's reign that the Marquis of Huntly went in 1639 for security, in the following regal state, according to Aberdeen's first historian, Spalding: "It was condescended among his friends that twenty-four gentlemen, whereof there should be three barons, should weekly attend and serve this Marquis in Aberdeen, week about; and when twenty-four went out, other twenty-four to come in, and daily to eat at the Marquis's table; and siclike there was eight gentlemen appointed to watch his lodging in the night, their time about, with fire and candle still burning within the house". Ten years later he lost his head at the Mercat Cross in Edinburgh.

Many years before, a no less splendid Huntly, his great grandfather, had been visible from the windows of Pitfodels' Lodging lying on the plainstanes before the Tolbooth. In 1562 the then Earl of Huntly died, some say of a stroke, some by the dirk of Stuart of Inchbreck, at the Battle of Corrichie, and his body was carried to Aberdeen and thrown down upon the pavement of the Castlegate. John Knox tells how "Lady Forbes among many others, came to see the body; and seeing him lying upon the cold stones, having only upon him a doublet of canvas, a pair of Scots grey hose, and covered with an arras work, she said, 'There lieth he that yesterday in the morning was esteemed the wisest, the richest and a man of the greatest power that was within Scotland' ". Knox adds, "she lied not, for in men's opinion, under a prince, there was not such an one these three hundred years in the realm produced".

It was a lively square in those days, if not altogether a happy one. From the Tolbooth itself a few days later tradition has it that Mary Queen of Scots was compelled by her half-brother, Moray, to witness the execution of the dead Huntly's eldest son, Sir John Gordon, who was reputed (as indeed were most personable men of high degree in those days) to be her lover. And from Pitfodels' Lodging in 1650, where Joseph Robertson surmises that Charles II stayed during his visit to Aberdeen, the merry monarch could see "a mangled limb of the great Montrose blackening in the air"—Montrose, whom Charles had sent to his death some months before. It is also recorded that during his stay Charles was admonished by one of the town's ministers to keep the curtains drawn when he was entertaining his girl friends; Lucy Walter, mother of the ill-fated Duke of Monmouth, was in his entourage, and she was not the only one.

But to return to our Provosts. After the first one, who was Gilbert, there was Andrew, twice Provost and once in Parliament, and then came his son Alexander, thrice Provost, during whose time there appeared on the scene the only family that ever really rivalled the Menzies in the days of their glory, the Rutherfords, and the mother of the first of these, Sir John Rutherford of Migvie and Tarland, is believed to have been a Menzies. Rutherford was eleven times Provost, and a great favourite with James III, who, when one of the Rutherford's elections was disputed by a Menzies, announced that the objection to "our lovet familiar servitour is right displeasand". Rutherford, however, was far from popular, one sweeping criticism of him alleging that he was "a masterful oppressour of the lieges, and for his oppressions there may nae merchante live within the burghe", which sounds like a bit of exaggeration. In fact he worked very hard for Aberdeen, going to Berwick to get lead for the roof of St. Nicholas Kirk, and with the Provost of Edinburgh making the journey to Flanders to arrange with the Austrian Archduke who ruled there for the import of Scottish goods into the Low Countries. Probably criticism of those in authority then as now was apt to be a little exaggerated. One citizen declared that Provost Alexander Menzies had found the price of a boll of meal at 4s. and would leave it at 20s. This was regarded as "perturbious" language and the critic was cast, as befitted such a cantankerous devil, out of the town.

The first Menzies provost of the sixteenth century was "Banison" Gib or Gilbert Menzies of Findon, who owed his nickname no doubt to "perturbious" language of another sort. Between 1505 and 1536 he was in the civic chair twenty-three times, and his ascendancy was such that on one occasion when he had to be away from home, he told the councillors to take their orders from his son Thomas, who was not even a baillie. Gilbert was Provost when James IV's young Queen Margaret made her first visit to Aberdeen, and when Aberdeen was immortalised by William Dunbar, who was in her train, in his famous and perhaps most sincere poem, "Blyth Aberdeen, thou beryl of all touns". It was a tremendous occasion. The Council decided to "receive our sovereign lady the Queen as honourably as any burgh of Scotland, except Edinburgh allenarly, and to make large expenses thereupon". The middens and pig cruives were removed from the streets, four of the handsomest of the burgesses carried the Queen into the town under a pall of "velvet cramase", the houses were hung with tapestry, there were pageants at every street corner, and a procession, consisting of a combined choir and orchestra of young ladies "all clad in green of marvellous beauty" and with "hair detressit" hanging down under their embroidered hats played on timbrels and sang "richt sweetly". At the Mercat Cross wine ran in abundance and the crowd in great good humour conveyed the distinguished visitor to her lodging.

With Thomas, however, the power of the family rose to its highest splendour. He was a believer in the traditions and "lovable consuetude" of the burgh, and upheld Aberdeen's rights against all outsiders, refusing to be cowed even by the all-powerful Earl of Huntly. After various shorter spells he returned to the provostship in 1547 and remained there without a break through all the troublous days of the Reformation until 1576, when he retired two months before his death. He continued, albeit remaining Roman Catholic at heart, to keep on good terms with the new dispensation, probably because he leaned to the English rather than the French side in the tug o' war that ensued between the two neighbouring powers for Scotland's favour.

Yet it was this man who must be held responsible for alienating the burgh's birthright. It was Robert the Bruce who in recognition of the town's unfailing support of his cause even during the years when he was a fugitive and a failure, bestowed upon the burgh the forest of Stocket with all rights therein in return for an annual feu-duty to the Exchequer of £213 6s. 8d. Scots. The Stocket property was extended later by the acquisition of the lands of Rubislaw, the Cruives, the Justice Mills and other subiects and rights. By the beginning of the sixteenth century the town's lands must have covered an area of over twenty square miles.

Gradually the practice developed of anticipating the revenue from the town's properties by, for example, letting the fishings for a longer lease at an actually lower annual rental provided the lessee paid a grassum or ready-money fine in advance. The value of the lands was fully appreciated and the title to them jealously guarded. As for instance when James IV bestowed the Stocket upon his successful pirate Sir Andrew Wood, and the Council, summoned by handbell to deal with this threat to the community's fortunes, sent a deputation to the Privy Council which "ripely advised" gave declaration that the "alderman, balzes and communitie sal breuk and joise the said burgh of Abirdene with the pertinence as thai bruikit abefor". So that was that.

Yet in 1557 the Town Council, inspired by the great Thomas Menzies himself, in effect threw away the whole property. A licence was obtained from the Crown, at a fee of 2,500 merks, to feu out the town's lands. At a meeting of the whole community, which meant the merchant guild more or less, the scheme was adopted, no doubt most of the burgesses present being sitting tenants of the subjects in question and therefore most likely to become the feuars. The subjects were then feued out for a total of £263 6s. 8d. for the lands, and £329 3s. 4d. for the fishings, or about £50 sterling in all plus about £170 sterling in grassums which, of course, did not recur like the feu-duties. Later sales raised the annual amount of the feu-duties to £70 sterling. In 1887 it was calculated that the annual revenue (not to the community) from the alienated lands and fishings was £40,000. In 1920 it cost the Council £40,000 to buy back Hazlehead, and in 1943 the much smaller estate of Raeden cost £19,434 10s. Attempts were made in the next forty years to have the decision set aside and the Privy Council was petitioned "that the small customes, commoun landis, takkis and utheris casualities, commoun rentis and gude of the said burgh, micht be yearlie roupit and sett to the best availl". But the petition failed and that was the end of it.

The Menzies family continued to fill the public eye for the best part of a century thereafter. Aberdeen's Commissioner in 1605 to the first Scots Parliament after the Union of the Crowns was a Menzies on his mother's side, Alexander Rutherford of Rubislaw, who received from the King a diamond ring for the eloquence of the speech, in Latin, French and "Scottish", which he delivered in a debate on the legislative union of the two kingdoms a hundred years before it took final effect. Thomas Menzies of Durn and Cults, nine times elected Provost, was responsible for the building of the new Tolbooth—the Mids of Mar—to replace the old one, whose steeple was blown down in 1589, and there still remains a portion of it. He was knighted in 1617. In 1620 he went to London and presented James VI with a beautiful black Ythan pearl found in the Ebrie burn, and at the same time showed the King some silver-ore from a mine in Sutherland. He died on his way home at Wooler, and no one knows where he is buried or where the silver mine was.

The last Menzies provost was twelve times elected Sir Paul of Kinmundy, knighted at Charles I's coronation in Edinburgh in 1633 and a younger brother of Sir Thomas. He was responsible for the introduction of a new water supply, distributed throughout the burgh by means of fountains and wells, the supply from the Loch, upon which the town had hitherto depended, being "filthilie defyllit and corruptit, not only by gutteris daylie rynning in the burne, but also by litsteris and the washing of clothes and abusing of the water in sindrie partis, with other sorts of uncleanness".

Sir Patrick Manson
the conqueror of the tropics

GREATEST of Aberdonians to live into the present century, greatest by virtue of the world-wide effects of his achievements, was the Oldmeldrum boy and Aberdeen medical graduate, Patrick Manson. In pursuance of his profession he made discoveries and initiated courses of research which have done probably more for the spread of civilisation and for the advancement of commerce than the work of any member of any other profession. Yet one does not often hear his name mentioned nowadays, and it is a sorry fact that when his body came to Aberdeen for burial in Allenvale, the only two doctors who were present at the railway station to receive it were the Professor of Medicine, the late Sir Ashley Mackintosh, and the late Dr. Alexander Rennie, the brother of Manson's partner in practice during part of his China days, Dr. Thomas Rennie. It may be mentioned that the latter's son was the Major-General Gordon Rennie, who was killed in 1945 at the crossing of the Rhine while in command of the 51st division.

Patrick Manson was born at Cromlethill, Oldmeldrum, in 1844, his father being a substantial agriculturist as well as agent of the British Linen Bank there, who afterwards became agent of the bank's Aberdeen branch. The Manson family are still worthily represented in the district of Patrick's birth. He at first intended to be an engineer and became an apprentice with that end in view, but during convalescence from a serious illness his fondness for natural history developed, and he decided to go in for medicine. Accordingly he matriculated in 1860 at Aberdeen University and graduated M.B. and C.M. in 1865 and M.D. the following year.

Going out to Formosa, where he became medical officer to the Chinese Imperial Maritime Customs, he got on the wrong side of the Japanese who even then were endeavouring to get a grip on the island which they eventually came to own. In 1871 he migrated to Amoy, where he engaged in practice and where he commenced the studies of parasitic diseases which eventually brought him fame.

In 1872 a Dr. Timothy R. Lewis, in Calcutta, and a medical graduate of Aberdeen in 1867, so that Manson must have known him, discovered the presence of microscopical worms in the blood of persons suffering from certain diseases. Manson, working from this basis, discovered that sufferers from elephantiasis, a very common Oriental disease, had this worm or filaris in their blood. He hit upon the mosquito as the carrier of this worm and found out a good deal more about it. But the principal advance he thus achieved lay in the knowledge he obtained of the mosquito itself.

In 1883 Manson went to Hong Kong, where he instituted what became eventually the University and School of Medicine in the colony. In 1889 he came home, having become an LL.D. of Aberdeen in 1886. In 1890 he set up as a consultant in London, being appointed in 1892 physician to the Seamen's Hospital Society. He had never ceased his researches, and while with the Society he observed that filaments broke loose from some malaria parasites (which had already been identified in 1880) and he deduced that these filaments must multiply and develop in an intermediate host. His acquaintance with that very hospitable insect the mosquito suggested it as the host. Other researchers, ending with Ronald Ross, carried Manson's findings and inspired suggestions to the triumphant conclusion that the mosquito disseminated malaria and that if the mosquito's breeding were prevented the disease would be brought under control.

To a great extent this has been done, the swamps in which the mosquito multiplied throughout the tropics have been drained, and malaria, that claimed so many pioneers and empire-builders, was checked and almost eliminated. Ross, to whom many commentators have ascribed the chief glory of the conquest of malaria, modestly and truly said that Manson " so accurately indicated the true line of research that it has been my part merely to follow its direction ".

The making of the Panama Canal has been cited as the classic example of what Manson's discovery has meant in the opening up of disease-ridden areas to the progress of man's enterprise, but *The Times*, in its obituary notice of Manson in 1922, put the whole story in noble phrases when it declared: " That Sir Patrick Manson was able to save millions of human lives, that he was able to banish disease from its immemorial fastnesses, that he was able to afford safe conducts to the missionary, the soldier and the merchant in many of the world's danger areas, are perhaps the least of his achievements. Greater by far than these is the moral support which his work has bestowed on what we speak of as Western civilisation."

Today, thanks to uninformed prejudices against colonialism and imperialism on the part of the ruling classes in both U.S.A. and Russia—strange bedfellows indeed!—what we speak of as Western civilisation in the backward areas of the earth has a less vulnerable enemy than the mosquito to implant disease and decay in its vitals. That, however, so far from lessening the magnitude of Manson's labours, only serves to indicate how perhaps, on an intellectual, psychological and social basis, this new menace may be confronted and perhaps in due time be eliminated.

Manson himself, whose lectures in tropical medicine had attracted the attention of Joe Chamberlain, then Colonial Secretary, was in 1897 appointed physician and medical adviser to the Colonial Office. On his suggestion and in conformity with a scheme of his the London School of Tropical Medicine was founded in 1899, and soon after Manson, knighted in 1903, retired from the Colonial Office in 1912, we find him described as the " father of tropical medicine ". The school was veritably his child, he was in it and thinking of it up to the day of his death in the spring of 1922.

He was a true man of science. " Never ", he once said, " refuse to see what you do not want to see or which might go against your own cherished hypothesis or against the views of authorities. . . . The thing you cannot get a pigeon-hole for is the finger-point showing the way to discovery." No more trustworthy guide could be imagined for the conduct of a young scientist. At the same time, no more glittering prize, no nobler aim could present itself to the young man than the enduring fame which was won by this country loon from Aberdeenshire.

Jaffrays of Kingswells

the oy of ane baxter and his adventurous son

No eminent Aberdonian in his career so strikingly illustrates how dull our modern lives can be than the third of the famous Alexander Jaffrays, and the fourth of them to be known to local history. But before recounting something of its variety, it may not be without interest to spend a paragraph or two upon his forebears.

The original Kingswells House

When Alexander Jaffray's father, the third Alexander, became Provost of Aberdeen in 1636, he was decried by certain of the citizens as being the "oy of ane baxter" (which means the grandson of a baker). But both political and social feeling ran high in those days, and the reporter of the saying was the historian Spalding, who as a Royalist and an Episcopalian had very little use for a Covenanter and Presbyterian like the Provost. The third Alexander's grandfather, the first Alexander, was indeed a baker, admitted a burgess of his craft in 1534. In 1549 and again in 1555 it is recorded that he, with others, was convicted of selling white bread of less measure and price than the standard laid down in the "common ordinance and statutis of this guid toune".

The Provost's father, Alexander the second, bought Kingswells, that delightful old manor, from one Robert Arthur in 1579; but apart from becoming a baillie and the father of the Provost, he is otherwise unknown to fame. The disapproval of the Jaffrays' rise to local eminence had no effect upon the target, the Provost himself, for when, the first Sunday after his elevation to the civic chair, he found a pie in his pew in St. Nicholas kirk, he "miskenit all and never querrellit the samen", in other words, paid no attention to the implied insult.

To Alexander the third Aberdeen owed its House of Correction, situated in what we still know as Correction Wynd, which took its name from the institution. This reformatory was founded in 1636, the magistrates authorising the levy of a tax of 2,000 merks upon the burgh to pay for the purchase and furnishing of the house, the idea being that thereafter, under the direction of a public company, the inmates should engage in the manufacture of "bred cloath, carseyis, seyis" and other goods. The baillies were empowered to consign to the House of Correction "all vagabonds, strong and sturdie beggares, idle and maisterles persones strong in bodie and habill to work, servants disobedient to maistris, children disobedient to parentis, leud leivars, pyikers, common scoldis, and uncorrigible harlottis not amending to the discipline of the kirk". The two disobedient categories alone would make many a full house today! It should be added that the conditions laid down for the establishment and conduct of the place, as set out in the Burgh Records for 1636, are an admirable example of business practice in those days.

Alexander the third seems to have been an excellent civic head, and in the hectic years of the Covenanting troubles around 1638, when he was again provost, and when Aberdeen was invaded first by the Covenanters under Montrose and then by the Royalists under Viscount Aboyne, he kept his head and the respect of the citizens. During his last term of office in 1641, the lack of a manufacturer of golf balls within the burgh was such a felt want that a maker of these articles in Leith came north and obtained a licence to set up in business in Aberdeen.

Alexander Jaffray the fourth, the subject of this sketch, who had been born in 1614, was educated at the Grammar School and at Banchory and matriculated in Marischal College in 1631 only to leave the following year. Whether his withdrawal was connected with his marriage on 30 April 1632 to Jean, daughter of the Principal, Patrick Dun, does not transpire although it looks as if there was some connection between the two events. In his celebrated diary, Jaffray is critical of his teachers whom he declares to have been incapable of bringing up the young. From Marischal he went to stay with his relative Robert Burnet, advocate in Edinburgh, the father of the famous Gilbert Burnet, historian of the Revolution and Bishop of Salisbury. Thereafter he went to the Continent, it is said in the company of Jamesone the painter. In Paris he had his first narrow escape from death, when a drunk soldier attacked and wounded him.

Jaffray returned to Aberdeen in 1636, and within two years he was apparently bankrupt, having "not only spent the rent of what was his estate, but four or five thousand merks of the stock". This inability to run his own affairs was, then as now, a common preamble to running the affairs of others. In 1638 he was a baillie and by sending to prison a servant of Sir John Gordon of Haddo he got into trouble that bothered him for years to come. Haddo first of all set upon Jaffray and his brother John and wounded them at Dalwearie, near Kintore, afterwards invading the burgh with a troop of horse and swaggering round the Market Cross in the Castlegate to the great scandal of the lieges. Haddo was fined 20,000 merks for this escapade. Later, in 1644, the same gang, headed this time by the Laird of Drum, came into Aberdeen early in the morning and carried off the two Jaffrays to Strathbogie, subsequently immuring them in Auchindoun, in the Cabrach, for several weeks. The shock killed Jaffray's wife, who had borne him ten children in their twelve years of wedlock.

By this time the Great Civil War (which, incidentally, began in Aberdeenshire) was in full cry and for prominent citizens the times were full of danger and escapes, of imprisonment, spoliation, wounds and death. Jaffray came through the battle of the Justice Mills in 1644, took refuge in Dunnottar Castle, then a Covenanting stronghold, managed to fall into the hands of the other side, and was shut up for six weeks with a few companions in Pitcaple Castle. By a stroke of luck they succeeded in locking out the garrison of the Castle, and were rescued by some of Argyll's troops, committing the castle to the flames when they left.

In 1647 Jaffray remarried, his second spouse being the daughter of that fanatical Covenanting divine, Andrew Cant, whose opponents no doubt thought he was well named. She bore him eight children. He became provost in 1649, and as he had already been Parliamentary Commissioner for the Burgh, he was appointed one of the Scottish deputation that crossed to The Hague to negotiate with Charles II for that dubious Monarch's occupancy of the throne of Scotland. Jaffray was never happy about this episode in his career, for he felt that the Commissioners "did sinfully both entangle the nation and ourselves, and that poor young prince". He actually advised Charles not to subscribe the Covenant if it was against his conscience, but Charles never had much of a conscience anyway, and like his grandfather Henri Quatre thought a crown worth swearing for whatever the mental reservations.

Jaffray went south with Charles and at Dunbar Drove he was badly wounded and taken prisoner. A meeting with Cromwell, however, put him in the good graces of the great soldier —who was not yet Protector—and he not only was released unconditionally, but became one of the five members from Scotland of Cromwell's Union Parliament, better known as Barebone's Parliament, and was appointed Director of the Chancery in Scotland. At the same time his intercourse with the Roundheads resulted in his renouncing the Presbyterian creed, first for that of the Independents and subsequently for that of the Fifth Monarchy men, who believed in the immediate personal reappearance of Christ upon earth. In 1651 Jaffray was again provost of Aberdeen, Scotland being incorporated in the Commonwealth during his second term of office.

At the Restoration Jaffray refused to bow the knee and was imprisoned in Edinburgh, but being "in ane infirm and valetudinarie condition" he was released after a few months and returned to Aberdeen. There he joined the Society of Friends, who were being much persecuted, and he suffered imprisonment in Banff jail and ill-treatment even in his native burgh. The Barclay of Ury immortalised in Whittier's poem was one of his Quaker associates, and his wife Sarah Cant went over to the Quaker faith also, a conversion which says more for Jaffray's sincerity and goodness of heart than any tribute paid him by a contemporary. He died in 1673 at Kingswells, the private burial ground of which he had put at the disposal of his co-religionists, who at that time were refused burial in the churchyards.

Alexander's brother John, of Dilspro (now known as Grandholm), was provost for three consecutive years, 1657-59. He lived and died a member of the Church of Scotland and on his demise in 1684 was buried in St. Nicholas kirkyard, where his stone, when still decipherable, carried a remarkable Latin tribute to his first wife, Janet Forbes, "most dutiful spouse of the most illustrious John Jaffray, provost of the Aberdeens, who, divinely endowed in mind and virtue, and grace beyond the lot of her age and the spirit of her time, freed from the irksome trammels of mortality, gained Heaven and immortality, 14th March, 1656". It was almost worth dying to receive such a testimonial as this. The last of the family seems to have died in Dublin in the middle of the last century.

The two provost Alexanders make an interesting contrast. The elder was a shrewd business man who as chief magistrate in a time of strife earned the respect of all parties "as ane loyal and gude subject to his majestie, and as a most cairfull and painefull magistratt for the weill and gude of the toune". The son, while not a trimmer, was a religious romanticist, whose diary is full of devotion, superstition and portents, armies marching in the heavens and the like, yet no weak or ignoble character.

When we consider the salient episodes of his career we cannot fail to be struck by his extraordinary vitality. In a catalogue of the prevailing weaknesses of the various Incorporated Trades of Aberdeen the vice ascribed to the bakers is "lowseness". Whether Alexander Jaffray's sudden withdrawal from college and that curious escapade in a Parisian street that left him with scars on his back and hand derived from an inherited wildness, we cannot know. After all, at no time in the world's history has the sowing of wild oats proved to unfit a man, if his heart is in the right place, for the sterner business of life. Jaffray's wide swing from Presbyterianism to the Millenarians reflected a tremendous inward revolution and revulsion from actual or fancied past misdemeanours and for us remains an unplumbed secret. He and his famous diary, which was not published until 1833, offer a happy hunting ground to the modern psychologist, but such speculations would not take us very far beyond where the normal experience of history conveys us.

Even more striking in their contrasts are his unconventional but downright honest boldness with Charles II, and his shrewd reading of that playboy's superficial character when he tackled him on the subject of subscribing the Covenant; and his intimacy with the great Protector, who, although a religious and political enthusiast, like most outstanding men of his time, was a pretty astute judge of men and did not allow supernatural agencies to blind him to the facts of life so completely as might appear from some of his military dispatches. It is very evident that Cromwell thought a good deal of Jaffray, and such esteem is not likely to have been engendered by any man of a shallow nature or an unpractical mind. That such a man should, at the very worst juncture for his own material prosperity, link his fortunes with a persecuted sect is not to be taken as an argument for his lack of common sense.

The whole portrait with its lights and shades makes a fascinating study. Alexander Jaffray placed side by side with his contemporary, Sir Thomas Urquhart, suggests an interesting picture in black and white, with both personalities partaking of the two extremes; but one was the laughing cavalier who actually died of laughing, and the other the restrained and rather sombre roundhead who died sighing.

The fabulous Chicago Smith

In the first article of this series, reference was made to its subject's celebrated cousin, George Smith, otherwise and more widely known as "Chicago Smith". He was born in 1808 in the farmhouse of Millhill, on the estate of Kinmundy, in Old Deer parish, that nursery of great men. Educated at Old Deer school and a private school in Udny (where, we rather think, the "Bayard of India", General Outram, was also educated) he went to Marischal College intending to study medicine, an uncle of his being doctor at Old Deer. However, he did not stay the course at medicine, perhaps on account of a weakness of the eyes; and he turned to farming, becoming tenant of Raecloch, near Turriff. At that also he failed to settle and in 1833, leaving his affairs and some of his money in the custody of his lawyer cousin, Alexander Anderson in Aberdeen, he set off to make a third start in life in the United States.

Once there he commenced business in Chicago as a seller of timber. The town was very small, being under a thousand of population, and the site was little better than a swamp. George Smith, however, was a strategist in commerce, and foresaw that the township was magnificently situated between New York and the established Eastern Seaboard and the great potential of the prairies and the West. He, therefore, bought land both at Chicago and further north at Milwaukee, which was destined to become a great railway centre. So rapidly did these towns expand that within three years Smith had sold out at a substantial profit and returned home, intending to retire on his gains. But the lure of land speculation had got him in its toils and he could not resist the temptation in 1837 to return to the scene of his first activities and commence banking as well as his own real estate business.

It is at this point that Smith steps upon the stage of Aberdeen history. We indicated in our sketch of Alexander Anderson that the great Provost's business methods were not infrequently open to criticism. In fact, some of his contemporaries would have used a harsher and sterner word. It would be interesting to discover, although that is probably impossible at this period of time, whether Anderson's initiation into the methods of Really Big Business was at the hands of his energetic cousin. Certainly it was in connection with George Smith's main finance venture in 1837 that Alexander Anderson laid himself open to the criticism which raged around him for more than two decades. And it came about in this way, which was to begin with quite innocent and in which no doubt there was at first no intention whatever to do anything but good to those who became associated with the two cousins.

George Smith had a fair amount of money in hand, but he probably realised that the opportunities of making a vast fortune in the Middle West were now boundless, all the more since there had been a bit of a slump, which he perceived was bound to be only temporary, but which made it possible to pick up greater bargains than before in land. He, therefore, suggested to his cousin that a company should be floated and this was done in the beginning of 1837 under the name of the Illinois Investment Company, with a capital which eventually reached the total of £95,000 actually subscribed and sent across the Atlantic to earn luscious dividends for the partners, of whom the principal member was George Smith himself, once more located now in Milwaukee and now in Chicago. As manager of the company, which was to deal in real estate, grant mortgages, and do insurance business, there was appointed the farmer of Mains of Laithers, near Turriff,

Patrick Strachan by name, who had been a neighbour of George Smith in the latter's farming days, but who otherwise had no apparent qualifications for so responsible a position. A clerk in the Aberdeen Fire & Life Assurance Company, William Donaldson Scott, was appointed accountant, but his job became more or less of a sinecure when, a little later, the directors sent out David Paterson to act as book-keeper. In 1839 a further company was launched in Aberdeen, in which both Smith and Anderson had an interest, called the Wisconsin Marine and Fire Insurance Company, towards the capital of which about £20,000 was subscribed in the city. Its manager from an early date in its history was Alexander Mitchell, an Ellon man who had been a clerk in the Peterhead branch of the old Aberdeen Bank, and who had gone out on a five year engagement with the Illinois Company but been taken over by George Smith in breach of his original agreement.

Strachan and Scott, at salaries that soon were fixed at £1,000 and £500 respectively, started off business in Chicago, but two years later, on the advice of George Smith, switched to New York, the reason adduced being that New York was a better centre for the company's activities. They sold the goodwill of their business to a Scottish immigrant, who, however, very soon found that George Smith was himself operating the Illinois Company's business in Chicago in place of its authorised officials. For a year or two the Illinois Company paid a dividend at the rate of 15 per cent., and the stock rose to a premium, but after the transfer to New York a change came over the aspect of the business and the partners in Aberdeen became so nervous that Alexander Anderson visited the United States in 1841, returning with assurances that the difficulties were only temporary and that all would soon be well again. That prediction was falsified during the next three years, when another director, Alexander Johnston, W.S., was sent across to make a thorough investigation, the result of which was to blow the whole venture sky high, and end in the company being liquidated, with a loss to the Aberdeen shareholders of approximately £75,000, as well as the bulk of their investment in the Wisconsin flotation.

Most unfortunately, just at the point when the Aberdeen directors had requested Messrs. Strachan and Scott to supply them with full particulars of their accounts, a fire on the opposite side of the New York street in which the Illinois company's offices were situated resulted, rather surprisingly, in the destruction of the company's documents. In consequence, it was never possible to ascertain exactly what had happened, and in the long run the only way the directors could see out of their difficulties was to sell the remaining assets of the company to Messrs. Strachan and Scott, who thereafter carried on the same business for their own behoof, and apparently did not so badly out of it.

Alexander Johnston's investigations, however, had revealed some extraordinary dealings with the company's money. In many cases the officials had been warned by George Smith not to do business, and had ignored the warning, only to lose large sums of the company's money. On the other hand there were cases in which Smith had played a very equivocal part. For example there was a deal in Chicago. A certain Archibald Clybourn appeared in the books of the company as being a debtor for a dollar amount equivalent to £3,613 10s. No interest was charged on this debt, which was secured by mortgage on some land near Chicago. On scrutiny in 1845, it transpired that Clybourn had done a land deal with George Smith but had been unable to pay the final instalments. Smith had then introducd him to Strachan, who lent the sum mentioned on security of the mortgage. The lands in question, however, turned out to be already mortgaged, and when Clybourn's loan from the Illinois Company proved to be insufficient to satisfy George Smith, the latter kept the real estate which was the subject of the original bargain, the Illinois Company lost its loan, and the holder of the prior mortgage on the bonded land stepped in and deprived the company of the security for its bond also.

We may well leave the Illinois Investment Company at that. It was a sorry story for

Aberdeen. George Smith used it as the first foundation of a financial career whose success eventually towered like the Empire State Building over all the other financial edifices of America. He used, as we have indicated, the Wisconsin Insurance Company, once he and Alexander Mitchell got clear of Aberdeen control, to challenge the banking houses of Wisconsin and Illinois on their own ground, and although according to the laws of each of these States his operations were quite illegal, the Federal system had not at that time been sufficiently perfected to enable the legislature of one State to make arrangements with that of another to prohibit such depredations as George Smith practised, with the result that he was able to pass off the paper currency of the Wisconsin Company as notes of the State banks. Indeed, he eventually bought up the State bank of far away Georgia as a defence against the encroachments of the authorities upon the activities of his Wisconsin concern.

In 1857 another recession set in throughout the United States. George Smith and his companies and associates successfully and easily weathered the storm, but he himself apparently never liked America, and in that year he began to pull out of his various businesses, returning to this country for good in 1861. He settled in London, after being for a short time proprietor of Westhall, Oyne, Aberdeenshire, and also of North College, Elgin. In 1851 he had been elected a member of the Reform Club in London, and he became fond of residence there to such an extent that he was allotted a special chamber in the Club for his own residence, where he dwelt during more than thirty years, much like a retired Captain Kidd or Paul Jones, surrounded by frock-coated and tile-hatted Liberal respectabilities. No one in Victorian London seemed to find any incongruity in this association, and it would ill become us to imagine any today. In his Reform Club chamber he read over and over again the novels of Walter Scott. Every day, weather permitting, he took a turn in one of the adjacent parks, and when the weather was bad he walked in the great gallery surrounding the central saloon of the Club. Such was the esteem in which the Club committee held him—he paid 15s. a day for his quarters—that they installed a lift (for which he paid) in the last year of his life to save him the trouble of toiling up, or what was probably worse at his age, toiling down the staircase. He died in November 1899 at the age of ninety-one.

He left a lot of money—thanks to the good Aberdonians of the Illinois and Wisconsin ventures, all of them by that time long since dead, including his cousin Alexander Anderson. His fortune was estimated at about £5 millions, which would mean at least six times that sum today. In his lifetime he had endowed an educational bequest to Old Deer, of which the capital at the time of his death amounted to £9,000. He also contributed to the extension fund of Aberdeen University, while his legatees were responsible for the presentation to Elgin of its attractive Cooper Park. Some eight years later James Henry Smith, otherwise and more popularly known as "Silent" Smith, of Kincraig, Tuxedo Park, Orange County, New York, and who died in Kyoto, Japan, the son of George Smith's cousin, left about £1¼ millions, which he had mostly inherited from his more retiring but also more adventurous relative. "Silent" Smith left nothing in this country.

Chicago Smith himself was buried on 11 November 1899, in the New Cemetery, Elgin.

Gibbs
five generations of engineering Gibbs

At least two of the prominent engineering families associated with Aberdeen were incomers: the first of which we have any records, and one of the most modern, John Crab, the Fleming who conducted the defence of Berwick against the English after the Battle of Bannockburn, appears to have been rewarded by Robert the Bruce with land in and around Aberdeen, as so many of the great king's friends were. He had a croft on the borders of the medieval burgh and Craibstone was his also. The family name crops up quite frequently for over a hundred years thereafter. One wonders whether John Crab had anything to do with the plans of the Brig o' Balgownie.

Sir Alexander Gibb

The other and very modern Aberdeen engineering family is that of the Gibbs, whose name has been familiar in the city and surrounding district for over a century and a half. The Gibb who is regarded as the founder of the line was William, who began as a mason and was one of the first men in this country to adopt the profession of civil engineer. He belonged to central Scotland, and added to his building work the science of the architect. He built the aqueduct which lifts the Forth and Clyde Canal over the river Kelvin. His son John, born in 1776, began the family connection with Aberdeen. He started as a civil engineer, learning the craft as an apprentice with John Rennie and with Alexander Easton, whose daughter he married. While he was working with Rennie in the making of Greenock harbour he got to know the great Thomas Telford, and when Telford, who had prepared the scheme for the improvement of Aberdeen harbour which was authorised by Parliament in 1810, looked around for a resident engineer, his choice fell upon Gibb.

Telford's plan involved the extension of both the North and South Piers by 300 feet—but the extension of the North Pier, which deepened the water in the harbour by 3 feet, was so successful that in 1812 a further 450 feet and in 1813 yet another stretch of 865 feet were sanctioned, the eventual length of the pier being 2,000 feet, which raised the depth of water from 14 to 20 feet. Gibb apparently substituted for the extension of the South Pier a breakwater running from the south shore for 800 feet and reaching to within 250 feet of the opposite pier. Telford seems to have favoured both pier and breakwater but finally adopted his resident engineer's proposal and the breakwater was completed in 1815. There was a good deal of opposition to the whole scheme, and when it was passed by Parliament its promoters gave a dinner, the cost of the ticket being £2 19s. 6d., which would mean at least 12 guineas today, and the principal objector, who did not carry his dislike of the scheme to the extent of avoiding the dinner, did not recover for some months!

After his six years in charge of the harbour reconstruction, John Gibb settled in Aberdeen, although his work, largely in conjunction with Telford, took him all over Scotland. He built, amongst local works, the Buchan Ness lighthouse, and when in 1845 the prospectus of the Great North of Scotland Railway was issued, John Gibb was the engineer. When he died in 1850 he was succeeded as head of the business and in that capacity by his son, Alexander, who in consequence was involved in 1857 quite involuntarily in an amusing action in the Court of Session. Like all the railways radiating outwards from Aberdeen, the G.N.S.R. was Alexander Anderson's child, and when it was well on its way he projected a further line through Buchan, of course with Gibb (who like his father was a director of the North of Scotland Bank) as engineer. One of Anderson's legal rivals, John Duncan, put up opposition plans for another railway through Buchan, and when his project was thrown out in Parliament, he rushed into print with allegations that the promoters of Anderson's Buchan line had only to put their hands into the North Bank's till in order to keep their railway in funds. "Mr. Gibb" ran Duncan's allegation, "is a civil engineer. It is not for his great talent in that line that he was selected for the Formartine and Buchan line; but for his influence as a financier at the North of Scotland Bank board." Four of the Bank's directors, Alexander Gibb being one of them, were awarded £250 damages each against Duncan. The action against him by the Bank itself was settled out of court, Duncan withdrawing his charges and paying the Bank's expenses.

Alexander Gibb served on the Town Council and the Harbour Board and was responsible for many years for the maintenance of the harbour, to which he introduced the first dredger. His father had become proprietor of Rubislaw Quarry and had sent its granite far and wide, to form part of many an edifice, including the Bell Rock lighthouse, Waterloo Bridge, and the terrace wall of the Houses of Parliament. Alexander, who began his career as an apprentice in Telford's office, was responsible for the construction of the new Bridge of Don of which the foundation stone was laid in March 1827, and which was opened in November 1830, the cost being £17,000, compared with about the same building period and ten times that cost which twentieth-century methods and work rules have decreed for the doubling of its width today.

Alexander Gibb married a daughter of William Smith, who ranks with Archibald Simpson in the hierarchy of Aberdeen architects and was responsible for the new Balmoral Castle, the South Church in Aberdeen, the old Girls' High School in Little Belmont Street now incorporated in the re-named Aberdeen Academy, and the steeple on the East Kirk replacing the fine old timber tower destroyed by fire in 1874. By the marriage the family included Easton Gibb, who probably first became prominent in Aberdeen opinion through his prowess as a cricketer. His principal contribution to the welfare of Aberdeen was the construction of the Cairnton reservoir for the city's water supply, which was sanctioned at a public meeting of the ratepayers under the chairmanship of the Provost, Alexander Anderson, in 1861. It may be of interest here to interpolate that in that year the population of Aberdeen was 75,198 and the consumption of water 16 gallons per head, or 1,250,000 gallons daily. The first sod of the lower Mannofield reservoir, on the farm of Braeside of Pitfodels, was cut in 1864, and the sluice at Cairnton was officially opened on 16 October 1866 by Queen Victoria. Three years before Her Majesty had made her first public appearance since her widowhood when on 9 October 1863 she unveiled Baron Marochetti's statue of the Prince Consort, knighted Alexander Anderson in memory of the occasion, and allowed the adjective Royal to be affixed to the title of the Northern Club, whose rooms, then at 1 Union Terrace, where the Northern Assurance Company's offices now are, she used on that day.

To revert for a moment to statistics: The Cairnton supply provided 5,000,000 gallons of water per diem, which was for a time ample, the population in 1871 being 89,554, using about 35 gallons a head or 3,130,000 gallons daily. Baths and indoor sanitation were becoming increasingly popular. By another ten years or so, however, Aberdeen had 133,000 inhabitants and 6,000,000 gallons a day were required so that further storage at Mannofield, Cattofield and Slopefield became necessary. The Cairnton supply is still " the stang o' the trump ", and it is a blessing that the Cairnton scheme should have been adopted, for of the four alternative suggestions of the consultant engineer, James Simpson, one provided for the intake of the supply at Potarch and one at Paradise, on the Don, and of these the latter simply will not bear thinking of!

Some of our readers will no doubt recall the rumpus over the most recent Dee scheme now nearly half a century ago, but in 1866 there were no doubts as to the purity of Dee water, and what in the circumstances was probably more important, there were several poets extant in the city to sing its praises. The opening ceremony was duly celebrated in verse, but we shall restrain our urge to quote after recording one verse from a poem recited in honour of Signorina Josephine, an equestrienne in Quaglieni's Circus (later the Palace Theatre) in Bridge Street, by Wallett, the Queen's Jester:

I gaze into your winning face and see
Truth pure and clear as runs yon river Dee—
Or Cairnton's stream set rushing full and free—
By our lov'd Queen—
(Liquid most excellent for Toddy or for Tea)—
My Josephine.

While the Gibb business as public works contractors greatly expanded under Easton Gibb's control, it was his son Alexander who brought the family upon the national and indeed the world stage. Alexander died as recently as the present year, having been knighted in 1918, like his cousin (son of his father Easton's brother William who remained in Aberdeen to run Rubislaw Quarry), Major-General Sir Ewan Gibb, who had a distinguished career on the Sapper side in the army. Alexander was born in the home of his mother's people at Broughty Ferry in 1872 and was as it were suckled on constructional engineering, for he used to look from his nursery window at the men working on that notorious Tay Bridge which fell so disastrously during the stormy night of 28 December 1879, and of whose security his father Easton, judging with professional insight, had never been satisfied. Born beside Dundee, brought up mostly in Yorkshire, educated at English schools, where his versatility in intellectual pursuits as well as in sport soon revealed itself, Alexander cannot be claimed as an Aberdonian.

Not that we need be too punctilious in that kind of thing; once an Aberdonian always an Aberdonian is a saying that tends to prove itself in practice. Certainly the qualities which the exacting North-East seems to instil into its inhabitants persist in their descendants wherever they are placed, and demonstrate their existence in an independence of character and originality of thought which, while not by any means confined to the people of the North-East corner, are very commonly met with in them. And while many born Aberdonians have made their mark in the wide world, nothing is more fascinating or remarkable in research into family history than the eminence of those who are at one or two removes from their Aberdeen connection. John Marshall, the jurist and Constitution-maker of the United States; Emmanuel Kant, the German philosopher; James Watt, the pioneer in British engineering; Barclay de Tolly, the Russian soldier ; perhaps Mackensen, the German general; Mackenzie King, the Canadian statesman ; Edvard Grieg, the Norwegian composer; van Tromp, the Dutch admiral—these are but a few of the distinguished Aberdonians, slightly " removed ".

Sir Alexander Gibb's career has been recounted by Godfrey Harrison in *Alexander Gibb: The Story of an Engineer,* published by Geoffrey Bles, of which firm, Alexander's second son, Jocelyn, is managing director, the firm of consulting engineers founded by Alexander and known as Sir Alexander Gibb and

Partners being now headed by his elder son Alistair. Alexander, notwithstanding his father's high position, came up the hard way, as pupil first of the celebrated civil engineer, Wolfe Barry, then as a resident engineer at £3 a week, a year or two later in a similar capacity on a section of London's Underground Railway at £300 a year; very soon after that he went back to his father's contracting firm for the building of Kew bridge, and by 1900 he was to all intents and purposes the executive head of Easton Gibb and Son. His biographer has contrived to bring out very suggestively all the conundrums, trials, vicissitudes, shifts and ingenuities of a contractor's life, as well as its hazards and its rewards. Gibb certainly made money, but he had to work for it like a galley slave.

Three of his early contracts were for the constructions of a dock eleven miles from the sea up the Orwell river for Ipswich, with treacherous sand to contend with as well as operations under water; for the building of a loop-line from Newcastle to Gateshead on the London and North-eastern Railway, of which his uncle Sir George Gibb was general manager; and the extension of the Newport Dock in Wales. All these engagements involved considerable problems, to which Gibb brought an original and rather unconventional but perhaps instinctively practical intelligence. He disagreed with authority at Ipswich when he built a cofferdam instead of caissons to accomplish the under-water work; in the Newcastle-Gateshead contract he contrived to tunnel beneath tramlines without disturbing the traffic; while Newport saw various new plant introduced on a job which twice hit back at the contractors, once when a buttress wall against the sea collapsed (as Gibb had dreaded but been unable to get measures taken to satisfy him), with a loss of thirty-nine men, and again when an exceptionally high tide surmounted a protecting dam.

The Newport battle, for such it was, led to the firm's securing the contract for the great new Rosyth Dockyard, covering 1,200 acres with 2½ miles of waterfront, in 1909. Here, again, Gibb's sense of engineering propriety came into conflict with official reaction or convention at the Admiralty, and again he carried the day. It is a pity that his biographer does little more than mention these many struggles with red-tape and hidebound officialdom. The reticence in regard to anything that affects the State's services, which is deemed nowadays to be seemly, results in each generation of the State's servants getting away with more mistakes and injustices, until today the greatest handicap the nation has to bear is the frustration caused by departmental ignorance, prejudice, and power. The dockyard was completed in 1916, but it is typical of official delays and pettifogging huckstering that he was not paid until 1922 after long dispute and arbitration by the Director of Works at the Admiralty, who " was not even moderately courteous to Gibb's representatives ", when judging a case in which he actually was the defendant!

Rosyth finished, Gibb went to the war with another " Aberdonian ", Eric Geddes, and when the war was over he served at the Ministry of Transport until 1921. He then set up as a consulting civil engineer, expanding within a year into the firm of Sir Alexander Gibb and Partners, in Queen Anne's Lodge, Westminster, which in other days had been the home of a succession of great engineers. Of the many world-famous schemes with which Sir Alexander was connected it is unnecessary here to write, but as exemplifying his versatility it may be mentioned that he was chairman of the Fine Arts Commission, Hon. President of the Burns Federation, Fellow of the Zoological Society, member of Cambridge University Appointments Board, Junior Grand Warden of the Grand Lodge of Scotland, member of the Royal Clyde Yacht Club, author of the biography of the greatest engineer of them all, *The Story of Telford,* and that he even presided at a Synod meeting of the Church of Scotland. Winston Churchill once gave an order to one of Gibb's workmen: " Gibb's ma maister. A tak' orders frae him," was the conclusive retort.

David Anderson

Davie do a'thing and his relatives and contemporaries

THE study of history is like keeping a cat: it preserves one's sense of proportion. Surrounded by dogs, men are tempted to regard themselves as superior beings, whereas one cat supplies the corrective to inordinate self-esteem. Absorption in the life of one's own generation tends to foster the belief that never has life been so wonderful or men so clever, but a knowledge of the past soon dissipates all illusions on that score.

We are very proud of ourselves in Aberdeen today and no doubt not without cause. But great men lived before Agamemnon, and the records of this city disclose several periods during which Aberdeen was very much in the forefront of the civilised world's attention and esteem. Never, however, in all its 800 years of recorded history has it attained to a higher eminence or boasted a richer body of great sons than in the years from 1590 to 1625. The long ruling family of Menzies was dying out, and its place was taken, not so much in civic politics as in intellectual ascendancy, by a brilliant coterie of which the central figure, and the source from which most of them derived, was David Anderson of Finzeauch, otherwise known to fame as "Davie do a'thing".

David Anderson belonged to a Donside family a branch of which at one time owned Candacraig. His own particular pendicle was Finzeauch in Keig parish, but like many another county laird he was associated with Aberdeen's trade and was a burgess of the burgh. We have reason to surmise that the family's connection with Aberdeen was an ancient one, that the Andersons in fact belonged to " the auld bluid o' the toun " ; certainly the patronymic is one of the most common in the North-east to this day.

There was a Baillie David Anderson, " one of the principall men " of the burgh, and " maister of Sanct Nicholace wark " (i.e. in charge of the building and repair of the toun's kirk) at the beginning of the sixteenth century. In 1527 he was master of the pier-work of the harbour, in 1529 on rumour of war he was one of the chief consultants who prepared a scheme of defence for the burgh, and the same year he was one of a trio in charge of the building of the Bridge of Dee. Another David Anderson was master of kirk work at the end of the century, and he may have been grandfather, uncle or cousin of the great David. The latter's father's name was Gilbert, and he must have had a fair share of brains, for he was also father of Alexander Anderson, Professor of Mathematics in Paris, of whom Sir Thomas Urquhart, in the course of a long and characteristic panegyric, says " he was excellently well skilled in the theory of the planets, and astronomy ; the optics, catoptricks, dioptricks ; the orthographical, stereographical, schenographical projections ; in cosmography, geography, trigonometry, and geodesie ; in the staticks, music and all other parts and pendicles, sciences, faculties or arts of or belonging to the disciplines mathematical in general, or any portions thereof in its essence or dependencies ". This would indicate that Sir Thomas, or Alexander Anderson, was a Department of Education in himself, and either would have made a valuable member of the Chamber's education committee.

" Having a body too weak to sustain the vehement intensiveness of so high a spirit, he died young ", Sir Thomas goes on to say. David likewise died in his prime in 1619, and the short life seems to have recurred in some of his noteworthy descendants, particularly his grandson the first and great James Gregory, the inventor of the reflecting telescope, who died of a cerebral haemorrhage which struck him in the midst of a lecture at the age of thirty-six. But these men, despite all the difficulties of travel and the lack of what we today regard as essential conveniences of life, contrived to do a very great deal in a comparatively short time. Of the contrast between the methods of their day and ours, David Anderson's principal achievement—or at least the principal one that has come down to us—supplies a striking example.

The early years of the seventeenth century, about the time of the Union of the Crowns, were like ours a formative period in the development of commerce and of the city. Ships were getting larger, cargoes bigger and more varied, the pulse of international trade faster. Aberdeen was then the principal port of Scotland, but its harbour, which was more or less the estuary of the Dee, could not accept any but ships of shallow draught because, although the channel was quite deep enough for contemporary shipping farther up the estuary, a big boulder called Craig Metellan or the Maitland Rock lay in the very middle of the fairway and blocked the passage. It was imperative that this rock be removed if Aberdeen's trade was to be preserved, much less expanded. The Town Council offered a fee of 300 merks, about sixteen guineas sterling value, for the shifting of Craig Metellan.

Davie do a'thing undertook the task, having closely observed the problem. Whether he was the originator of the method he employed, which became fairly common practice about then or shortly after, we do not know ; but we have to remember that Aberdeen was then frequented by mariners and merchants from the Baltic and the German Hanse ports, from the Low Countries and Bordeaux and the Mediterranean, and that therefore David's feat would be widely recounted in Europe and the expedient he employed would soon become known elsewhere. At all events having measured the rise and fall of the tide, fifteen feet at the springs and ten at the neaps, he attached a number of empty barrels by stout ropes to the rock at low water, and when the tide rose the barrels by their buoyancy lifted the great stone and carried it up channel, where it was steered to the bank and got out of the way. Aberdeen's greatest historian says David seated himself on one of the barrels and sailed up the estuary with the rock. If not true, this addendum deserves to be, as would be the further picture of the banks lined with cheering spectators.

So was Aberdeen's harbour modernised in 1610 at a cost of sixteen guineas by the use of sheer brains and very little else. Two hundred years later, when the harbour was again modernised, the cost of that part of Thomas Telford's scheme which was adopted was £80,000. Today the smallest improvement costs about the Telford figure, and a complete overhaul of the harbour, after a delay of a year or two while awaiting Treasury sanction and of at least as much to allow of the job to be done, would cost the best part of a million pounds. Davie took about an hour! If it should be objected that he did not do so much, it may be pointed out that he did all that was necessary, which is about as certain a yardstick of achievement as can be imagined.

Self portrait of George Jamesone

No doubt it was David Anderson who was mainly responsible for the construction about the same time of the Bulwark, or breakwater, to protect the mouth of the Dee. He had much to do as a baillie and Dean of Guild—local government officials then, fortunately or unfortunately, being conspicuous by their absence—with various undertakings considered desirable by the council. He was responsible for the sundial on the wall of the Tolbooth, he made " ane orloge " or clock for the " common clerkis chalmer ", he designed a steeple for St. Nicholas Kirk, and he probably had the oversight, on behalf of the Council, of the construction of a new twin-arched Bow Brig over the Denburn for which the contractor was his own brother-in-law, Andrew Jamesone, who rebuilt the Brig o' Balgownie and was also father of " the Scottish Vandyck ", George Jamesone.

While Davie do a'thing was the finest flower of his family, and himself assisted, as we shall see, to transmit its remarkable intellectual qualities, it is evident that the Anderson genius was conveyed in other channels as well. His sister Marjory was the wife of Andrew Jamesone and by him the mother of the great George. He deserves to be regarded as the Father of Scottish Art, just as that other ancient Aberdonian, John Barbour is accepted as the Father of Scottish letters. We are sadly lacking in the arts of self-advertisement in the North-east. Who today would believe that families within our bounds have produced the premier baronet, the premier baron, the premier earl and the premier marquis of Scotland? Who realises that it was Aberdeen that opened up originally Scotland's overseas trade and that until long after the Union of the Crowns our chief export was men who themselves or in their progeny materially influenced the development of civilisation in war, in politics, in philosophy, in law, in finance, music, commerce and literature? Someday someone may tell the thrilling story of the wandering Aberdonian.

George Jamesone, after being educated as a good son of a worthy burgess, is said to have gone to the Low Countries, where Aberdonians were almost as common as Flemings, to study art at Antwerp. There he was the pupil of the great Rubens and fellow-student of the successful portrait painter Vandyck. Before going on his travels Jamesone painted portraits of several eminent Aberdonians, including his uncle Davie do a'thing, and after he came home he had his studio in his house on the Schoolhill, just east of where Harriet Street now stands. Jamesone's house was pulled down about three-quarters of a century ago, during one of those spasms of vandalism which occasionally afflict Aberdeen Town Council, and during another of which the lovely old Greyfriars Kirk was desecrated by a face-lifting operation. Jamesone in 1633 was in Edinburgh for the Scottish coronation of Charles I, and received a commission to execute a portrait of the king. This was subsequent to his old friend Vandyck's famous full-length of Charles and his family (1632) and before the finest of the latter's efforts, the National Gallery portrait of the king done some years afterwards. Jamesone's patron was one of the Campbells of Breadalbane, for whom he did a long series of paintings that hung (perhaps still hang) in Taymouth Castle. In his prosperity Jamesone built a canopy to protect the famous Well of Spa, and feued from the town an adjacent piece of land called the Playfield, where the Incorporated Trades had been wont to stage their plays. He turned the space into a semi-public pleasance which came to be known as the "Four Neukit Garden". The old Infirmary buildings and grounds now cover it.

George Jamesone died wealthy and honoured in 1644, in Edinburgh, and was buried in Greyfriars Kirkyard. Of his family, his daughter Mary is the only one to be remembered now, for she it was who did the fine tapestries that hang in the West Kirk today and are, with her father's portraits, and the oak stalls at King's College Chapel, the armorial roof of St. Machar's Cathedral, and the early printed books of Edward Raban, the evidence now remaining to us of the intellectual and artistic distinction of the old burgh.

Coeval with David Anderson and George Jamesone there were several other illustrious Aberdonians, who were not related to the Anderson family but whose transcendant abilities show that the town in those days could boast of citizens of international repute. There was George Keith, the fifth Earl Marischal, and of all that line the most distinguished until the last Earl, also a George, was attainted after the 1715 rebellion. George Keith was a scholar of repute, pupil of the great Theodore Beza at Genoa. He was the wealthiest noble in the land, and having gone to Denmark to procure a bride for James VI, he provided the money for his mission and was never repaid, any more than was Aberdeen Town Council for the powder it lent James to capture old Slains Castle.

Of all the noble families associated with Aberdeen, the Earl Marischal's was the only one that gave the burgh something in return for what they took out. In 1593 the Earl founded Marischal College and presented it to the town. It is interesting to recall that as a young man, doing the Grand Tour of the Continent, he stayed with the Landgrave of Hesse, and the two nobles toasted one another as the respective heads, in Scotland and Germany, of the family that traced its origins to that Hermann or Arminius who annihilated the legions of Augustus Caesar under Varro. The fifth Earl died in 1623.

Another important Aberdeen figure was Arthur Johnston (1587-1641), born at Caskieben (now Keith Hall) and educated at Kintore School and King's College, of which he became rector ; physician to Charles I, and (unlike doctors nowadays) an elegant poet who translated the Psalms into Latin verse and wrote other Latin poetry which entitled him to be regarded as George Buchanan's successor as the leading humanist of his day. Another Aberdeen Latinist was Thomas Reid, who was one of the secretaries of James VI and I, who borrowed from St. Paul's Cathedral library certain volumes which he passed on to Reid and both (after the fashion of borrowers in all ages) forgot to send them back. Instead, five of them found their way to King's College, Aberdeen, which thus today owns the sole relics (with one exception) of the old St. Paul's library to survive the Great Fire of 1666.

Amongst the practitioners of medicine the outstanding name is that of Duncan Liddell (1561-1613), graduate of the Grammar School and King's College, a professor in a German university, physician to the Court of Brunswick, and author of many medical and mathematical works. He bought the estate of Pitmedden on the Don, in whose haughs stands a monument to him, and he conveyed the lands to help poor students in Aberdeen and his other wealth to found a Chair of Mathematics at Marischal College. There is a brass of him in the West Kirk and a benefaction annually recalls his name in Aberdeen University.

There were many more great Aberdonians at that time but we must return to our Andersons. Davie himself was married to Jean Guild, sister of the munificent benefactor of the Incorporated Trades, Dr. William Guild, who requires an essay to himself. David and his wife had amongst other family a daughter Jane, who married the Rev. John Gregory of Drumoak, and became the mother of James Gregory the mathematician and thus matriarch of the most fabulous academic family of all time, who also will require an article to themselves. Here it may be mentioned, however, that James Gregory married his kinswoman Mary Jamesone already mentioned, thus reinforcing the Anderson blood in the pedigree of his family and perhaps—who knows?—by this device of in-breeding well known in the animal world, imparting to his line the impetus which carried its remarkable genius on for 200 years.

Aberdeen Harbour in the days of Davie do a'thing

Sir James Taggart

Aberdeen's *most popular Lord Provost*

THOSE who remember Sir James Taggart in his prime will have difficulty in persuading themselves that he was born at the end of " the hungry Forties "—for contrary to history, in Aberdeen at least the years after the Repeal of the Corn Laws were leaner than those that preceded it—that Sir Robert Peel and the Duke of Wellington were both alive when he first saw the light, and that he was close on his tenth birthday when Alexander Anderson took his seat in the Lord Provost's chair. But so it was. He was a youth during the great transition period when the trains began to run south, north and north-west from Aberdeen, when the first steamboats were challenging the early clippers, and when many of the city's great enterprises were taking shape, while others like Leys, Masson & Co.'s famous factory at Grandholm were on their last legs.

He was a Donside loon, born on a croft at Coldwells, near Inverurie, overlooking a bend of the Don where the river makes a right-angled turn to the west, and its waters, on propitious summer evenings, slip into vision out of sunsets breath-taking in their loveliness. His birth-date was 6 December 1849 and when his father died six years later, he had to assist his mother to keep the croft going, and no doubt did not trouble his head very much about schooling at Inverurie, a couple of miles away. One cannot but be fascinated by the change in our habits in respect of education. It would be shocking to the public conscience, let alone a grave misdemeanour, for a parent to be so lost to responsibility as not to send his children regularly to school; probably James Taggart when he was grown up and famous saw no reason for not blessing his mother for failing to shoe him again for school. Two of the best educated men we have known, and successful in their lives, had less than three years' schooling before they were thrown on the world and their own resources. But James Taggart, when he elected to be a mason and came to Aberdeen to serve his apprenticeship, attended the Mechanics' Institute in Market Street, where many an Aberdonian eminent in those days got a solid grounding in good substantial knowledge.

He was apprenticed to Birnie and Stewart, in Crimon Place, and later went to Legge's yard as a sculptor, after which for a short time he was in U.S.A., whither many a score of Aberdeen and Aberdeenshire granite-workers migrated in those days. But he was back in Aberdeen in 1879 in partnership with a John Macgregor, and in 1883 he started on his own at 92 Great Western Road, where he built up the fine business which, now in other hands, still flourishes. If ever a man resembled the material in which he worked, it was James Taggart. That strong, sharp, eagle face seemed to have been chipped and carved out of granite. His portrait by Ambrose McEvoy in the Art Gallery, however, while it conveys something of the granite quality of the features, fails to reproduce that animation which lighted them up when, as so often happened, the Provost was making or enjoying a joke or a duel of wits.

In 1899 he entered the Town Council, defeating the sitting member in Ruthrieston Ward. There were no "politics" in those days, and the issue of a contest depended upon brains and character. In 1901 he became sixth baillie, in 1902 under Lord Provost James Walker he was senior magistrate, in 1905 he took the first of his many convenerships, that of the Tramways Committee. When in November 1914 he was raised to the civic chair, he had intimate experience of all facets of municipal activity. The autumn of 1914 was the days when heaven was falling. The public were dispirited by the heavy losses in the early battles of the war, everything seemed to be going wrong, a nation accustomed to liberty and personal freedom unknown elsewhere was beginning to find the harness of wartime restrictions more than a little irksome. At the same time, a dour courage was taking the place of the "March on to Berlin" light-heartedness of August 1914, and the horrors of the Somme and of Passchendaele were hidden in the future.

In such an atmosphere Taggart was in his element. He was always ready—indeed rough and ready—with a heartening speech, a timely joke, a reminder of what Scotsmen were traditionally capable of in an emergency. Such gay elevation of mind over untoward circumstances is a wonderful asset in an emergency, and Aberdeen has reason to be grateful to the Fates who have bestowed upon her in two great wars two laughing philosophers like James Taggart and Thomas Mitchell. The great need when the former became Lord Provost was for keen young volunteers for the services, and the brigade of artillery which was raised in Aberdeen in those early months was known throughout the war as Taggart's Own in tribute to the incomparable recruiting officer who raised the unit. "The Provost" and "lang Jimmy Smith" of St. George's in the West were kenspeckle warriors on the streets of Aberdeen in those days, doughty characters both and neither likely to be mistaken for anyone else or to feel the need of imitating anyone else. During his Provostship, which was extended by another term to 1920 so that it terminated almost coincidentally with the official ends of the various wars we had had on our hands since 1914, Sir James was described as "the most popular Lord Provost the city ever had", and when he received the K.B.E. in 1918 the whole town rejoiced.

On retiring from office and the Council Sir James continued his public work in many directions. He had been raising funds to build a new Sick Children's Hospital where it now stands, then known as Burnside. He was president or chairman or member of public and private bodies, industrial, charitable and social, too numerous to catalogue, though we may mention, besides his own Granite Association, such diverse societies as the Scottish Cyclists' Union, the Aberdeen Burns Club and the Home for Widowers' Children. He was laureated LL.D. by the University in 1919. His efforts to raise money for what was in those days abbreviated into "the Sick Kids" provided the material for one of the most characteristic samples of his quick irresistible wit.

Looking around for possible subscribers on a large scale, he naturally fixed his eye upon the first Lord Cowdray, who even then had proved himself a good friend to Aberdeen although the full extent of his eventual generosity to the city could hardly have been guessed at. So to Dunecht House set off the Lord Provost, and being known to the butler had himself announced at the door of Lord Cowdray's study. The opening civilities having been disposed of his lordship told Sir James that he wished he would call oftener as the friend he would like him to be, and not as on this occasion when he no doubt was wanting something. And Lord Cowdray proceeded to ask somewhat testily what that something was. Quite unabashed by this unconventional reception, the Provost told his story. "And how much do you want from me?" demanded his lordship. Only lips moved in the block of granite facing him as the instant reply shot out, "How much have ye got?" As the episode was related, Lord Cowdray reached over for his cheque book, wrote out a substantial donation (we forget what it was), rang the bell and ordered the footman to bring in a bottle of champagne.

In the twenties, and after he retired from local politics, Sir James achieved what almost amounted to notoriety by reason of his story-telling contests with the Marquis of Aberdeen and Temair. If the truth be admitted, neither exponent of a great art, now very much in decline, was at his best in these duels. The very fact that they were duels deprived the anecdotes of spontaneity, and the telling of stories in any case is not for the public platform but for the select company of friends. Even with these handicaps, however, the two protagonists succeeded from time to time in producing a good one, but in Sir James's case even his best stories were never quite so memorable as his own witty remarks. In any case, it has to be recorded that neither he nor Lord Aberdeen could in respect of anecdotage have competed, for the real Scottish stuff, with Charles Murray or Dr. J. F. Tocher, or in the empyrean realms with Dr. David Rorie or Sir Alexander Gray. All four, however—and only the last, alas! is still alive—maintained their light, as it were, under a bushel and shunned the glare of publicity.

But in what the late Professor Sanford Terry, endeavouring to score a little point at the expense of a colleague, described as "what I have no doubt are his very wise and witty remarks", Taggart had few equals. Once in proposing a vote of thanks to a transatlantic lecturer in the Mitchell Hall whose English had the nasal ring and the nutty flavour that one associates with the log cabins of Tennessee or the blue grass of Kentucky, the Provost, speaking in pretty broad Doric, remarked that the British and the Americans were bound to get on well, "seein' we baith speak the same wye". On another occasion he found himself in pursuance of his civic duties upon a temperance platform listening to a dissertation upon the evils of alcohol. Proposing the vote of thanks to the speaker, the Lord Provost said the speech had disabused him of one misconception. "The speaker told us that alcohol is really sugar, and that the average human body requires an ounce of sugar a day, and I minded there's saxteen drams to the ounce."

Another story of him he used to tell against himself. One of his devices for raising money for some charitable project was to ask people to give him their empty bottles, which at the end of the first, as of the second, Great War commanded a certain fee. Twa wifies, so his story ran, passing along Great Western Road by his residence, Ashley Lodge, were struck by the huge pyramid of empty bottles reared against the gable. Neither knowing the reason of the hooick, one wifie said (according to Sir James) to the other, "Mercy be here, I'd aye heard the Provost liket a dram but I never kent he wis sic a drooth as that". Perhaps the most dramatic of his interventions was when Douglas Haig was made a Freeman of the City at the end of the first war. Haig had in the morning been laureated LL.D. by the University, along with Sir Roger Keyes, the dare-devil leader of the Dover Patrol, who when a young officer commanding a destroyer took his ship up the canal to Aintree so that his crew could see the Grand National. When Sir Douglas Haig went forward to sign the Burgess Roll, Keyes, who did realise the significance of the signature, moved forward behind him, only to be restrained by the Provost's muscular arm, and the admonition, "Nae you; we've got to draw the line some wye!"

In those now dim and distant years we once found ourselves in Dundee addressing in that celebrated city the Aberdeen, Banff and Kincardine Association. Some little time before,

Sir James had performed the same task of bringing manna from home to the exiles. We were told he began his address by saying that although he had often passed through Dundee in the train, he had never until that day set foot in it. "And noo I've seen the place, Gweed kens fit wye you Aiberdeen fowk can bide in't." That, although to a great extent a libel upon a respectable city, and a rather unusual way of expressing the Aberdonian's reaction to all other towns, also very sincerely revealed his great love for "Aiberdeen awa". Although, apart from his raising of Taggart's Own and his collection of the funds for the new hospital for sick children, there was nothing spectacular in his service to the city, it was nevertheless a very real service in practically all departments of civic activity, for in his convenerships he was painstaking, thorough, and progressive, and he had the gift of leadership.

Rev Dr William Guild

perpetual patron of the seven incorporated trades

No doubt most knowledgeable Aberdonians, if asked to name some one who had been an outstanding benefactor of the city, would name Dr. William Guild, if not at first go, certainly as one of those who by their filial generosity deserve to be remembered. And indeed he was a very good friend to the city, for apart from his historic gift to the Incorporated Trades, he was liberal to the University and to the poor of Aberdeen. Yet he is a most evasive personality when one tries to lay hold of the skirts of his ghostly robes. There is no difficulty in recapturing the essence of his brother-in-law, Davie do a'thing, but William Guild eludes analysis—though he is not like Shakespeare, "out-topping knowledge".

Joseph Robertson indeed, who of all Aberdeen historians was the most erudite, despite religious prejudices that almost equalled those of the city's first annalist, John Spalding, dismissed Guild far too cavalierly. "A vain, weak man, with no constancy of principle, a writer of many volumes of little note, and indebted to his wealth and ostentatious charity for a reputation which neither his learning nor talents would have gained." This was going rather far, as will perhaps transpire from this essay, and it is surprising that Robertson, who was an ardent Episcopalian, should have been so caustic on this occasion, for Guild, had he been alive today, would have been side by side with the Iona Community's leader in the campaign for a merger of the Church of Scotland with the Church of England.

William Guild was born at Aberdeen in 1586, son of Matthew Guild a sweird-slipper or armourer who is described as a "worthy deacon" of the Hammermen craft, and who for a fleeting instant appears in history when on 14 May 1565 he and some of his friends were convicted and imprisoned in the tolbooth for " coming through the town with a minstrel playing before them through the Gallowgate" the previous Sunday afternoon in defiance of the burgh regulations and of sundry acts of Parliament. It is, by the way, rather interesting that the Act which they broke was passed in 1555, before the Reformers gained the ascendancy, and prohibited the presentation of the plays and pageants so beloved of the people then, in which Robin Hood, Little John, the Abbot of Unreason, the Queen of the May and other dignitaries were portrayed in Aberdeen by the crafts in the Fowr-Neukit Field at the Woolmanhill upon which the old Infirmary Buildings now stand.

The Guilds seem to have been a fairly tough family. Two years before our William was born, a brother, also William, had been slain in a brawl by a burgess named John Leslie. Then in 1604 one Robert Guild, alleged to have been a younger brother, was convicted of murdering Alexander Blair, the capital sentence being "his heid to be taken off, and his richt hand, quhilk committed the said slaughter and big knife put thairin and set on the Tolbooth in example to others in tym to cum". These family extravagances may have been the first inducements towards charity which affected the great Patron of the Trades.

He himself was one of the early students at the recently founded Marischal College, and applied himself to Divinity. In 1608, at the age of 22, a bit late for those days, he was appointed Minister of King-Edward, where one of his younger parishioners would have been Sir Thomas Urquhart of Cromartie, then residing at the family mansion of Craigston. It may be doubted if they would have understood each other, for although they were both all their lives what were called King's men, the great translator of Rabelais was a wayward genius in thought and word, to whom the prosaic and conventional talents of the parish minister might, even in those early years, have been uncongenial.

The year Guild went to King-Edward he published his first tract, resoundingly entitled "The New Sacrifice of Christian Incense; or The True Entry to the Tree of Life, and Gracious Gate of Glorious Paradise". It was published in London, and dedicated with true Aberdonian comprehensiveness to the Prince of Wales, that Prince Henry whose untimely death is so deeply mourned by historians who think he would have made a better King than his brother; to Charles Duke of York, later Charles I, and to the Princess Elizabeth, the much sung Winter Queen whose misfortunes were in no long time to be the talk of Europe. "The New Sacrifice" was the first of Guild's many writings, all of them evangelical or polemical and all in theology, then the most popular of subjects. Thirteen of his works were printed by Edward Raban, Aberdeen's own printer, but many more issued from London, though probably printed nearer home.

No one who has not felt impelled to seek solace in Dr. Guild's writings is in a position to assess the value or discuss the comparative merits of what he wrote. He was not one of the celebrated Aberdeen Doctors whose doctrinal disputes with some of the Covenanting enthusiasts enlivened the days before the sword took the place of the pen in the Great Civil War. He never wrote anything so moving and enduring as Henry Scougal's "The Life of God in the Soul of Man", Scougal being an Aberdonian by virtue of his father's tenure of the bishopric of Aberdeen. Duncan Liddel in medicine, John Barclay in philosophy, Arthur Johnston in Latin verse, Thomas Dempster in philology, Sir John Skene in law, these and several others of his Aberdeen contemporaries were much more eminent in authorship than he. His best effort, which went through several editions, was "The Harmony of all the Prophets" usually printed along with his most popular production of somewhat the same tenour entitled "Moses Unveiled". A denunciation of salmon fishing on the Sabbath during kirk-time is described by Kellas Johnstone, Aberdeen's most exhaustive bibliographer, as the first of its kind.

Guild did not, however, trust solely to his pen for advancement. Having married a daughter of James Rolland of Disblair, a substantial burgess, he began, although still no more than minister of a remote parish, to take a prominent part in Church affairs, so much so that when in 1617 the Bishop of Ely, Dr. Lancelot Andrewes, came to Scotland to explore the possibilities of approximating the Church of Scotland more nearly to the Anglican system, which James I wished to extend over all his possessions, Guild was one of the men with whom the visiting prelate conferred, and one of the few with whom he became friendly. A liturgy of Scotland was decided upon and prepared at an Assembly held at Aberdeen and no doubt Guild was not remiss in pressing forward the idea. Otherwise the scheme collapsed, but Guild dedicated "Moses Unveiled" to Andrewes, who incidentally was a very esteemed man and on his death won the guerdon of a sonnet by John Milton, who was not over-fond of bishops. Another of Guild's influential friends was Dr. John Young, Dean of Winchester and a native of Arbroath, whose father was King James's librarian and through whom the minister of King-Edward got into the good graces of royalty.

In 1631 Guild became one of the Ministers of Aberdeen itself, but he had never allowed his intimacy with his native burgh to lapse, and in 1623 he had bought a house in the Broadgate and given it to the Town Council so that the gateway to Marischal College might be enlarged. Those who can recall the modest pend which formed the entry to the College at the beginning of this century may feel inclined to think that it could not have been a very big house. Although the late Sir Robert Rait, Historiographer-Royal of Scotland, says the gateway lasted until 1893 we think it was still in existence ten years later.

Guild's career in Aberdeen was destined to be chequered. In 1683 the first of the Bishops' Wars was blowing up and Scotland's reactions to King Charles's attempts to impose episcopacy at English strength upon the country was being opposed everywhere save in Aberdeen. The National League and Covenant, based upon the Negative Confession of Faith signed by King James in 1581, was drawn up and subscribed throughout the country. In Aberdeen Guild and another minister would only sign with reservations, and their scruples were accepted by the Covenanting Commissioners. Almost at once Guild found himself in Glasgow at the famous General Assembly which abolished the Scottish Bishops. Quite possibly he allowed himself to be swayed by the majority for on his return he deemed it wise to take a holiday in Holland, after which he published an appeal for something like Gandhi's philosophy of non-violence, but without Gandhi's idea of resistance.

And then in 1640, the General Assembly having deposed the Principal and other officials of King's College because they were royalists and episcopalians, what does Dr. Guild do but accept an invitation to take the vacant principalship, simultaneously subscribing the Covenant without any reservations whatever. Why he should have taken a step so little in accord with the logic of his previous attitude has never been explained and probably cannot be explained except in terms of Joseph Robertson's contemptuous verdict. Even so, it brought no assurance to Guild, for in 1649 he was deposed along with several of his colleagues by an Assembly Commission of Inquiry, apparently because he was still too much of a royalist. The Commissioners, however, were unable to agree on a successor and reinstated him. Two years later he was finally ejected by a Cromwellian Commission which included the notorious Colonel Desborough. He failed to regain his post as one of Aberdeen's ministers, and retired into a private and no doubt studious existence, dying on 9 August 1657, and being buried in St. Nicholas Kirkyard where his monument, erected by his wife and restored by the Incorporated Trades, is conspicuous.

In 1631 Guild purchased the monastery and chapel of the Trinity Friars, which had been wrecked at the Reformation. The property stood at what was then the west end of the Shiprow, now the south-east angle between Market Street and Guild Street, where until a few decades ago the Alhambra Music Hall was. Guild's intention, which he carried through, was to found a hospital and erect a meeting-house of the Incorporated Trades: he raised contributions from the trades themselves, from the Town Council, and from private citizens; and for over a century the Trades used the old chapel for a place of worship, while the hospital, with its quota of bedesmen, persisted until about the time that Union Street began to be built—1803, to be precise. The old Trades Hall was doomed when the railway mania came on. The first proposals for Aberdeen's railway station located it approximately where Hadden Street, Exchange Street and

Stirling Street now are. The Incorporated Trades felt it imperative to move, our modern Tarnty Ha' was built at the south-east end of

Gateway of old Trades Hall

Union Bridge, and the last of the old buildings disappeared in 1857, to the skittish strains of a song by Deacon Robb:

Nae mair the cheerfu' sang amusin'
Will re-echo through those wa's;
Nae mair the bursts of elocution
Bring down thunders o' applause.
My heart is sad when I consider,
Ere anither year or twa
That nae ae stane upon anither
Will be left o' a' this ha'.

But whare's the use o' waefu' skirlin',
Lat us a' be happy yet,
Altho' rail trains will soon be dirlin'
O'er the spot whare now we sit.
O never lat us be down-hearted,
Let us drive dull care awa',
Nor think our glory is departed
When we leave our ancient ha'.

John Spalding the historian reserved some of the most vitriolic expressions of his splenetic, exaggerated and wholly charming records of the Troubles in Aberdeen for Dr. William Guild.

> He dang down the walls of the Snow Kirk to big the College dykes. Now he is demolishing the Bishop's house, pitiful and lamentable to behold; kirks and stately buildings first casten down by ruffians and rascals, and next by churchmen under colour of religion. . . . Dr. Guild at his own hand cause break down the great oaken joists within the bishop's house, and transported them therefrae for reparation of the college. Pitiful to see so glorious a building thus thrown down by despiteful soldiers, and then demolished by Doctors of Divinity.

Apart from the fact that the bishop's house happened to be Guild's own personal property his actions in Old Aberdeen were similar to the ideas which guided him in his dealings with the Incorporated Trades. He used old and decaying and superseded material within his ownership and jurisdiction to rebuild or to found more modern institutions and enterprises. His acts of spoilation in the Aulton gave a fresh start to King's College, of which he was a progressive principal. Yet because he liked to sit on the ideological fence, he gained in his own time a reputation for weakness and duplicity that his fame has never quite lost!

Archibald Simpson
architect in granite

FAMILIARITY tends to breed forgetfulness. We, as we traverse the streets of our city, seeing without observing the buildings around us, are inclined to take them for granted, almost as if they were phenomena of nature. But there are brains and skill behind them all, and sometimes there is also art. The art may be the product of talent, or it may be born of genius. No one responsible to any considerable degree for the building of Aberdeen is more generally conceded, by those competent to judge, to have possessed something of the divine spark of genius than Archibald Simpson. If to Alexander Anderson we owe our modern Aberdeen as a civic entity, to Archibald Simpson more than to any other architect that city has been indebted for the variety of its fine building and for much of the spaciousness of its layout.

When medieval Aberdeen was taking shape, the directing brains behind the planning of buildings and communities were those of churchmen. Times have indeed changed, for today all the forces of authority crack down upon any member of the clergy (except perhaps a dignitary of the Church of England) if he dare to express an opinion upon a subject that is not theological or ecclesiastical. The first Aberdeen clergyman whom we know to have taken a practical formative part in the building of the city was Alexander Galloway, the parson of Kinkell, to whom both Bishop Elphinstone and Bishop Dunbar entrusted the supervision of the completion of St. Machar's Cathedral and the construction of King's College, the Snow Church (now demolished), the Bridge of Dee and Greyfriars Kirk (no longer like the original of the fifteenth century).

With a record such as his, it is almost impossible for Galloway not to have been a draughtsman and designer of a calibre sufficient to qualify him for description as an architect. But by and large in medieval and early modern Aberdeen there was not much building in stone to be done at any given time; the "St. Nicholas wark" or construction of the town's church, took generations. The result was that for quite a long time indeed until stone houses became fairly common after (though not because of) the Union of the Parliaments in 1707, a good master mason was quite capable of initiating and seeing through a whole building job. The second edition of the Tolbooth, of which a part still guards the southern entrance to Lodge Walk, and the Market Cross were both the work of master masons, both located at Auld Rayne, the former about the beginning and the latter about the end of the seventeenth century.

Although Aberdeen began to cross the Denburn about the same time, it was not until the great period of expansion opened in 1800 with the Union Street and King Street projects that there was much scope for the architectural profession in Aberdeen: but of course we must not forget James Gibbs, who was responsible for the original part of Gordon's College and the new building of the West Kirk; James Burn, for the now defunct Bridewell in Rose Street and the office of the Aberdeen Bank (now Bank of Scotland incorporating the Union) at the top of Marischal Street; and Charles Beveridge, who designed the old Grammar School in the Schoolhill. Needless to say, there were others, but the three practitioners mentioned are sufficient to indicate that the city was not without its artists in stone before Archibald Simpson commenced his all-too-short career.

Nor was he alone amongst his contemporaries. Greatest of them, and greatest of all Aberdeen architects in the opinion of critics and of his own profession, he undoubtedly proved himself to be. But we need only mention John Smith, who "did" the old Crimonmogate House, until recently the home of the Royal Northern Club, the South Parish Church in Belmont Street, only recently superseded, the improvements to Galloway's Bridge of Dee in 1841-2; the St. Nicholas façade on the Union Street frontage of the burgh kirkyard; the two wings added to Gordon's College in 1834; and many other monuments to his high talent, even including (if one looks at it the right way) Balmoral Castle. A little later than Smith, came a pupil and friend of the subject of our sketch, James Matthews, Lord Provost from 1883 to 1885 (another architect, William Leslie, to whom Dunrobin Castle is due, having preceded him in the civic chair 1869-73), whose eventual partnership with the late A. Marshall Mackenzie, creator of the beautiful frontage of Marischal College, links the old school of the profession with the new. Matthews was responsible for the Grammar School in Skene Street, what is now Christ's College at Babbie Law, the West Church of St. Andrew, the Palace Hotel block destroyed by fire during the last war, the St. Nicholas branch of the Clydesdale and North Bank, at one time the head office of the Town and County Bank, and many country houses. He was perhaps rather more inclined to the ornate and to massive effect than his master.

Archibald Simpson came of good Aberdonian stock. His father was a merchant of standing in the town, while his mother belonged to a family hailing from Deeside named Dauney, one of whom was a professor and another edited one of the earliest of Scotland's collections of folk-music, the Skene MSS. of about 1620. It is probably worthy of record now that the Guestrow, or what little remains of it, is doomed, that the chief begetter of modern Aberdeen was born there, at No. 15. His birth-date was 4 May 1790, at which time the burgh had scarcely dared to overspill its walls, and its beauty, wealth and fashion dwelt in the comparatively confined and congested areas that are today being gutted and transformed into boulevards and civic squares and bus stances (if not, alas! into car-parks). A decade or so after Simpson's birth the better-class folk of the burgh who sought new houseroom were finding it in such salubrious localities as Wales Street and Constitution Street.

From the Grammar School he went to Marischal College, but it appears that his father's death terminated his academic career almost before it had begun, when he was only 14 years of age, the old Scottish precocity in learning combined with the traditional secondary school function of a Scottish University in those days being still in full swing. A cripple left arm and a maternal architect uncle who may have laid out the then comparatively new Marischal Street were probably, with the loss of his parent, the directive forces that sent him to seek his living in the architectural profession. He began as an apprentice in a mason's yard in the Castlegate, then contrived to go to London, where he studied under one Robert Lugar (no doubt a Scot, perhaps from Ayrshire—"Behind yon hills where Lugar flows") in Holborn, the author of "Villa Architecture" and probably a good teacher. To him Simpson went in 1810, and before long was turning out his own designs, including his first Aberdeen job, Union Chambers, which includes McCombie's Court. Before returning to Aberdeen he made a visit to Italy and spent some time in Rome.

Simpson set up in business in his native city

and house in 1813. These were the spacious days of Aberdeen's civic history. Despite the existence of public nuisances like Napoleon, who later was to be the indirect and unconscious cause of the almost complete disruption of Aberdeen's economy, the town had got an act through Parliament in 1800 for the making of King Street as far south as Love Lane (or Advocates Road) and of Union Street as far west as "the Damhead Road towards the Chapel of Ease" (now the southern end of Summer Street). In the first quarter of last century, the population doubled and the area of the burgh more than doubled. The foundation stone of Union Bridge was laid in 1801 and the keystone was in place before the end of summer in 1803. With the completion of the bridge the way to unlimited expansion was open. The first house built beyond the bridge was Crimonmogate's already mentioned, but what we now know as Union Street, with its ancillaries and continuations, was still in a very inchoate condition, when Archibald Simpson came home.

Victoria Street *Aberdeen Corporation*

Although he died five weeks short of completing his fifty-seventh year, Simpson accomplished so much in so many different kinds of building, and projected so much more not merely in individual constructions but in the lay-out of streets that it is difficult within short compass to know where to begin and how logically to group his work. One might take his town-planning ideas first, his public buildings next, his private residences separately. Or one might collect and discuss his contributions to the modernisation and improvement of the old "four quarters" of the burgh and balance that with his impress upon the new Aberdeen west of Union Bridge. Or one might deal with him progressively throughout his career, tracing and endeavouring to analyse his artistic development. Or one might adopt the sensible line taken by Dr. W. Douglas Simpson in his centenary oration twelve years ago and approach the subject by considering first the Classical and then the Gothic examples in the Archibald Simpson career.

Some things, however, may be said by way of general commentary, not in any sense critically, for it would not become an utter layman to express such opinions, but as one might say, historically and factually. Perhaps Simpson's greatest achievement was his mastery of his not very tractable material, granite. Before his time even in Aberdeen it was far from popular—except perhaps for causey-stones. Our ancient buildings were and are almost wholly fashioned in freestone, the nave of St. Machar's Cathedral being the outstanding granite exception. We used constantly to hear that it was impossible to do more than a very limited number of styles in granite—and if we hear less of that nowadays it is perhaps because contemporary designs tend to reproduce the outlines of boxes and because new techniques involving facings rather than blocks have made granite less stubborn to control. But thirty years ago or so architectural exponents—from outside the city—might never have heard of Simpson or applied their observation and their minds to the study of his work.

And because he achieved that mastery, he at

once became and has ever since remained an inspiration to the architects of his native city. In Scotland south of the Tay one probably hears more talk of Charles Mackintosh, especially in Glasgow, and it may be that of all Scottish architects he was the boldest innovator. But he had not the granite to deal with and—again without any pretensions to more than personal preference—one may hazard the opinion that he was inferior in pure art to Simpson. Apart from contemporaries—and Aberdeen for a couple of hundred years has always been fortunate in having a few more than merely competent architects within her bounds — there is no Aberdeen architect so generally recognised in lay memory, while, as has already been said, his primacy is a matter far above discussion in the circles of his profession. The urge to achieve and maintain an artistic integrity in architecture has clearly and most happily animated all our subsequent native-born architects.

28 Albyn Place

And in the third place, it is difficult to conceive of the appearance of modern Aberdeen had there been no Archibald Simpson. It is hardly practicable to run over all his work in the city, but the main specimens may be recalled, working more or less from east to west. In King Street we have facing each other the Medico-Chirurgical Hall in severe Ionic style, and St. Andrew's Cathedral, in ornate Gothic. At the corner of Castle Street he built the head office of Alexander Anderson's North of Scotland Bank, on the site of the New Inn. Many critics regard it as the finest fruit of his genius. Over against it on the other side of the Castlegate is the Athenaeum designed for Provost Brown's library and reading room, whose dignity compares very strikingly with the same quality which by a very different method Simpson infused into the assembly rooms which we now term the Music Hall. A comparison by contrast is supplied by the eastern end of Marischal College quadrangle with the lower part of the Mitchell Tower, which partakes of the Tudor style and somehow is the right design for a college; and by the Market Street frontage of the Newmarket which is very certainly apt for a market, but a great deal superior to most experiments in that direction.

One of Simpson's exercises with a quaintly bijou effect which is coyly hidden from sight in a byway is the old Girls' High School, now part of the Central School recently snobbishly renamed the Aberdeen Academy, in Little Belmont Street. There is probably not much in it and it is no doubt conventional within its type, but it has a most appealing charm. Anything but conventional is one of its designer's most ambitious and daring efforts, namely the group of three churches at the northern end of Belmont Street, erected on the site of the old cotton factory of Gordon, Barron & Co. (where William Thom the poet had worked) when the Disruption took place in 1843. All Aberdeen's city ministers "went out" at that time, and ten new churches were required for the enthusiastic Free congregations. The spire, which like the windows is in brick, is the only spire Simpson built, for when he had raised the present East Church of St. Nicholas after the old building was pulled down in the middle thirties, he did not add the spire. Last of his notable buildings east of the Denburn is the old Infirmary Building, whose mass is remarkably prevented by his sense of variety from appearing to the onlooker as unbearably heavy.

In addition to his buildings, Simpson had the opportunity of submitting numerous plans for the laying out of the new Granite City. He was consulted when Messrs. Adam and Anderson undertook the provision of the Newmarket, entailing a fresh street lay-out which involved Market Street, Hadden Street and Exchange Street. It is thought that Simpson may have been the architect of the double arcade at the top of the street, the more westerly of which may still linger in the memory of readers. The western side of the Denburn, however, afforded him greater scope. There is much of his thought in Union Terrace; away south in Ferryhill part of Marine Terrace is an unfinished vestige of another plan; Bon-Accord Square, Terrace and Crescent are also his monuments, and in the Square he lived and worked, respectively at Nos. 1 and 15, his last residence being No. 1 East Craibstone Street. It seems strange that he did not design the lay-out of Bon-Accord Street itself, for the northern part of the street proper looks much like his style. Then again he projected a scheme for west of Babbie Law, which gave us Rubislaw Place, Waverley Place, and Victoria Street, the last named of which that very fastidious artist of our own day, James Cromar Watt, used to maintain against all comers, was the loveliest street in Aberdeen and the most delightful manifestation of his genius. Rubislaw and Queen's Terraces, with the elegant Albyn Place Gardens, were not Simpson's conception, but are due to Walter Scott's friend James Skene of Rubislaw, to whom Aberdeen and Scotland owe rather more than is generally recognised. The actual plan was that of James Giles, the artist whose pictures of Aberdeenshire castles in the Haddo House collection were published by the Third Spalding Club; he was associated in the making of the plan with Messrs. Mackenzie and Matthews, the instruction coming from Skene.

On Albyn Place Simpson built a series of villas or suburban residences of which that now inhabited by the Conservative Club, formerly the home of Sir John Marnoch the surgeon, and the present home of the Royal Northern Club at No. 9 are two of the most interesting examples. He built much more, both in Aberdeen and elsewhere mostly in the North-East and always with taste and originality despite his loyalty to mainly classical thought. For the rest, he seems to have been a merry if not altogether conciliatory kind of person, fond of fiddling and his glass and the Scots tongue and a dinner party of convivial and congenial souls. Whether this was due to his persistence in remaining a bachelor may be left to the argumentative to discuss. He died of a chill on 2 March 1847, one of the very greatest of Aberdonians and with Sir Alexander Anderson the source of much more that is spacious and enduring in modern Aberdeen than any other individual.

Robert Gordon

merchant in Danzig and founder of Gordon's College

THE use of the adjective "unique" is always dangerous, and especially when applied to persons, for while on the one hand every human being is an individual, on the other hand we are a' John Tamson's bairns. But the epithet may surely be permitted as the correct description of Robert Gordon's standing in the history of our community, for not only is it the good he did that lives after him, but in no other case of Aberdonian benevolence has the testator's initiative been carried so far under its own impetus. Dr. William Guild's legacy to the Incorporated Trades was in truth on a restricted scale. The fifth Earl Marischal's endowment of our town's college has been merged and lost its original identity in the process. And the several bursaries and similar mortifications that in the calendar of the university still persist, serve only to perpetuate names that to the generality have no meaning.

Robert Gordon

But Robert Gordon's bequest still flourishes, and the seminary which owes its existence to him is now, nearly 230 years after his death, still in vigorous health and vastly expanded in scope and influence beyond what he envisaged, although, it is true, it does not in every detail follow the plan he laid down. England, as the noble foundations in Oxford and Cambridge so magnificently bear witness, has been rich in gifts of the kind, and both there and in Scotland it is interesting to observe how such munificence has often germinated in the minds of uncommon characters. It was the Elizabethan play-actor Edward Alleyn who founded Dulwich College; Edinburgh's very famous educational establishment (as we can, we hope, with impunity, so term it at this distance from the lovely city that one of our friends, native of Glasgow, once described as the Necropolis of Scotland) arose out of the fruits of the usury of the Jacobean Jingling Geordie Heriot; and Robert Gordon's College sprang from the shekels amassed by the founder from whom it takes its name through selling merchandise to the East Germans and Poles and by taking bonds on the landed property of cash-hungry Aberdeenshire lairds.

For long it was believed that Robert Gordon, albeit of Aberdonian parents, had suffered the double misfortune of being born and educated "in the sooth", which, we need hardly pause to remark, is a heathenish way of embarking upon existence. But it has now been established that he was not only born in Aberdeen—in 1668, but that he was actually a student at Marischal College and graduated there in 1689, the year of the Glorious Revolution. He came in fact of a branch of the great Gordon family that was more distinguished than most septs of that house for its interest in intellectual pursuits. His great-great-grandfather had been slain at Pinkie-cleugh; his great-grandfather, Sir John Gordon of Pitlurg, had been member of the Scottish Parliament for Aberdeenshire; his grandfather, Robert Gordon of Straloch, was the first M.A. of Marischal College, and an internationally famous geographer whose Scottish Atlas of 1648 was one of the most notable accomplishments of our nation in a noteworthy age; his uncle was the Parson of Rothiemay, James Gordon, to whom Aberdeen owes its first topographical description. Robert Gordon's father, Arthur Gordon, was a lawyer, his mother a daughter of Thomas Menzies of Balgownie, and so a member of the great family of Aberdeen Provosts of the sixteenth and seventeenth centuries. His sister Mary was to become the wife of Sir James Abercromby of Birkenbog, and through her the blood of this Gordon sept continues to this day.

While Robert Gordon was still a youngster his father died, and his share of the inheritance was £1,100 and some shillings and pence. After graduation his movements have not been very accurately ascertained. One account has it that he set off with a friend on the Grand Tour of the Continent and spent all his patrimony. This statement rather loses force because it fails to explain where his fortune came from. His name crops up in various Aberdeen documents from 1699 onwards and while Queen Anne was still on the throne he was lending money in his native city. Another account sends him to the Baltic where his successful intromissions in commerce were said to supply him with the necessary finance for his moneylending and eventual great bequest. The probability is that his mercantile adventures and excursions by the Baltic shore enabled him to amass the capital required by his lending activities in Aberdeen. Today something of a stigma seems to be attached to the term "moneylender", but in Robert Gordon's days banks as we recognise them, although a few existed, had neither the range nor the quality of their modern business. The moneylender performed at least one of their present-day functions, on terms probably less usurious than those which have obtained of late.

Amongst the subjects upon which History Honours students of Aberdeen University might profitably direct their attention, with respect to the community of which the university is a part—that is, on the assumption that it is indeed still Aberdeen University and not merely a university—is the connection of the North-East with Scandinavia, the Baltic littoral, the Low Countries, France, and the Mediterranean in the late fifteenth, sixteenth and seventeenth and the early eighteenth centuries. The human export of our area to these countries was very considerable and exercised a decidedly formative influence upon European civilisation and by its recoil upon Scottish culture and the Scots economy. Until the Union of the Crowns England—the prospect of the road south—was pretty well closed to Scotsmen. Those who followed James the Sixth resembled a flock of cormorants rather than a migration of ambitious young men, and the Union of the Parliaments and the Jacobite Rebellions had diverse repercussions upon the affections of the wandering Scot.

From the Reformation and 1560 to the Revolution and 1689 the magnet to the Scot who went abroad for a living was above all Poland, then a huge territory which included the Ukraine (our generation will recall that the modern Polish brigand dictator, Marshal Pilsudski, attempted to resume his nation's long abolished sovereignty there). Aberdeen, as the principal trading post and the second largest town in Scotland, had a long and close connection with Danzig, through which Poland and all the adjacent lands had been conquered with some Scots in their ranks by the Knights of the Teutonic Order. The Poles were Catholics, the Scots for the most part were Protestants, but some Catholic Scots went to Poland as to congenial company, while to the Protestants, who in outward show at least partook of the immemorial Scottish cosmopolitanism, the Poles were fair game in business and need not be antagonised by any display of Reformed bigotry.

All the authorities upon this fascinating aspect of the history of the Scot abroad are agreed that during the seventeenth century, that is, for half a century before Robert Gordon's birth and during his youth and earlier manhood, the number of Scots trading in the territories we have mentioned was legion. Several of these authorities put the number of Scots engaged in trade in Poland at any given date during that period at the well-nigh incredible figure of 40,000, a staggering total even assuming that it covers the families as well as the traders, for the population of Scotland itself was then under the million. Even those historians who demur to the figure mentioned never sink below 10,000 and sometimes admit to 30,000. They were in fact so numerous and so financially warm that after the execution of Charles I, both Cromwell and Charles II sent collectors to Poland to raise funds for their respective causes from the Scots and English merchants there, an interesting inversion of the practice today of raising funds from the United Kingdom for refugees elsewhere. And there is every reason to believe that not only did the Scots outnumber the English, but the Scots from Aberdeen and the North-East were more numerous than their compatriots from any other district perhaps actually as well as proportionately to population.

We know a good deal about some of these wandering Caledonians, particularly of the soldiers of fortune. The fighting man usually held up as the beau ideal of the strong silent male, has in all ages had a happy knack of telling the world about himself. The merchant, on the other hand, is of necessity more interested in making a living than in cutting a dash. So it comes about that whereas we have next to no knowledge of Robert Gordon's intromissions in those foreign lands, we hear no end of the escapades of that other scion of the family, Patrick Gordon of Auchleuchries who in the wars of those days changed sides half a dozen times, and who, no doubt acting upon the higher intelligence of his Aberdonian companion who rejoiced in the name of Alexander Keith, contrived to make war pay for itself by levying a species of blackmail upon friend and foe alike. Of Robert Gordon we do not even know whether he conducted his operations from a warehouse in Danzig or graduated to some such centralised depository through the discipline of a few years on the road with a pack upon his back. Probably the former is the case. With his pedigree he could hardly have failed to possess some kinsman who had established his emporium in delectable Baltic trading haunts and who after the genial custom of Scots abroad, then and even to a certain extent now, would take him in and eventually spare him a share in the business. Or the £1,100 patrimony may have purchased what blood relationship failed to conjure up.

Be the source of his affluence what it may, we find Robert Gordon fairly early in the eighteenth century lending money in Aberdeen to those small lairds in the neighbourhood who, like their "bonnet" and parvenu prototypes today, never commanded enough cash to meet the appetite of a rapidly developing agricultural economy. When he died in 1731, the great bulk of his estate of £10,000 to £12,000 proved to be invested in this way. And we should remember that it was a terrific amount of money for an indweller in a small and remote town like Aberdeen to have amassed in those days. We ourselves have seen in half a century the purchasing power of the pound drop to about one-sixth of what it was before the First World War, and in the two centuries or so between Robert Gordon's death and 1914 a similar declension took place. We may therefore calculate the present-day value of his estate at not far short of half-a-million in the depleted currency of 1960.

It is perhaps advisable here, this being intended as a fairly complete chronicle, to mention the legend of Robert Gordon's parsimony, but in doing so we would point out that there is in some misers a grandeur of character that springs from their heroic submission to a discipline of thrift which weaker natures simply could not support and in addition, however unbecoming in the eyes of a normal man Robert Gordon's avarice may seem, it cannot be alleged against him that he practised it for base purposes. We recall being told of an Aberdeenshire farmer who two or three decades ago died leaving nearly quarter of a million, and who was upbraided by a friend for meanness because he neglected to have his boots soled. "Foo nae spen' your siller," said the friend; "Ye canna tak it wi' ye." "No, man," came the instant rejoinder, "isn't it an awfu' peety!" Robert Gordon most emphatically would not have subscribed to that philosophy.

It is said of him that he lived on milk and "breid", otherwise oatcakes, the cheapest forms of subsistence in his day. It is related that once, finding a mouse in his milk (the more ambitious imagery of recent repetition enlarges it to a rat), he squeezed the intruder dry, over the bowl, pointing out that the milk would be none the worse. It is said that, seated with a friend at night, he refused to light a candle, since they did not require light to talk. He is credited with pacing back and forth in his room carrying a bag of coal in order to warm himself: better that than burn the coal, for "coals burnt are coals wasted". And there is an apparently silly story that he bored a hole in the floor of his room so that he might read beside the aperture by the light of the candle or cruisie in the room beneath—a tale which only requires to be analysed to be revealed as nonsense. It is true that he shocked a contemporary Provost of Aberdeen by refusing to leave anything to his sister Mary or her Abercromby children, but there may have been valid reasons for that. Actually, the Laird of Birkenbog after his brother-in-law's death applied to the Town Council and persuaded them to part with 7,000 merks for Mary, and mourning suits, shoes and swords for himself and his two sons. But on the other side, quite apart from his grand design of a boys' hospital we have the fact that Robert Gordon left a quite respectable collection of engravings and some books which suggest that, had his philanthropy been less he might have been numbered with the Hebers and Christie-Millers of bibliomania.

The original hospital building of 1746 still dominates the modern additions

In 1730 Robert Gordon got the feu of the manse of the Black Friars and two gardens for £10 per annum. This was next door on the west to the Grammar School, whose location there for many years gave its name to Schoolhill. It stood where Gray's School of Art now is, and the new school was opened in its present location in 1863. To Robert Gordon's feu the Town Council subsequently added the whole of the croft of land, with houses and yards, that had belonged to the Black Friars, and having purchased a grey horse, a black horse, and a horse with a switch tail to cart stones, proceeded to build the Hospital in terms of Robert Gordon's mortification and of plans prepared by William Adam, the Edinburgh architect who was father of the brothers who built London's Adelphi and were responsible for some only of the innumerable Adam mantlepieces and bits of furniture which are regarded today with such awe by collectors.

In his will Gordon described his wish as "a pious Mortification of my whole substance and effects . . . and that towards the building of an Hospital, and for Maintenance, Aliment, Entertainment and Education of young Boys, whose parents are poor and indigent and not able to maintain them at Schools, and put them to Trades and Employments, which Resolution purely proceeds from the zeal I bear and carry to the Glory and Honour of God; and that the true Principles of our holy and Christian Religion may be the more effectually propagated in Young Ones; and that the Knowledge of Letters, of lawful Employments and Callings may flourish and be advanced in all succeeding Generations". All of which was handsome talk indeed for a Gordon, a family which had never before given anything to the burgh. Having been a lodger all his life Robert Gordon enjoined that no woman should be employed in the Hospital, which to begin with housed and educated twenty-six boys.

But although the school was roofed in during 1732, it was long before it was opened for its stated purpose. Various causes combined to postpone the commencement of its work, and when Aberdeen in 1745 became one of the key points in the Jacobite campaign, its inauguration must have seemed farther off than ever. In 1746 as "every schoolboy" knows (we hope), George II's "Martial boy" the Butcher Duke of Cumberland, who incidentally had been Lord Rector of Marischal College, came to the burgh in pursuit of the Young Pretender's forces, and when he moved on in early spring to what in a few days was to be the decisive battle of Culloden, he left his sick and a few other troops, some 200 men all told, in garrison. This detachment occupied the Hospital building (which still stands as the central block), and digging up the garden and levelling the dykes, surrounded the house by "a trench and earthen rampart, faced with palisades", the whole being designated Fort Cumberland. The Town Council later succeeded in extracting £300 from the Government in solatium for the damage then done.

And so in 1750 at long last Robert Gordon's Hospital was opened, and its twenty-six boys paraded in all the glory of "tailed coat of good blue cloth, a blue woollen bonnet, and knee breeches of corduroy, the coat and waistcoat handsomely furnished with full gilt brass buttons". They were known then and for many years thereafter as "Sillerton" loons, the school having been named Silvertown Hospital in Paterson's map of Aberdeen dated 1746. No one has been able to explain the origin of the name, and a newspaper correspondence some years ago proved singularly unproductive of plausible ideas for solving the puzzle. All we know is that for nearly 200 years the boys at Gordon's have been known as Sillerton loons. It proved immediately impracticable to run a boarding school without at least a matron, and Gordon's wishes in this respect were set aside, as was later his further intention that when the boys made their way in life they should repay the cost of their education. At one time there was a crisis in the staff owing to one of the hazards of having women in the establishment; Gordon may have foreseen just such a contretemps, the character of which, it should be mentioned, was not of the "Young Woodley" variety, which modern suspiciousness might expect. Eventually, even the conception of the boarding school had to be abandoned, and in 1882 the last boy left the Hospital, which then became Robert Gordon's College.

The temptation is strong to forget that this series is entitled "Eminent Aberdonians" and is not intended to deal with Aberdeen institutions, for Robert Gordon's College has had a noble history. A word or two about the headmasters may be permitted—present and almost present company excepted as is the rule in good social conversation. The head of 1802-7, Alexander Simpson, succeeded Sir Alexander Anderson's father as minister of Strichen. John Ramsay, A.M., later editor of the *Aberdeen Journal*, was on the staff from 1826 to 1831 when he resigned owing, in his own words, "to a disordered state of the viscera and an irregular distribution of nervous influence", which was a good excuse for getting out of teaching. Robert Simpson, later minister of Kintore and founder of its more than century-old savings bank, was head from 1826 to 1829 when he was succeeded by the great James Robertson, who introduced superphosphates to Scotland while minister at Ellon, became an inspiring Moderator of the Auld Kirk about the Disruption time, was the energetic originator of her Endowments scheme, and ended as Professor of Divinity at Edinburgh. He was succeeded by George Melvin, brother of the more famous James, Rector of the Grammar School; and in 1842 there came to the College Andrew Findlater, native of New Aberdour and still remembered as the first editor of *Chambers's Encyclopaedia*. In 1859 after many years of fine service as Maths master there retired John

Ogilvie, uncle of no fewer than four LL.D.'s—George, headmaster of George Watson's, Edinburgh; Alexander, headmaster of Gordon's College; Joseph, Director of the Church of Scotland Training College; and Robert, Inspector of Schools.

Today Robert Gordon's College is the only independent school of any considerable age left in the North and North-East of Scotland. Old boys of its once next-door neighbour, the Aberdeen Grammar School, may well today regard its status with envy and reflect with bitterness that their own glorious institution has been betrayed by the very body that should have been the guardian of its integrity. The good fortune that has thus attended Robert Gordon's College has added to its claims upon the patriotic spirit of Aberdonians, and will no doubt inspire them to assist the school in its appeal for financial aid, even if they do not emulate its pious founder in the methods he employed to endow it with the means of existence.

The Gregory professors
from the reflecting telescope to the famous powder

A SCOTTISH antiquary of about two hundred years ago included in one of his publications a ballad relating to an eminent Aberdonian which ought to be engraved in letters of lead above the desk of every student of genetics. Substantially the same ballad is found in Germany, and it does not matter very much whether Scotland or the Rhineland gave birth to it, for in the days before proletarian school children were given trips to Europe at the public expense, Aberdeen actually enjoyed a much more intimate acquaintance with the countries of the Continent than it does today.

Professor James Gregory

The ballad in question tells how there lived in Aberdeen a man, a professor, of great intellectual eminence but with no pretensions to physical attraction. When the professor addressed himself to the problem of securing a suitable wife, he chose a young lady who, if her intelligence was negligible, was (and it happens) a remarkably beautiful woman. For he reasoned, tempted thereto by what he fancied was the logic of science, that their progeny would have her beauty and his brains. But alas! the burden of the ballad was the recording of the unhappy fact that the issue of the union had her brains and his beauty.

This somewhat lengthy exordium is deemed necessary as a corrective to any false assumptions to be lightly drawn from the quite extraordinary, though not quite unique, record of the Aberdeen family of the Gregories. Their case has been well known and very widely commented upon in the last hundred years, and it is most unlikely that any fresh light can now be thrown upon it, either in the way of scientific exposition since the great Francis Galton considered it, or of additional facts since—to mention the two most recent though not the most exhaustive accounts—the late P. J. Anderson and Walter R. Humphries wrote their essays on it. Or perhaps two observations may be hazarded: one, that the blood of the Gregories still courses in the North-east within the castles of Fyvie and of Drum, and the other that while genetics and eugenics in the practical mating of human beings have never been seriously studied, those who have applied knowledge of the laws regulating such matters to the breeding of birds and animals are only too sadly aware how much of the outcome is vanity and vexation of spirit.

The Gregories were, of course, originally MacGregors, like their distant cousin who gave that great musician Edvard Grieg to Norway, and that greatest of all folk-song collectors, Gavin Greig, to Aberdeenshire. According to family tradition, "A Gentleman of the Name of McGregor, a son of the Family of Rora in Glen

Lyon", made his way to Banffshire and married a daughter of the Laird of Findlater. One of their ten sons "James was surnamed Gregory" and was made by Findlater chamberlain or factor of Woodland, in Udny parish. He married a sister of William Moir of Ferryhill, and the one of his family who counts is James, who became a saddler in Aberdeen and was Deacon-Convener of the Incorporated Trades, and who died in 1623. His son John, born 1598, M.A. of Marischal College in 1616, inducted minister of Drumoak in 1620, was more successful in correcting the vagaries of genetics than the fabled professor, and with him the real tale of the marvellous Gregories commences. Before dealing with his marriage and the blood lines it drew together, it may be mentioned that John Gregory was not the only minister to display business acumen. He no doubt inherited a bit of money and may have collected more with his wife, but like Robert Gordon he found plenty of lairds in sad need of financial accommodation and provided it to such purpose that when he died in 1652, having survived fines and imprisonment in 1640 and further suspension in 1649 for failure to conform with the Covenant, he was proprietor of Kinnairdy and Netherdale in Banffshire, and of Frendraught in the parish of Forgue, which had fallen to him by reason of non-payment of a debt by James Crichton, Viscount Frendraught.

The Rev. John Gregory selected as his spouse Janet, daughter of David Anderson of Finzeauch, our old friend Davie Do a'thing, and granddaughter of Matthew Guild, the sword-slipper. Her maternal uncle was thus Dr. William Guild and on her father's side there was Alexander Anderson the celebrated mathematician, in Paris. Her cousin was George Jamesone the painter. The controlling blood in the wealth of talent that thus became the heritage of the Gregory family was probably that of the Andersons; the fact that Alexander Anderson the mathematician was only a half-brother of Davie rules out the Guild claim, and the pretensions of the Gregories must be qualified by the eminence of later Andersons during the hundred years or so after the Rev. John Gregory's death. David Anderson was Professor of Divinity at King's College from 1711 to 1733; James was the author of "Royal Genealogies" in 1732; and Adam wrote a "History of Commerce" in 1764.

Having got John Gregory and Janet Anderson married and their forebears redd up, we proceed to consider their family. They had three sons and two daughters. A daughter of the younger girl became an ancestress of the present Irvines of Drum. The eldest son Alexander succeeded to Frendraught, but in 1664 he was decoyed, wounded, and conveyed a prisoner by Francis Crichton to the House of Bognie, where Viscount Frendraught was then living. In terms of the libel in the subsequent trial, "the said Viscount Frendraught did maist inhumanely and barbarouslie drag the said unqule Mr. Alex. out of his bed as he was lying bleiding in his woundes and did cast him overthwart ane horse, upon his breast, his head and arms hanging on the ane side and his legs on the other syde and so carryed him away in ane cold and stormy morning to ane obscure place myles distant, where they keiped him prisoner three days and then deserting and leaving him". Alexander Gregory died as a result, but the Crichtons were Catholics and were pardoned by the Duke of York, later James II and VII.

Alexander was succeeded in his father's properties by the next brother David, to whom we shall return after dealing with the third and youngest, James, one of the brightest ornaments not only of Aberdeen and Scottish genius, but of human erudition. Born in 1638, and educated as befitted a true Aberdonian then at the Grammar School and the toun's college of Marischal, he was led by a suggestion from his brother David to concentrate upon mathematics for his life's work. In 1659, when he had occasion to appear on behalf of his mother's claim to the lands of Bainshole, he was described as "ane discrete young man". His first book was published in London in 1663, with the title *Optica Promota,* in which he gave sufficient details of the reflecting telescope to be regarded as its inventor; Isaac Newton, who perfected the discovery, acknowledging as much. James then went on to Padua, where he issued his conclusions on the quadrature of the circle, a subject which, like his observations in astronomy, is a little too much up in the air for the present writer to interpret here. In 1668 he was appointed Professor of Mathematics at St. Andrews, and five years later he was given the corresponding chair at Edinburgh. Soon afterwards he was struck with blindness while demonstrating to his students, and he died in a few days in his 37th year. He left a year-old son James, of whom more shortly, by his wife Mary Jamesone, daughter of George the portrait painter and thus a close relation of his own. This in-breeding was fairly successful but not sufficiently so to improve the family significantly. Mary, whose monument are the tapestries in the West Kirk of St. Nicholas, was a widow when James espoused her, having married Baillie John Burnett of Elrick, Newmachar. She was not enamoured of single blessedness, for after her second bereavement she married Baillie George Adie of Aberdeen, whose house was almost to our own day one of the architectural treasures of the city.

James lived a good deal less than half the time spent on earth by his older brother David, who must now be subjected to our scrutiny. If the man's the gowd for a' that, and academic success or material prosperity regarded as merely incidentals, David Gregory, laird of Kinnairdy, would occupy a very high place in history. He went out to Campvere in the Low Countries as a merchant in his youth, but returned to Aberdeen about the time of his father's death and became Librarian at Marischal College. He was twice married, in both cases to Aberdeen girls, and is credited with anything from twenty-nine to thirty-two children lawfully begotten. Uncertainty in a matter of such fertility is pardonable, and the astronomical interests of the family become understandable. He lived to be ninety-five, and as he was a discursive student who took all human activity for his province and was in the habit of doing his mental work in the small hours of the morning and then having an hour or two of sleep before breakfast, he may be cited as an argument against specialisation and in favour of early rising.

He appears to have been an exceptionally enlightened man. He practised medicine apparently without fee, and at the same time taught his sons in the mathematics by which they became famous. He was an ardent meteorologist and possessed a barometer, then regarded at both kirk and market with superstitious terror. On one occasion the "glass" gave him warning of an approaching storm and being thus forewarned he got his crops in safely —we could wish some of our weather prophets were as reliable today; and he had some difficulty in explaining away his foreknowledge to the Presbytery who strongly suspected him of witchcraft. He seems to have had about him not a little of the gay spirit of Sir Thomas Urquhart, for during Marlborough's war he invented a new gun, and proposed to take it to Flanders and conduct a campaign there on his own; but on submitting it to Sir Isaac Newton, he was dissuaded from his purpose by the great English scientist, who recommended that it be consigned to oblivion as too likely to be destructive to the human race. One wonders what the Aberdonian's idea was; one has little need to wonder what would have happened to it today (barring of course submission to the War Office which would have ensured its condemnation) had it become known to our higher civilisation! The story is, however, interesting as adding a third Aberdeen inventor of firearms to Ferguson and Forsyth.

Let us now return to the progeny of James of the telescope. So far he is the only professor of the name we have encountered, but there is a mob of them close on his heels. His only son James was educated in Aberdeen and studied medicine in Edinburgh and abroad. He came to Aberdeen to practise in 1699, married firstly a daughter of Sir John Forbes of Monymusk and secondly the only daughter of Principal George Chalmers of King's College where eventually in 1725 he himself became Professor of Medicine. He it was who was visited in 1715 by his distant relative Rob Roy MacGregor, sent to recruit supporters for the Jacobites by the Earl of Mar. Rob, so the story goes, offered Gregory to take his young son James away with him "and make a man of him", but the doctor probably felt that for "man" he should read "cateran" and pleaded the lad's extreme youth and so saved him from enlistment in the clan "that is nameless by day". Scott tells the story and the late Sir Francis Burnand, the editor of *Punch*, had (if memory is to be trusted) a skit on the incident.

This first of the Gregory medical professors is chiefly notable for a feat quite unconnected with his profession. In 1727 he, as it were, put the banks on the Don. Perhaps this enterprise arose out of his interest in salmon fishing. It is not generally known that the river from which the city takes its name once ran on such a course that the town was actually at the mouth of the Don, as its name implies. After passing the Brig o' Balgownie the Don turned in an almost southerly direction, past the birth-place of the father of Adam Smith, himself the Father of Economic Science, and through the Links to the foot of the Broad Hill, whence it turned eastwards to debouch into the sea about where the Bathing Station now stands. With the help of soldiers and salmon fishers, Gregory cut a new channel due east, which the river still (with occasional digressions) follows, but its old course may be traced today through the Links in very wet weather by the pools that form along it.

The James that escaped enlistment into the Children of the Mist succeeded his father in 1732 as Professor of Medicine at King's, and proceeded to follow his grandfather's example by a bit of in-breeding, marrying a Burnett of Elrick. James Gregory died in 1755, when he was succeeded in the chair by his half-brother John, who was appointed eleven years later to the Chair of the Practice of Medicine in Edinburgh, and who was active in securing the foundation of the Royal Infirmary there, besides being the author of *A Father's Legacy to his Daughters* 1774, which had the distinction of being translated into several European languages, the advice it contains being worldly enough, but not quite in the sense of the word as applied to Lord Chesterfield's "Letters to his Son". John Gregory must have been an amiable person, for in *The Minstrel* James Beattie thus describes him:

He, whom each virtue fired, each grace refined,
Friend, teacher, pattern, darling of Mankind.

He died in 1773.

By his wife, a daughter of the 15th Lord Forbes, John had a son and two daughters. One of these, Anna Margaretta, who married John Forbes of Blackford, and brought the Gregory blood eventually to Fyvie, was god-daughter to Mrs. Elizabeth Montagu, Queen of the Bluestockings, as learned ladies were then nicknamed. This relationship, as it were by font, is rather surprising and amusing, in view of her father's warning in the *Legacy* against the display of high intelligence by women. Another daughter, Dorothea, became the mother of William Pulteney Alison, who occupied three Edinburgh medical chairs between 1820 and 1855, and of Sir Archibald Alison (1792-1867), author of a once highly popular *History of Europe*. John Gregory's son, another James, was Professor of the Institutes of Medicine 1786-89, and of the Practice of Medicine 1790-1821 in Edinburgh. He invented that abominable but drastically efficient concoction so bitterly remembered by children for a century after his time—Dr. Gregory's Powder. His sons were William, who was Professor of Medicine at King's 1839-44 and of Chemistry at Edinburgh 1844-58; and Duncan who was a mathematician. With these the line from the great James Gregory disappears.

From David of Kinnairdy, there sprang seven professors, as compared with the six from James, making fourteen from the whole Gregory family. His eldest son David was elected Professor of Mathematics at Edinburgh in 1683 a month before he graduated. In 1691 he was appointed to the Savilean Chair of Astronomy at Oxford. His son, also David, became Dean of Christ Church and Regius Professor of Modern History at Oxford. The elder David's Chair of Mathematics at Edinburgh was filled, when he left for Oxford, by his brother James, who had been Professor of Mathematics at St. Andrews;

and yet another brother, Charles, occupied the same St. Andrew's chair from 1707-1739, being succeeded there by his son David, who held it until 1763. Upon this David, Robert Ferguson wrote an elegy of a humorous character, as may be gauged by the following verse:

He could, by Euclid, prove langsyne
A ganging point compos'd a line;
By numbers too he cou'd devine,
When he did read,
That three times three just made up nine;
But now he's dead.

Of the Kinnairdy daughters, the sixth child Isabel married Patrick Innes of Belnaboth, later of Tillyfour, and her grandson Alexander Innes was Professor of Philosophy at Marischal 1739-42. The sixteenth Kinnairdy child, Margaret, married Lewis Reid, minister of Strachan, and her son was Thomas Reid (1710-96), Regent at King's College 1751-64 and Professor of Moral Philosophy at Glasgow 1764-96. Next to the first James he made the greatest academic stir of all the family when he published his *Inquiry into the Human Mind on the Principles of Common Sense,* which was intended to dispose once and for all of what were considered to be subversive reasonings of the infidel David Hume. For a generation Reid's arguments on the whole commanded the favour of the philosophers, but his theories lacked that masculine quality which inspired the ideas of Hume, and it is rather curious that Reid should have deprecated the scientific treatment of moral subjects despite the pronounced scientific bent of his mother's family. Today the weight of evidence is probably more decisively behind Hume's than any other theory of philosophy.

William Tawse

child of the renaissance in the modern age

An Aberdonian who, if he did not labour under the handicap of being still alive, would qualify to be described as eminent, once committed himself to the opinion that in the modern age two Aberdonians have been outstanding for their vision and their business genius, Sir Alexander Anderson and William Tawse. It is now twenty years and a little over since William Tawse died. Of his close associates more than half are no longer here. The phoney war ended on the morning of his funeral when the Germans invaded Norway and Denmark, and all the serious part of the conflict followed by the most concentrated social, political, economic and scientific revolution in the world's history has intervened between that date and this. Yet never even to this day do two or more of his old friends find themselves in company but their talk for some period of their meeting veers round to him and the years of his maturity, as to a golden age, an epoch more spacious than ours.

William Tawse

It is difficult for anyone who has lived in intimacy with another to write objectively and judicially. It is more than usually difficult in this case, for absence indeed has not made the heart less fond. Of few men were such conflicting assessments made, mainly because the man himself was such an extraordinary bundle of contrasting qualities, good and bad but never commonplace, black and white but never grey. There were those who would scarcely hear a redeeming word about him, and there were those who would have considered the forfeiture of his friendship as an intolerable calamity. Time and again he would disconcert, often he would annoy, frequently he would exasperate, sometimes he would even alienate his friends, but never for long and never in such a way as to alter their fundamental admiration of him. Shortly after his death an Aberdeen lawyer who knew him well, who was not friendly with him, and who in fact seldom condescended to speak well even of his own friends, replied in conversation to a remark about William Tawse having his faults, "Yes, but they were a man's faults". It will, therefore, be appreciated that this sketch will not be lacking in colour emphasis.

Although it is, and was, difficult to believe, William Tawse was born in Yorkshire of a Scottish father whose family had been for long in the Howe o' the Mearns, and an English mother who hailed from the county whose sons are wont to boast that its closest connection with the Scriptures derives from its having as many acres as the Bible has words. He was born in

1880, his father Peter Tawse being cashier-book-keeper-correspondent with that Easton Gibb the contractor whose name cropped up in a previous article in this series. About 1890, the Gibb firm being short of contracts, Peter Tawse joined the staff of John Fyfe as foreman or manager of Kemnay Quarry, and at Kemnay school William received the first part of his serious education, which no doubt became even more serious when he began to travel "oot an' in" to Robert Gordon's College with a piece in's pooch, the traditional sustenance of young Scottish students when the idea of education was to train the mind.

But already William had established his reputation as a character, as a rebel, probably as "an ill-tricket deevil", and certainly as one who had no intention of going anyone's way but his own. Very early in his career, during one of his frequent visits to an affectionate and indulgent aunt in Dundee, he became namely for his pranks, the earliest of which—and it was very early indeed—was to march up the aisle of the kirk one Sunday morning clad in his birthday suit. One wonders how many of the douce frequenters of the Aberdeen church of which he eventually became an elder were aware of this escapade—or indeed how many of them ever realised that he was an elder at all! Yet the complete lack of inhibitions which the juvenile prank revealed was an integral part of the character of the man. He was a creature of moods and impulses that were inextricably entangled with business aptitude and practical sense. He uttered the thought that was uppermost in his mind at the moment, did what happened to be before him to do, and if he found himself in difficulties he usually though sometimes only eventually contrived to get out of them, although it was seldom that he did not show repentance for an indiscretion or regret when he had done himself a disservice by a miscalculation.

In 1896 John Fyfe the elder handed over business affairs to his sons and Peter Tawse set up for himself in Aberdeen with a lum hat, a horse, a gig, a whip and a yard at the Clayhills near Portland Street, now used as a coal store by the Electricity Board. William, now sixteen, was taken from school and set to his first job wheeling kerbs and causey-stones to the paviors working for his father on the docks railway in Aberdeen. It was a rough introduction to the harsher realities of what was to be his life's work, and it was difficult to associate with such navvy-labour the finely-shaped, expressive and artistic hands of the mature man. But it taught men to appreciate him, as they will always appreciate those who have worked at their job, and it taught him the worth of the deeper loyalties and sympathies that, in an ideal relationship, should bind master and man, that make the men recognise the master and the master appreciate the men.

Long years later, on a sewage job, at the end of a tunnel a break-through of water occurred which threatened to drown the squad on the job. An Irish navvy stuck his arm in the aperture, like Katherine Douglas when she used her arm as a door-bar in the cellarage of the Perth abbey, and he kept it there for a long time until measures had been taken to control the torrent. The prolonged exposure and immersion set up rheumatic or arthritic trouble in the arm, and he could not work again, but by orders he continued to present himself week after week for his usual pay packet. On the morning after William Tawse's death one of his sorely upset staff told the present writer how the men were wont to take their personal problems, domestic and economic, to their boss for advice and if possible solution. Yet there were occasions when he would abuse them with a command of coruscating language not unworthy to be compared with that of the poet Swinburne, who was reckoned in that line to be the greatest of the Victorians.

Peter Tawse died in 1908, by which time William, along with Howard Anderson, was actively associated in the direction of the firm. When William became head of the firm its operations were gradually and greatly extended. Even then contracts had been won from Dundee on the one hand to the Northern Highlands on the other, with the laying of Aberdeen's principal streets with setts and the construction of Aberdeen's main drainage system as the chief jobs at home. William, however, was gifted with remarkable commercial imagination and great aesthetic resources. His suggestions of civil engineering projects for modernising the area could be extraordinarily graphic and eloquent; the hearer got the impression somehow of a landscape picture being built up and filled in, as idea after idea was presented in language which would have done credit to an orator or professor. His flair for combining the practical with the attractive was quite unusual, and it was translated into reality best perhaps of all by the work he did along the Great Glen and, still better, in Glencoe. Of the Glencoe road there was much criticism from "arty" quarters before it was completed, but that died down when eventually the whole project was presented with its skilful utilisation of natural features and its constant exploitation of those features to enhance the majesty of the rapidly changing view. He was not, of course, the architect of the road, but his influence on its development, his suggestions for the solution of the problems that arose in both planning and construction, had a very great deal to do with the beauty, as well as the efficiency, of the finished product.

As an example of the boldness of his ideas his scheme for the improvement of A92, the Buchan road, may be instanced in one part at least. Incidentally, he did not agree with, and was caustically critical of, the planning of the double carriageway from the Bridge of Don to Denmore. He had himself built the Barracks and his picture of what ought to be was quite different from what the siting of the road made it. When the dual carriageway was undertaken, there was a good deal of talk of further alterations, which have, in one shape or another, only been put in hand during the last three or four years. They have certainly been improvements, although it is not so certain that they will not be as urgently requiring improvement themselves fifty years hence as the old road was five years ago. William Tawse's idea included a completely new section cutting straight across country from Fontainebleau via Tarty and over the Ythan at Logie-Buchan to rejoin the old line of road approximately at the northern end of the recent improvements near Auchmacoy and Crawheid. This, of course, would have cut out Ellon altogether, and Ellon is not an unimportant or voiceless community, and for quite a time behind the scenes there was a battle royal. Perhaps his project never had a chance of being adopted; perhaps it was not sociologically suitable; but it was characteristic of the Tawse boldness and thoroughness.

There was another aspect of this pictorial imagination of his. He had an equally unusual capacity for impromptu composition, not infrequently satirical. In company one day a prominent member of Aberdeen's business community was enlarging upon the success with which he had conducted the affairs of a local charity. Another individual said he wished the speaker would organise success for him. Whereupon William Tawse intervened. "That is perfectly simple, my friend. All you've got to do is to invent something—let's say a bicycle that goes without propulsion. Take it to A—(mentioning the successful one). He'll float a company, £300,000 capital. He's a J.P., an LL.D., an elder, he is this and that, and everyone will subscribe seeing his name on the prospectus. (Here ensued a synopsis of the prospectus, full of digs and innuendos and sly slaps). Then, my friend, after about six months, having heard nothing more, you'll call on A—and ask how things are going, and perhaps some day you'll get a cheque for maybe £25,000, which will set you on your feet. The expenses of floating the company will have absorbed the rest of the £300,000."

One of the most interesting of William Tawse's earlier contracts was the construction of the "blimp" aerodrome at Lenabo near Longside, during the first World War, which involved the linking of the aerodrome with the railway at Longside Station. He also doubled the line between Parkhill and Newmachar. For Aberdeen he built the Invercannie waterworks and most of the aqueduct to the city. The pontoon dock at Aberdeen, the swimming pool at Stonehaven and most of the work at Gordon's College swimming pool, which he along with Dr. James A. Mackie and the late Dr. Walter A. Reid gave to the College, were other examples of his versatility. He pioneered the building of concrete bridges in this part of the country, and he was in the forefront of roadmaking. The surface of the road which he laid from the old Suburban Tramway terminus to Haudagain, nearly forty years ago, has withstood all the incessant traffic of Aberdeen's principal arterial highway to the north. Time and again the knowledgeable traveller in the Highlands is moved to thank Providence for Bill Tawse.

In the interval between the two World Wars Aberdeen was an enviable place to live in for the extrovert and those whose social proclivities were based upon sound human fellowship and were not too much expressed in fancy. Away back at the beginning of the century the young manhood of the West-end was curiously concentrated about the activities of the boating club on the Dee. Between the wars, apart from the muscular mountaineers of the Cairngorm Club and those who found intellectual satisfaction indoors at bridge, probably the most characteristically individual associations were the Life Preserving Society and the Sit Siccar Club. The former, founded during the first war, and consecrated to country and mountain rambles of a not too exhausting nature, passed through several vicissitudes until William Tawse took it over and made it his own. The Sit Siccar Club (Sit siccar being the Scots for Ranunculus repens, the creeping buttercup, the idea being in Charles Murray's words, "You're safe on your doup") was devoted to semi-learned talk and highly-polished anecdote.

The two associations were linked loosely by having one or two members in common, and by their contrast in character. For whereas in the Life Preservers it was all high living and low thinking, with the Sit Siccars the living was low and the thinking high. William Tawse's literary taste was eclectic. His intimates on one occasion presented him with sets of some of his favourite novelists—Jane Austen, Thomas Hardy, and Anatole France, a somewhat curious range in taste. And he used his knowledge of literature to good effect. One of his friends he habitually addressed, for instance, as Prince Istar; and he found other associations. But he was, for no reason at all, not a member of the Sit Siccar Club, notwithstanding that it was a common custom for that Club to be represented when the Life Preservers having reached the end of a perambulation, rested the soles of their feet and extended the wings of their hospitality. Of the Life Preserving Society William Tawse was the life and soul. He knit together the very disparate (he would have insisted they be called desperate) characters of its members. They all had some link with him, but few had links with other members. When he died the Society, after a few spasmodic efforts to remain in being, quietly expired.

The Society in the main constituted a principal relaxation of an important section of the industrial and commercial life of the city, leavened by a few representatives of the professions. There were industrialists, contractors, engineers, merchants, professors, scientists, public officials, accountants, lawyers, journalists, even farmers. The Society operated every Saturday from the first after the New Year until four weeks before the Twelfth, the exercise consisting of walks, short and by the sea to begin with, then gradually getting longer and working upwards to the hills as the days lengthened and the weather became more dependable. Cars took the party to the starting point and went round to meet them at the finish. The walk might be anything from ten to over twenty miles. Each week-end William Tawse pored over his map, studying contours and the dotted lines that (sometimes) represent "well-defined paths". He then compiled a route with descriptive notes, indicated when the car would call, and posted off the notices. There were eighteen members of the fraternity besides himself, but as in those civilised days twenty or more identical notices could be carried for a half-penny, he addressed one to himself and one to the Postmaster-General, thereby saving himself ninepence.

The Society was well-known and favourably regarded in the whole North-east countryside. It could be sure of a welcome, whenever it made one of its usually unheralded visits, in castle, country-house and cottage. "Ye're jolly lads, haste ye back" was the usual parting word, while at one of the castles a piper suitably equipped and backed by a butler hospitably armed, was not unknown. William Tawse would talk couthily or learnedly or critically according to the quality of his hosts, and the good wife of the cottage at least was always fluttered by the generosity with which the visit ended. But much scandal and even slander was talked en route. Once a stranger to the society's customs, who had been invited to the walk, was thunderstruck by the appalling allegations against the character of a member present in person, and in a quiet moment expressed his horror at the remarks. "They can't be true", he said, and retired into complete dumbness when he got the answer, "If that was all the truth, it wouldn't be so bad". One member, now in the House of Lords, has recorded his opinion that the talk of the Life Preservers contained more sense than that of all the potentates, princes, cabinet ministers and politicians he has encountered.

It may seem to be exaggeration to say that the death of William Tawse brought a darkness to the life of Aberdeen that was like the sudden descent of night in the tropics. The war was bad enough, and was forgotten only in the feverish but completely unconstructive activities of war-time. But death in taking away William Tawse abstracted a gaiety from the life of the city—what the French call *le gai savoir*. Those of his close friends who still survive can vouch for it that existence now even when it seems most enjoyable is more than a little commonplace without him. His vitality communicated itself to all who knew him. His brusque dynamic masculinity was as powerful as the latest device in prairie-busters. He ordered his last suit from a country whip-the-cat whom he called the Court Tailor of the village he worked in, and to help the man he proposed to buy suits for the whole company. The last snapshot taken of him showed him wheeling a baby in a pram down a village street. He had the seeing eye for character. Two men came into a restaurant for lunch. "I'll bet these boys take their peas with a knife." The manager was requested to serve the pair with a dish of green peas, and sure enough, the peas disappeared off their knife-blades. When a prosy after-dinner speaker wearied him, a waiter was summoned to be told to tell the orator his wife was dead. When a leading citizen got his portrait done, there had to be a dinner at which the organisers were entertained. "The Octotoddle", in celebrating an eightieth birthday, was organised by him; the actionable strouds of "The Lass of Rheinaharn" and "The Roup at Eastie's Toun" were inspired by his remarks. Nothing relating to mankind did he regard as unworthy of his notice and he lived his life with a Renaissance zest that, while it probably shortened his days, gave him fullness of experience and his friends a joy and a catholicity of interests that had to be felt personally to be thoroughly savoured.

George Keith
the noble founder of Marischal College

George Keith

Of all the county families who begged, borrowed or stole from the community of Aberdeen—the Gordons, Forbeses, Irvines, Setons—only one condescended to pay anything back. "The toun's college", Marischal College and University, the centenary of whose amalgamation with King's College to make the University of Aberdeen has just been celebrated, represents the *quid pro quo* of the Keiths for their acquisition after the Reformation of certain assets of the White Friars in the Green and the Black Friars in the Woolmanhill, and perhaps also in recompense for material assistance granted, some years before the foundation of the College, by the town to the Earl Marischal in 1590, when "four hagbutters" were sent to oust his obstreperous brother Robert Keith of Benholm from the Abbey of Deer. It may here be interpolated that the military stores advanced by the burgh to James the Sixth when he blew up the Hays' castle of Slains were never paid for, a reminder that those who sup with Governments require at all times a very long spoon.

George Keith, who gave the college to the town in 1593, thus deserves to be remembered amongst the eminent Aberdonians. Whether he was born at Inverugie, near Peterhead, or Dunnottar, near Stonehaven, or at any other of the numerous castles or country houses possessed by the family, he associated himself for many years very closely with the fortunes of the burgh, and at Marischal Hall, the house which on being pulled down gave its name to Marischal Street, he spent as much of his time as could be spared from the king's business, in which he was active, and the care of his extensive estates. Born in 1553 he succeeded his grandfather the fourth Earl in 1581, and lived until 1623. His grandfather had been very much to the forefront during the Reformation, and although he, and his successor in the earldom, did pretty well out of the spoils of the old church, there is some reason to believe that both his and his grandson George's adhesion to the new dispensation was perfectly sincere.

This may be a little hard to believe in view of the public outcry that arose in connection with the Abbacy of Deer. A brother of the fourth Earl had been appointed Abbot in 1544 by the Queen Regent, Mary of Guise. He was succeeded in 1551 by the fourth Earl's second son Robert, who became known as the Commendator of Deer, and who was a rascal, a hypocrite and a time-server. On his death some forty years later, King James VI gave the property to the fifth Earl, who was the Commendator's heir-at-law, to repay him for his outlays while acting as ambassador to Denmark in connection with the king's marriage. No doubt the adherents of the old faith, who were very strong in the North-East, being headed by the Earls of Huntly and Erroll, made the most of the transaction, perhaps hoping that Marischal, whose mother was a Catholic and one of the Hays of Erroll, might be deflected from accepting the gift. Patrick Gordon of Ruthven, a Catholic propagandist of the next generation, while describing the Earl George as "a learned, wise and upright good man", alleges that "fourteen score chalders of meal and bere were a sore tentation, and he could not weel endure the rendering back of such a morsel", although his wife "forbids her husband to leave such a consuming moch in his house". It is believed to have been in answer to his wife's repetition of the public criticism of his action that the Earl coined the contemptuous brushing-off epigram which superseded "Veritas vincit" as the motto of his family and which, having been inscribed on the first buildings of his College, has been adopted as the motto of Marischal College also, "They haif sayd: Quhat say they? Lat Yame Say".

Arising out of this interesting piece of Jacobean business there was recorded a further anecdote. The Earl's lady, as has been indicated, was much disturbed by the whole affair and dreamed a dreary dream. "In her sleep she saw a great number of religious men in their habit come forth of that Abbey (Deer) to the strong Craig of Dunnottar. . . . She saw them also sett themselves around about the rock to get it down and demolish it, having no instruments nor tools wherewith to perform this work, but only penknives, wherewith they foolishly (as it seemed to her) began to pick at the craigie. She smiled to see them intend so fruitless an enterprise", but when she called her husband to clear them off "behold the whole craigie, with all his strong and stately buildings was by their penknives undermined . . . so as there remained nothing but the wrack of their rich furniture and stuff floating on the waves of a raging and tempestuous sea".

Those who put credence in such freits interpret the monks' use of penknives as indicating the length of time that elapsed between the dream and the fall of the house of Marischal nearly 150 years later. And while we are on this macabre subject we may mention that the other principal home of the family had its fortune "redd" thus by the celebrated and lugubrious Thomas the Rhymer:

> Inverugie by the sea,
> Lairdless shall thy lands be,
> And aneath thy cauld hearth-stane
> The tod shall bring her bairns hame.

As however, Thomas was dead long before the Keiths owned or had built Inverugie Castle, his prophecy had reference to a previous shadowy building known as the Craig of Inverugie built by the Cheynes, whose lands passed to the Keiths by marriage and were thus at no time "lairdless".

George Keith was sent to King's College, where he studied the Classics and Hebrew, and is said to have shown considerable interest in history and to have appreciated literature. The auld college, although by this time the Reformers ruled the land, had contrived under its resourceful and determined Principal, Alexander Anderson, to continue very much in the old ways, until 1569, which would have been about the year when Keith left, when he was deposed. Thence, with his brother William, the future Earl Marischal went to Geneva, where he studied under Beza, and his brother William was killed in a brawl. Beza, a member of a noble Burgundian family, poet, scholar, lawyer, military chaplain, diplomat, administrator, theologian, historian and professor, had an extraordinarily varied and exciting career. He was the associate, biographer and successor of John Calvin, who had been dead only a few years when Keith reached Geneva, but Beza appears to have mitigated the severity of his master's rule. He had several Scottish pupils, the most eminent of whom was Andrew Melville, to whom, even more than to John Knox, the Church of Scotland owes its present constitution.

When he had concluded his studies at Geneva, the young scholar set off on the Grand Tour of Europe, during the course of which he spent some time with the Landgrave of Hesse, chief of the descendants of the celebrated Catti or Chatti, whose leader Arminius had destroyed the legions of Augustus Caesar under his general Varus, A.D. 9. The story goes that the Saxon and the Scot toasted one another as the respective heads of the family in Scotland and Germany.

On his return home George Keith appears to have been involved in quite a few of the feuds of the period. After his succession to the title in 1581 he was absolved for being art and part in the murder of his kinsman, William Keith of Ludquharn, and after he founded Marischal College he was before the Privy Council for his share in a deadly feud with the laird of Meldrum. And the quarrel with his brother Robert over the Abbey of Deer may not have been wholly his brother's fault. On the other hand, he was highly regarded by the king, who chose him to go as his ambassador to Denmark in connection with James VI's wooing of the Princess Anne, in which duty "he behaved to the great admiration of the Danes and glory of the Scottish nation". But it was a costly trip even for a nobleman whose inherited rental of 270,000 merks a year (£15,000 sterling) made him the richest subject in Scotland, whose lands mainly in the Lothians, Angus, the Mearns, Aberdeenshire, Moray and Caithness were so extensive that he could travel from Berwick-on-Tweed to John o' Groats and never take a meal or spend a night in a house not his own.

The Reformation was just as much a revolution as the Renaissance, and its effects were political and social as well as religious. George Keith with his training, could scarcely avoid being deeply involved with the new ideas that the spirit of the age had liberated. There was a similar ferment in the minds of men in 1560 and subsequent years as there is today in 1960. Values changed overnight, ideas had suddenly become fluid and struck civilisation with all the irresistible impetus of the waves of the sea. It is not possible within the limits of a page or two to do justice to the extraordinary upsurging of intellectual power in the Scotland of those days. Aberdeen was especially active in this respect. There was not a seaport or university town, not a military camp or a commercial community on the Continent where the Aberdeen accent could not be heard, and on the plainstones of the Castlegate one could encounter as many Aberdonians of European celebrity as one may meet Englishmen of like distinction today on the pavements of Whitehall. The history of the century following 1560 teems with the names of such eminent Aberdonians, and our comparative insignificance in contemporary affairs is a humbling thought.

In these circumstances it was almost impossible that a high-spirited and rich nobleman like George Keith should not be inspired to do something for his country. And so in 1593, having got the succession of his patriarchal estates straightened out and his fortunes, insofar as the Danish matrimonial embassy went, in part restored by the grant of the lordship of Altries with the abbacy of Deer, he embarked upon two projects and was entrusted with another royal commission. By virtue of this last he was appointed Lieutenant of the North to keep an eye on the Catholic Gordons and Hays who were embroiled in the mysterious episode of the Spanish Blanks and were regarded at Court as only too capable of staging a rebellion in favour of the old faith. At the same time George Keith entered into a contract with the feuars of Peterhead, which he had erected into a burgh of barony six years before, and laid in effect the foundations of the corporate community there. He was also responsible for the first harbour.

But the Earl's gift to Aberdeen was the crowning glory of his career. A year or two before, Edinburgh had somewhat belatedly got its university, and in 1592 Sir Alexander Fraser of Philorth had secured permission from the crown to erect a college at Fraserburgh which, after a chequered existence, was closed down in 1605. Marischal College was thus the last of the six universities, or colleges to be founded in Scotland. The Earl had acquired the property of the Carmelite or White Friars in the Green and of the Preaching or Black Friars in the Woolmanhill, the Deer properties had come to him by royal charter, and he had persuaded the Town Council to make over to him the buildings and some of the property of the Franciscan or Grey Friars in the Broadgate. All or most of these subjects or their proceeds he conveyed "freely and for nocht" to endow his foundation and he stipulated (perhaps having in mind the town's alienation of its common lands) "that there should be no perpetual leasing out of land or feus, whether on pretext of augmentation or improvement, or for any other reason, or under any name whatsoever". But this strict injunction did not avail, and within five years a perpetual feu had been granted. On 25 April 1593 the General Assembly passed the Charter which was ratified by the Estates three months later.

When, a hundred years before, Bishop Elphinstone had won royal and papal authority for the establishment of King's College, the argument for the foundation was that this was a remote part of Scotland cut off from the rest of the country by arms of the sea and mountains and inhabited by "rude, unlettered and almost barbarous men" to whom a university in Aberdeen would make knowledge available to the ignorant and culture to the uncivilised. But things apparently were not much better in 1593, for the Earl Marischal opens his foundation charter with the lament, "observing and seriously considering with ourselves in what darkness and ignorance most men lie, so that they exist in misery, erring most shamefully and wickedly as to the method of a good and happy life, and hence failing grievously, so that, stained from natural depravity with every crime, they often suffer the most complete ruin and shipwreck". His solution is "an honourable, liberal and christian education and training", wherefore he has resolved to found a "gymnasium" in Aberdeen, "a city which has deserved well at our hands" in the old Greyfriars buildings, "where young men may be thoroughly trained and instructed, both in the other humane arts and also in Philosophy and a purer piety, under the charge of competent and learned teachers".

The original staff of the College consisted of a principal, three regents (that is professors who carried their respective classes through their full course from start to finish), six alumni or bursars, a steward and a cook, all living in, students not bursars being permitted to live out. It was not until about the end of the eighteenth century that the Scottish Universities ceased to be predominantly collegiate and the personnel both teachers and students to find their own lodgings outside. The opening of the hostel at King's College this autumn marks the course of the return to the older fashion. At Marischal College to begin with there was a distinct atmosphere of cleavage from the older tradition at King's for the Earl Marischal had been a member of a committee of inquiry into conditions at the seminary in the old town, he was a close friend of Andrew Melville, whose reforming zeal did not confine itself to the church, and he was of course a strong Protestant himself.

Many famous men were connected with old Marischal College in the two-and-three quarter centuries of its independence. There was Duncan Liddell, mathematician and doctor, who generously endowed it with bursaries which still bear his name, otherwise commemorated by the monument in the haughs of Pitmedden of Dyce and by a plaque in St. Nicholas Kirk. There was William Forbes, for some years Principal who was wont to preach for four or five hours at a stretch, and whom Charles I made first Bishop of Edinburgh because of his advocacy of a reconciliation with Rome. There were Bishop Gilbert Burnet, historian of the Revolution, and the great James Gregory; Thomas Reid, James VI's Latin Secretary, whose gift of books to the library made it "the best library that ever the north parts of Scotland saw" and whose benefactions included five of the six volumes of St. Paul's Cathedral library to survive the Great Fire of London; the last and greatest Earl Marischal and his brother Field Marshal James Keith; John Skinner, author of *Tullochgorum*; Principal George Campbell, author of *The Philosophy of Rhetoric*, 1776, and the *Dissertation on Miracles*, 1762; James Beattie, author of *The Minstrel*; Sir William Fordyce, "father" of the North of Scotland College of Agriculture; Sir James McGrigor, Wellington's chief medical officer; and James Clark Maxwell, probably the leading physicist of his time, to whom a comparative nonentity at King's was preferred for the joint chair at the union in 1860.

The fifth Earl Marischal died in 1623 at Dunnottar, plagued by his second wife, who belonged to the Ogilvy family of Airlie and who at his death carried off a quantity of her deceased husband's property and whose acts and character including her "clandestine and night work" were trenchantly stigmatised by King James, "out of the regard we had to the memory of that man who had to our honour and contentment served us at home and abroad in greatest charges".

William Alexander
or *Johnny Gibb of Gushetneuk*

THE city of Aberdeen was founded and built up principally by Flemings and Saxons. Its hinterland, upon which it peculiarly depends for an important section of its activity and prosperity, and from which over many centuries it has drawn great reinforcements to its population, consisted originally of Taexali and Beaker men and "clannyt men from Birse", to which were later added Scandinavians, Saxons and Flemings, with a few Normans in the higher social strata, and a handful of Huguenots from France.

William Alexander

That being so, and since Aberdeen's gates have always been open to the stranger to take him in, even from the lesser breeds south of the Dee and from "our auld enemies of England" (as the burgh minutes used to have it), the town has a cosmopolitan provenance, which its inhabitants have endeavoured to temper, if not altogether to conceal, by a very intense pride and interest in Aberdonians' achievement, particularly when that achievement happens to emphasise the differences and distinction between inhabitants and natives of the North-east of Scotland and those who have been so unfortunate as to be born outside the charmed area.

On the whole, these characteristics, although perhaps nowadays hardly so strongly marked as in past generations, have survived amongst Aberdonians with a surprising tenacity. They account beyond a doubt for the enthusiasm that at intervals over a period of a hundred years, with every testimony invariably prognosticating the early and complete demise of the doric or braid Buchan dialect as a medium of speech, has greeted some outstanding example of literature in that tongue. *Johnny Gibb of Gushetneuk*, first published serially in the (then weekly) *Free Press*, 1869-70, *Hamewith* in 1900, and *Eppie Elrick* in our more recent days, have all been acclaimed by a public with no bounds of social status or distinction of academic training, but most aggressively Aberdonian at heart.

Johnny Gibb and *Hamewith* have within the area of Scotland's North-east acquired something of the reverential atmosphere that in Oxbridge and Camford circles surrounds Homer and Virgil and Horace. Phrases and lines are quoted from them with unction to describe or elucidate all manner of incidents and problems of experience and conduct. The authors of both were men of outstanding quality: here we deal only with *Johnny Gibb*'s creator, William Alexander (1826-94). He was born on the farm of Rescivet, near Legatesden, Pitcaple, where his father combined crofting with a smiddy. From Rescivet his father James, complete with family (eventually there were ten), migrated to a nearby holding called Damhead, where William, who intended to be a farmer also, came by an accident that cost him a leg, and had to look out for another form of livelihood.

At this juncture he came under the notice of William McCombie, the farmer of Cairnballoch, Alford, and not the only agriculturist of Aberdeenshire to become the proprietor of a newspaper—in his case the *North of Scotland Gazette*, succeeded in 1853 by the *Free Press*. In 1852 William Alexander joined the staff of the *Gazette* as a reporter and sub-editor—the present writer possesses his letter of acceptance of the post, presented by Alexander's nephew and namesake. In Aberdeen, and throughout the surrounding area where the Aberdeen newspapers circulated, Alexander became, at presbytery and ploughing match, social or local authority meeting, one of a great trio of reporters, James Valentine for the *Aberdeen Journal*, William Carnie for the *Aberdeen Herald* and himself of course for the *Free Press*.

Carnie in his *Reporting Reminiscences* has many anecdotes of their individual prowess and collective exploits. They arranged to have a school of shorthand started in a room in Correction Wynd. The hour of tuition was from 6 to 7 a.m., and the attendance of young men was from 50 to 60! In 1856 a Head Court of the citizens was convened by the Lord Provost on the Castlegate to decide upon the views of the inhabitants on the respective merits of the Buchan railway schemes propounded by Alexander Anderson and John Duncan, the plan of the latter providing for the line to traverse the town's links. In the heat of the debate, the three reporters being seated at a table close to that which constituted the official platform, the press was such that the Fourth Estate might have suffered three serious casualties had Alexander not inserted his wooden leg between the tables and saved them from being crushed.

Parenthetically, with what gay efficiency our predecessors carried off their disputes. Of the chief promoter of this scheme the rhyme ran:

He sent them up to London town
  In first-class by the train;
He feasted them on turtle soup,
  And claret and champagne.
Turtle soup, champagne and claret—
  All the best of meat and drinks,
So they went before the Parliament,
  And sold the people's Links;
The only ground for miles around
  For exercise or play,
The people's only heritage
  These traitors gave away.

Compulsory education has put an end to the mental agility that composed and appreciated that sort of thing.

At Town Council meetings where the Three Musketeers sat together at a little table in a corner, Alexander had a habit, when a spicy passage occurred, "of pressing the thumb and forefinger of his right hand tightly upon his eyes and bending down, becoming wholly enveloped in the joke, while Valentine seemed to be seized with a fit, and throwing himself suddenly backwards gave a sharp bark of a laugh. The other worthy affected to be very grave." The Town Clerk, John Angus, was wont to pull them up with an admonitory "Gentlemen, gentlemen, remember we are at business".

In due course William Alexander succeeded William McCombie in the editorial chair of the *Free Press*, and two years later in 1872, it became a daily newspaper. More permanently important, as it proved, was that when he became editor, *Johnny Gibb* was running as a serial. He had built the house 19 Watson Street to which in 1867 he brought his wife from Chapel of Garioch. She was a first cousin of Sir Theodore Martin, part-author of the *Bon Gaultier Ballads*, biographer of the Prince Consort, and husband of Helen Faucit, one of the greatest of Shakespearean actresses. A younger sister of William Alexander was destined to be the grandmother of Sir James I. C. Crombie, one of the few recent Aberdeen graduates to rise to high distinction in the Civil Service.

William Alexander's younger brother Henry, who served his apprenticeship as an engineer, came into journalism after losing an eye in the "shops" at St. Rollox and married a daughter of William McCombie of the *Free Press,* whose mother was a relative of Sir Johnston Forbes Robertson the actor and of the greatest of Aberdeen's historians, Joseph Robertson. Henry, when William on the starting of the *Evening Gazette* in 1882 took control of that venture, became editor of the *Free Press,* and was succeeded in the chair by his eldest son Henry who was knighted when Lord Provost of Aberdeen, and who died in 1940. Sir Henry was partly responsible for the introduction of town and country planning though not for the course it eventually took.

The younger son, William McCombie Alexander, who died in 1959, was one of the most versatile scholars of his time, master of several languages—he went to Russia as interpreter with a team of British scientists to study an eclipse of the sun in Siberia between the wars—a competent mathematician, a historian of Aberdeen University, and author of one of the few sensible books on the derivation of place-names. Had he not been above all a dilettante and an amateur of life, had he applied himself to the development of but one of his many gifts, he would have made a very great name for himself.

The first edition of *Johnny Gibb* was published by Robert Walker and James Murray, Aberdeen, in 1871. From that date to the novelist's centenary in 1926 no fewer than nineteen editions were published, a record which few novels, no matter how manfully "cried up" in the London press, have equalled, and to which certainly very few domiciled (as it were) in Scotland have been able to aspire. Amongst the editions may be specially mentioned the noble de luxe issue, with twenty illustrations by that great artist Sir George Reid, and the seventeenth, which appeared in 1912, with twelve illustrations and an introduction by Alexander Mackie, whose lectures on Alexander's works in the country districts vied with those of Professor J. Arthur Thomson in popularity during the early years of this century. Anyone who wishes to become acquainted with *Johnny Gibb* from scratch cannot do better than to devote a few of his leisure hours to a search for a copy of this edition.

Amongst other works by William Alexander, only two need be mentioned, one of them probably the most authoritative of all commentaries on the civilisation of the North-east in that period —*Notes and Sketches illustrative of Northern Rural Life in the Eighteenth Century,* and the other, first published in 1875, is fiction again, *Sketches of Life Among my Ain Folk.* There are many who regard *Life Among my Ain Folk* with more affection and appreciation than *Johnny Gibb.*

But *Johnny* is surely immortal. Not even the opening sentence of Xenophon's *Anabasis,* or Caesar's *Gallic Wars,* or the first lines of Virgil's *Aeneid* are more quoted or more generally known amongst the normal academes than, with the normal reading public in our midst, the "Heely, heely, Tam, ye glaiket stirk—ye hinna on the hin shelvin' o' the cairt" with which Johnny sets out for the "walls" of Tarlair and William Alexander made his entry into the Hall of the Immortals. Thereafter with majestic decorum the story is unfolded of the Disruption, in all the realism of life in the landward areas in the first years of Victoria's reign.

The characters are distilled out of the very heart of the Aberdeenshire tradition. There's Johnny himself, cautious, capable, well-doing, upright even to harshness: there's his dramatic opposite Peter Birse, foosionless, henpecked, malleable; his redoubtable wife, who need not lower her colours to any tough lady in fiction, not even to John Galt's Lady Grippy herself; Dauvid Hadden the laird's man and ground officer; Jonathan Tawse the stickit minister and dominie; Meg Raffan the hen-wife; Hairy Muggart the joiner and Sandy Peterkin the smith; the farm servant Tam Meerison (the "glaiket-stirk" himself) and Johnny's red-haired kitchen-quine Jinse Deans; Roderick McAul the souter and his ill-tricket imp of a son Willy; and many another type, if not quite so easily encountered nowadays in a country walk, that used to be thick on the ground half a century ago.

Life among my Ain Folk consists of four short stories which delve rather more deeply into the emotions than is the case in any of the episodes described in *Johnny Gibb*. The longer novel has nothing of the pathos and tenderness with which *Mary Malcolmson's Wee Maggie* and *Francie Herrigerie's Shargar Laddie* are suffused; while *Couper Sandy* is a good-going rural comedy and *Baubie Huie's Bastard Geet* deals with a problem about which, when it was written, it was not considered quite the thing to write or even to speak. The four tales each offer something of their own to enrich the colours of *Johnny Gibb*.

William Alexander himself was a man of very strong views—Free Kirker, Radical, friend and defender of Robertson Smith, another most eminent Aberdonian, when the latter was hounded out of the Free Church on a charge of heresy. The story is told that Dr. Davidson, of Wartle, a formidable character, who had operated on Alexander after his accident as a young man, half-humorously challenged the editor after an election with the retrospective threat, "Ay, they tell me, Willie Elshiner, ye've turn't oot a terrible Radical. Man, if I'd kent, it's nae yer leg but yer heid I'd cuttit aff." Davidson was a holy terror. As he was leaving a country house after being upstairs attending the laird, he was being assisted into his ulster by the butler, a man notorious for his meanness. The latter, hoping to get free advice, said, "I wonder, Doctor, what I'd better do for a sore throat". "Cut it", was the succinct answer as the medico wrathfully stumped over the doorstep.

Alexander was not of that habit of mind. All testimonies are of the sweetness and kindliness of his nature, the infinite trouble he would take to assist the needy or the deserving, the geniality of his discourse, and the impregnable broadness of his dialect. He had the reputation of being an uncannily shrewd judge of character, and could see further into a stone wall than most. Thus he regarded Sir Alexander Anderson, despite that worthy's many and blatant lapses which might have been expected to repel the uncompromising churchman, as the greatest of contemporary Aberdonians. He himself, for all his manifold and valuable gifts as a journalist, depends for his immortality upon what were after all merely recreations. It is a warning to those, now as heretofore, to whom the Fourth Estate presents an appearance of permanence and power.

James Chalmers
and the founding of the *Journal*

LOCAL tradition has it that Aberdeen had its news of the Battle of Culloden in a news-sheet issued by the town's printer James Chalmers, a couple of days after the battle; and that this print, the first in point of time of the long series of the *Aberdeen Journal,* was burnt and its author forced to fly for his life by a band of Jacobites who took possession of the burgh in their retreat from Culloden. It is always a thankless duty to dispel pleasant legends, but there is only a little grain of truth, if indeed any at all, in the story. James Chalmers quite probably was with the Hanoverian army at Culloden, whither it had marched from Aberdeen, for he appears to have had some kind of quasi-official civilian appointment under the Government. He may have sent an account of the battle to Aberdeen in a letter, and it may have been printed as a sort of bulletin, but the elaboration of the burning and Chalmers's flight for life is romantic fiction typical of the kind of nonsense that for over two centuries has been written about that sorry episode in the history of Scotland. Such Jacobites as may have fled from the battle to Aberdeen did so in ones and twos, and made haste to get further away or to hide themselves immediately. From the time when the Duke of Cumberland took up his quarters in the burgh in the spring of 1746, the Jacobites, who under Lord Lewis Gordon and Moir of Lonmay had for five months lorded it over the inhabitants, were conspicuous by their absence.

James Chalmers

The tradition at least is true in this respect that it presents James Chalmers to posterity as a very wide-awake gentleman indeed. He belonged to a family that was (unlike the Jaffreys) of the auld blood and aristocracy of the town. The Chalmerses of Balnacraig, in Cromar, and of Balbithan and other properties were prominent in burghal history very early, William de Camera (which is the Latin for Chalmers) of Findon having been the Alderman or Provost of Aberdeen for at least two terms before 1400. In all, the family gave seven provosts to our city, and the name is prominent in its records for five hundred years. James Chalmers's father was minister of Dyke, in Morayshire, when the future printer was born—he was baptised on 8 January 1713; so that strictly speaking he is not to be described as an Aberdonian. In 1728 his father was transferred to Greyfriars Kirk in Aberdeen, and became at the same time Professor of Divinity at Marischal College, filling both offices until 1744.

It had been decided to make James a printer, which then as now occupied an intermediate position between the trades and the professions, combining (let us hope) the rewarding emoluments of the one with the at least theoretical intellectual freedom of the other. Accordingly he was apprenticed to James Nicol, who was the town's printer in more senses than one, for he was officially appointed by the town as well as by the town's college, Marischal, and he was the only printer in town. After serving his time he went south to continue his training with a famous London Metropolitan printer named Watts in Lincoln's Inn Fields. This was the printing house where Benjamin Franklin improved his knowledge of his own trade when, encouraged by the Governor of Pennsylvania, William Keith of Ludquharn, he made his first trip to London in 1725. The story that Chalmers and Franklin worked side by side is, however, another legend, for Franklin had left long before the Chalmerses had migrated from Dyke to Aberdeen. James Chalmers worked in London until 1736.

Nicol meanwhile was getting old. He was fifth in succession of the Aberdeen printers, for although the art was introduced into Scotland in 1507 in order that the Aberdeen Breviary might be printed to the order of the Bishop of Aberdeen, and although the second of the Scots printers who are known by name was a Deeside man named Thomas Davidson, it was not until 1622 that Edward Raban set up his press in Aberdeen. Raban was a pretty good printer, some of whose productions are still esteemed by bibliophiles. He was succeeded in 1650 by a much inferior craftsman, James Brown, son of the minister of Invernochty, who filled the bill until 1661, when he died. It seemed that he printed or was intended to print in 1657 the "Weekly diurnall to be sellit for the use of the inhabitants", John Forbes stationer "to fernish" (i.e. publish) "the samen weekly." This John Forbes followed Nicol, his son, also John Forbes, being styled printer in the licence from the town. The book by which the names of Forbes is remembered is the *Cantus, Songs and Fancies* of 1662, with subsequent editions in 1666 and 1682, the first song-book published in this country. The older Forbes was probably the author. Forbes died in 1704, and for the next few years only one book was issued from the Aberdeen printing-press apart from official matter from the town and university, the licence being held by Forbes's widow Margaret Cuthbord, who was not an enterprising person. But her daughter Margaret Forbes in 1710 married James Nicol, and the following year the town conferred the privilege on Mr. and Mrs. Nicol. Of Nicol we know little. The very day he resigned in 1736 James Chalmers, who having no doubt heard what was toward had hastened home from London, applied to the Town Council to be permitted to succeed him. His prayer being granted, a new era of better printing opened in Aberdeen.

For some time life was reasonably plain sailing in Scotland in those days. Chalmers, like most educated men of his time, was a competent musician, and in 1740 we find the Town Council appointing him Master of the Sang School, which functioned then in a building in the north-west corner of St. Nicholas churchyard, not very far from the Grammar School. While the appointment does not seem to have been wholly eleemosynary, Chalmers desired to have Andrew Tait, a professional musician, as teacher in the school, whilst he himself discharged the associated duties of precentor of the West Parish Church. It is, however, more than a little curious that when the Aberdeen Musical Society was founded in January, 1748, one of the six founders was Andrew Tait, then and from 1743 organist in St. Paul's Church, whereas James Chalmers never became even an ordinary member, although socially as well as artistically the society was the highlight of the town.

When the Jacobite Rebellion was so brusquely stamped out at Culloden and during the subsequent summer, Chalmers, who was "far ben" with the Government, was appointed a commissioner for the sequestrated estates, and had amongst others Hallhead and Esslemont in his charge. There is even some reason to believe that he had Government assistance in founding his new paper whose first number, with the title of *Aberdeen's Journal*, appeared on 5 January 1748. Though not in point of time the first published Scottish newspaper, the *Journal* eventually became the oldest newspaper continuously published north of the border, and its suppression in 1957 like the discontinuance a year or two earlier of the *Northern Almanack*, the lineal and almost continuous successor of the *Aberdeen Almanac* of 1623, while no doubt arising out of the economic background to newspaper and periodical publishing in the 1950s, might have been postponed had the proprietors been steeped in the Aberdeen tradition. It should be pointed out that while the claim is made that the *Aberdeen Journal* was converted into a daily as the *Aberdeen Daily Journal* in 1876, the old weekly newspaper actually never ceased to appear and never lost its individuality until it ceased publication in 1957.

We do not know much more about Aberdeen's first newspaper proprietor and journalist. During a trip to London by sea after 1746 he seems to have been captured by a French privateer and released within a week without his belongings. He married in 1739 a granddaughter of John Allardes, who had been Provost of Aberdeen 1700-1. He printed in 1755, *A Plan of Education in the Marischal College and University of Aberdeen* which enjoyed a considerable reputation on the Continent, although Marischal's foundation had already attained to sufficient celebrity in the New World to form the basis for the charters of at least two American universities. In view of James Chalmers's paternal and official connection with Marischal College, there was a real recognition of the Aberdeen tradition in the will of his great-grandson, John Gray Chalmers, who in 1890 left £10,000 to Aberdeen University to found the Chalmers Chair of English Literature in 1893. For the rest, the original James seems to have been a witty fellow who could turn a competent rhyming stave, and even on occasion in his newspaper addressed his readers in verse that is more intelligible than some of the subsequent prose that has appeared in it.

The first issue of the paper was produced in Raban's old printing house on the north side of Castle Street in a building belonging to the town, just behind what is now the back wall of the Aberdeen Head Office of the Clydesdale and North Bank. In 1798 the printing works were transferred to a disused ribbon factory behind the Townhouse; in 1813, they migrated to the Adelphi, where they remained until 1894, when they were established in the quarters where the old weekly was to be laid to rest, in Broad Street. The first number of the newspaper contained nothing that could be termed original but the solitary advertisement which announced "that on the 29th of last month were amissing three promissory notes of the Aberdeen Company, one for £10 and two for 20s. each; and of the Bank of Scotland two for twenty shillings. Whoever brings them to the publisher of this paper shall have two guineas reward, and no questions asked." The paper consisted of four pages of three columns each, folio size, and the price was twopence.

James Chalmers died in 1764, having triumphantly survived one challenge to his monopoly in a rival sheet named the *Aberdeen Intelligencer,* which lasted from January 1752 to February 1757, one of the causes of whose failure being the disinclination of virtuous Aberdonians to pay double for their advertisements. James was succeeded by his son James, born in 1742, married to a member of the Douglas family that still in our day own Tilwhilly, and trained to his job in Cambridge after having studied at Marischal College. He carried on the paper and the printing business until his death in 1810. He tried, unsuccessfully, to expand his publishing business in 1787 by launching the *Northern Gazette and Literary Chronicle and Review of the Month,* but this literary digest failed to find favour with the Aberdonian of the time, and expired after eight months. Soon after, leading articles were introduced into the *Journal* and the price raised to 3½d. though whether there was a connection between the two innovations has not transpired. Chalmers also tried an *Aberdeen Magazine* which persisted with a fair amount of success in the late 1780s and early 1790s.

James the second's claim to fame has come actually to rest upon a quite fortuitous circumstance, to wit, the appearance in Aberdeen in the course of a Highland tour of Robert Burns who spent a convivial hour in Chalmers's office with the printer himself, "a facetious fellow" according to the poet; Bishop Skinner, son of John Skinner the author of *Tullochgorum* and *The Ewie with the Crookit Horn,* who has left an account of the session; Andrew Sheriffs, M.A., "a little decrepid body with some abilities" as Burns described him, the author of various poems and plays and of the popular song "A Cogie o' Yill an' a pickle ait-meal", who had been editor of a rival newspaper, the *Chronicle* that soon expired, and was at the time of the historic meeting editor and proprietor of an excellent periodical called the *Caledonian Magazine*; an uncertainly identified Mr. Ross; and John Marshall, a lawyer, who was credited with the authorship of "Logie o' Buchan" and was the improver, if not the original author, of that "Thainy Menzies" song which set Burns off on his "In coming by the Brig o' Dye". A picture of the celebrated meeting still hangs in *The Press and Journal* office.

James Chalmers's second son, David, succeeded to the ownership and control of the *Journal* in 1810. His elder brother, James the third, had migrated to Dundee, started an unsuccessful paper called the *Dundee Mail,* and for a time printed the *Dundee Advertiser.* David, who had been born in 1788, had just come to man's estate when he stepped into his father's shoes. He proved to be the most progressive member of the family. At once he turned the firm into a company—D. Chalmers & Co. He shifted within three years to more commodious premises. In 1830 he introduced steam printing, the first newspaper proprietor in Scotland to do so. Under his energetic and careful management the *Journal* became the leading newspaper in Scotland. In 1832, when it was increased in size to forty-eight columns, considerably larger than any Scottish newspaper up to that time, it also had the largest number of advertisements. When Queen Victoria came to reside at Balmoral, it was claimed that she made an exception in favour of the *Journal* to her practice of having the newspapers filleted for her; the *Journal* she saw as it was delivered.

David Chalmers served for two spells of duty on the Town Council, and two of his daughters married future Provosts—John Webster, 1856-59, and Alexander Nicol, 1866-69, respectively predecessor and successor of Sir Alexander Anderson in the civic chair. Chalmers bought the estate of Westburn, and built the house; the estate was acquired by the Corporation in 1900. In 1854 he retired and handed over the management of his business to his sons James and John Gray Chalmers. He died in 1859. His sons carried on as a private firm until May 1876, when they sold the paper, premises and plant to a limited liability company formed to establish a Conservative daily newspaper in Aberdeen in opposition to the Liberal daily *Free Press.* James died in 1896, and his elder son, D. M. A. Chalmers, of the legal firm founded by Charles, fifth son of the second James, was secretary of the newspaper company almost until his death in 1929. He would have been perfectly at home in the circles in which James the first Chalmers printer moved. He was a survival of the eighteenth century, a *bon viveur,* cultivated, courteous and a kenspeckle figure in the streets of the city. Towards the end of his life he bought Thorngrove, in the Mannofield district, and the present writer spent some happy hours with him there planning a new lay-out of the attractive grounds. A third member of the party one Sunday afternoon in May 1929 was John Buchan (later Lord Tweedsmuir), who was due that week to enter on his duties as Lord High Commissioner to the General Assembly. He wished to write his address and asked his host if he might have some paper, preferably sermon paper. "I'm sorry," said D. M. A., "I can only give you deed paper, but that may do as well."

Only a few weeks later he was dead, and with him died the Chalmers family name in Aberdeen, although the blood of the pioneer newspaper printer is maintained in one who until a few years ago was a member of the Council of the Chamber and is still in business, although not in residence, in Aberdeen—William Littlejohn Cook, whose grandfather William Littlejohn, manager of the Town and County Bank for forty years to 1878, was a son of one of Charles Chalmers's bevy of five daughters.

Home Guard

the men of the *Chamber's Own*

IT may be that members of the Aberdeen Chamber of Commerce are unaware that they share, in their corporate capacity, with the most distinguished personages in the land the honour, if not the title, of having a military unit associated with their name. History, it has long been appreciated, is a fickle jade, and many a body far less deserving of immortality in human memory than that which might quite accurately have been designated the Chamber's Own has been accorded a niche in the Temple of Fame. The theme might be considerably elaborated, but as this is an article in a reputable journal and as such is expected to present brevity with or without wit, the cryptic spirit of those opening sentences will here and now be abandoned and we shall "return to our muttons".

Aberdeen Journals Ltd.

One of the acts which, psychologically, deterred Hitler from insisting on the invasion of the United Kingdom, and which in consequence played a part in the eventual winning of the war was, no doubt, quite unknown to the British Cabinet that made the decision, the raising of the Local Defence Volunteers, later to be renamed the Home Guard, in May 1940. The reason why it was so important was that the appeal for a home defence force was made to and heard by the men who had served in 1914-18; and whatever the Germans may say and however kind we may be in retrospect to our Allies, there is no doubt that every German who fought in that first war, including Hitler, knew who beat him, and that "who" was the British soldier. We may, and do, make jokes about the Breathless Army; one misguided relative of the present writer who endured all the horrors of war in the H.L.I. has even gone so far as to say that the L.D.V.s' "as there was little likelihood of them having to fight, were renamed Guards". It was, as has just been stated, the fact that they were embodied that contributed to the likelihood of their not having to fight.

When the 4th City of Aberdeen Battalion L.D.V. was raised, firms in the city with large numbers of employees were encouraged to form so-called utility platoons which were to be incorporated in this Battalion. Soon afterwards several Ministries were persuaded that it would be advisable for firms engaged in the work they were commissioning all over the country, to be able, if necessary, to defend their own premises. This aspiration resulted in little more than the appearance of strange architectural pimples upon the face of some industrial buildings in the city. At the same time large numbers of employees in these works were joining the Home Guard and more could be expected, particularly if facilities were developed for enabling them to be grouped according to their places of employment.

Accordingly, about the beginning of October 1940, there began to take shape out of chaos what was to be known as the 7th (City of Aberdeen) (Works) Battalion Home Guard. Its Commanding Officer and second-in-command were both associated with firms who were and are members of the Chamber, one of the adjutants was a member, two of its officers have been Presidents of the Chamber and, with one or two exceptions, all of the score or so of establishments brought together under the Battalion's aegis were members of the Chamber. It therefore implies no straining of language to call it The Chamber's Own. As such, those who composed all its ranks may remain in this account of their adventures anonymous; it would be invidious to single out any unit for special mention where all did their bit manfully. The Battalion continued in being as a Works Battalion until the Home Guard was ordered to stand down in 1944, and it is believed that, with one doubtful rival in Leeds, it was the only Battalion of its kind in the country that did so survive to the end.

A Battalion of two or three thousand men divided as this was at one time, into twenty-three "private armies", could hardly be expected to be popular in conventional military circles. And there were occasions when the brass hats could not be blamed for their opinion, although the Battalion was fortunate in always having as good friends the Garrison Commander (also with links with the Chamber), Highland District, and Scottish Command. As late as the autumn of 1942 there were rumours that influences were at work in more exalted circles to put a period to the Battalion's activities and existence; but if these rumours were true, the Battalion survived to win a still greater measure of official confidence. Even in 1944, after D-Day, it came safely through a difficult period. Jerry having had recourse to guided missiles, which were aimed only at the London area, and when, very properly, measures were taken to strengthen the anti-aircraft defences of the metropolitan sector, the official mind, fettered by immutable regulation, made identical arrangements for Aberdeen and Londonderry and Stornoway as for London, just as in civil life a few years later it was to make the Catering and Wages Act indiscriminately applicable to Applecross and Mayfair, Appleby and Piccadilly. A special board was appointed in Aberdeen to take the cream off the Home Guard for Ack-Ack duties but in the 7th Battalion units whose commanders kept their heads, this resulted in reorganisation in a more compact and efficient body.

This is in no way intended as a history of the Battalion. Its members retired into private life unhonoured and unsung, and they were unwept for the simple reason that there was nothing to weep about either in what they did or what they left undone. For the most part, although not in every case, the works units were under the command of a senior executive, and in several cases of the head, of the firm. As the reason for the units' existence was first and all the time the defence of their own establishments, there were obviously strong grounds why unit commanders should put the interests of their firms' war effort before that of mere military exigencies. This was eventually recognised by an arrangement announced at the end of 1942, that the Battalion was not to be called out in the event of a raid, but this decision was apparently cancelled six months later when there was allocated to the Battalion a long stretch of the perimeter defence of Aberdeen. Obviously the whole *modus vivendi* was of a delicate nature, which no doubt explains why other works battalions proved to be unworkable, while the survival of the Aberdeen Battalion testifies all the more emphatically to the good sense of those who had the most intimate dealings with it—the Garrison Commander, the G.S.O. whose sphere of influence embraced the Home Guard, the Battalion commander, and those in charge of the Units it comprised.

Even so, difficulties cropped up. Generally, if a visiting brass hat at a unit commanders' conference failed to couch his instructions in terms that softened them into suggestions, a grin would ripple round the room which said, without a word spoken, "You're telling me". When in the course of time it was decreed, rightly or wrongly, that the units should be brought together in groups, under the commander of one of them who got the rank of major, there was a danger that ancient firm loyalties and rivalries might rear their heads, and co-operation between the members of a group might run the risk of being less hearty than would be the case as between equals. That this did not develop to any serious extent was due to the sound business sense that was directing the various units. In one group indeed the commanders, who were all captains—the selection of a major being left to their own choice—decided to do without a major altogether, on the dual ground that they had managed all right hitherto and that in any case, while there had never in history been a Major who earned the epithet Great, there had been a Great Captain, they continued to operate in perfect humour and amity to the end of the chapter.

The public impression that the Home Guard offered an easy way out of the strenuous duties of civilian war work is not borne out by the facts, at least so far as the Aberdeen Works Battalion is concerned. A unit commander's diary which has been made available for the purposes of this article shows that during the four years of the Battalion's active existence, there was a parade every Sunday (with very few exceptions) and two or more unit drills, lectures or demonstrations every week; while officers had, if unit commanders, to attend a battalion conference roughly once a fortnight, conducted proficiency tests, the work on which occupied a goodly number of hours for two or three weeks twice a year, had to take courses on various subjects as and when these were offered, and had week in week out to arrange rota of duties and courses of training, to keep registers and generally to do Orderly Room work at odd hours. Apart from the Battalion conferences, other officers had to take their share of such chores, while n.c.o.s, besides their supervisory work at parades and drills, were frequently required to attend refresher courses. It says a great deal for the keenness and good citizenship of the men that these proficiency courses, which brought no increase of non-existent pay and no kudos except the consciousness of efficiency in a job, attracted hundreds of entrants.

Most of the firms put themselves about to ensure that their Home Guard units had reasonably adequate facilities for the performance of their duties. Some had small-bore rifle ranges; some had lecture-rooms, in one or two sumptuous, with first-rate equipment such as a large sand-table with sufficient lay figures to make toy warfare interesting, magnetic blackboards, epidiascopes for showing films, and other appointments. Some of the Battalion officers, after special courses, went the rounds of the units and lectured and demonstrated. Again the keenness of the rank-and-file should be mentioned. One unit commander reported how, having asked a man to procure some twigs of whin for a sand-table lay-out, the private braved a dreadful storm on Tullos Hill to procure these small adjuncts to realism in time for the demonstration. Whilst the rifle-range, small-bore shooting, street fighting, patrols, Smith guns, unarmed combat and similar excitements were naturally most attractive, there was little skulking of drearier subjects like Tewts, messages, gas drill, map-reading and so on, even that extraordinary allegory of real warfare known as battle drill which was introduced in the spring of 1942.

There were, of course, route marches, for which in due course the Battalion was endowed with a pipe band. There were shoots not only at the Black Dog but at other disused ranges near Aberdeen where patrols, distance judging, and other exercises could be undertaken. One ingenious engineer unit rigged up at one of these ranges a moving tank, marked with bull's eyes at the vulnerable points, which was drawn slowly across the butts and fired at from 100 and 200 yards. Some companies contrived to have week-end camps, with night patrols, dawn attacks, and other amenities which appear to have extended to the social aspect, for in one tent occupied by half-a-dozen visitor members of a unit which belonged to a service that is now nationalised, no fewer than eighty-seven empty bottles were counted on the Sunday morning. When the Battalion was assigned its share in the perimeter defences of the city, its various units carefully reconnoitred their sectors, prepared schemes of defence (as indeed they had done for their business premises long before), and tested these out not only by getting other units to attack them but also by attacking other units in them.

The issue of pikes, officially designated bayonet standards, in the early days of the war was the subject of much ribald comment at the time. The facetiousness was rather misplaced in a nation so bound by tradition as ours; after all, pikes have been issued to the defenders of these shores in every case of apprehended invasion since the Norman Conquest. After the pikes came the Ross rifles, and after that very little indeed in the way of armaments for a long time. The artillery of the Home Guard, until the very mobile Smith gun made its appearance in the spring of 1943, was confined to the Blacker bombard, otherwise known as the Spigot mortar, and so far as the Works Battalion was concerned the issue of these was more promissory than actual. This led to an interesting dialogue during one of the Battalion exercises when, in the absence of the bombards themselves, men were detailed to represent them. A highly placed officer who was inspecting the arrangements called a private to order who had passed without paying attention to him. The private, who had spent the first war in the Senior Service, had naturally no very exalted opinion of the Army in any case. "Didn't you see me?" asked the officer. "No, sir," said the private. "But you looked straight at me. You were bound to have seen me." "No, sir." "But you're not blind." "I'm a token Spigot, sir" replied the erstwhile matelot to bring the conversation to a triumphant end. The officer was understood to have recommended urgently an issue of bombards to the Battalion.

The Battalion was called upon to fight many "battles". The most picturesque was an early one laid on in the wooded area on the north bank of the Don beyond Stoneywood. This exercise was planned with all the care that its originator, a unit commander in the Battalion, was wont to lavish in civil life upon theatrical performances. It was noteworthy in that one patrol actually waded, in some parts up to their shoulders, in the Don to gain cover from its overhanging banks, and from the decision of one of the umpires, a Regular n.c.o. who had trained part of the opposing side, who had a detachment of the Battalion "shot" by its own men when he saw they were rounding up the men he had trained. Another exciting encounter was with a company from a county Battalion whose headquarters were captured by two youngsters who persuaded a farm servant to run his tractor beside the building with them crouched in the shelter of its high mudguards.

Several night attacks were also staged. The most exacting of these exercises took place on the south bank of the Dee and in the railway marshalling yards at Craigshaw, on a wild October night of rain and tempest, the pitch darkness being thick enough even to shroud the red lights that were all the recognition signs of shunting engines and vagrant waggons. It was at Craigshaw also that one of the Battalion groups was entrusted with a try out of walkie-talkie communications, the officers who used the instruments being somewhat surprised when, having exhausted their stock of military intelligence and become anecdotal, the Voice of Authority interrupted their conversation with a criticism of the subject of it. On yet another occasion, when a platoon of one unit was posted in a cemetery during a particularly hard winter morning when no movement developed on their sector, the officer in charge later reported that his men stood till they were as stiff as the poor coves underneath.

But the greatest of all the engagements was the celebrated Battle of Bonaccord on 31 May 1942. Aberdeen was attacked by two Battalions of the 52nd Division, the 9th Cameronians and the 4/5th Royal Scots Fusiliers, and a Recce Company. The perimeter defence of the city was then in the hands of the 4th Battalion Home Guard, while the Works Battalion was distributed on its own various premises. The great majority of the Home Guard were naturally old 51st Division men, and inevitably they were out to teach the Lowland Division the art of war. Umpires were to be allocated by the Army to both sides, but for some reason those who were said to have been assigned to the Home Guard never materialised. Nevertheless the umpires who accompanied the assault admitted that the invaders would have been wiped out, tanks and all, several times before they reached the centre of the city, where the exercise was called off.

At one works the attackers were lured into a cul-de-sac. At another a hose was turned on them and one of the armoured vehicles ran into a wall. Several of the principal spires in the city were used as look-out points from which observation of the invading host was maintained. On Union Street, on the pavement, a canvas shelter such as Electricity Department workmen used when repairing underground cables was rigged up to cover an anti-tank gun which, the umpires conceded, knocked out three tanks. On the southern part of the battle-front the Home Guard, founding on a notorious historical precedent, used a sewer to get in the rear of the attackers. In another sector, sharp-shooters with cardboard chimneys over their heads and shoulders were able undetected to cover an assaulting party from a long roof top. When many months later the 52nd Division carried a German town in fine style, Home Guard critics (or sceptics as the case might be) in Aberdeen ascribed the success to the lessons of the Battle of Bonaccord.

Such then, in part at least, were what Alfred de Vigny called the "grandeurs et servitudes militaires" which the Chamber's Own Battalion of the Home Guard experienced in 1940-44; not so much grandeur and plenty of servitude. But probably the steady routine and the remarkably varied range of subjects which were studied helped to make tolerable a period when thinking people, unless their attention was well occupied, might have been tempted to despair. One man earned two wound stripes while serving with the Battalion. Another, while still with it, contrived to be sent to Achnacarry Commando School, where he proved himself as tough as the hardest cases there. A less meritorious notoriety accrued to an officer who, at a training course, was discovered by the President of the School drilling a squad of English majors, one of each couple carried on the other's shoulders, in what he apparently conceived to be the evolutions of cavalry in their classic days.

Peter Williamson
vintner *from the other world*

ABOUT the time when, as was recorded in this series a couple of articles ago, James Chalmers was assuming his responsibilities as printer to Aberdeen Town Council and the Marischal College, there was a douce well-doing and respected citizen in the town, William Fordyce by name, a double baillie in that he held that position both in the royal burgh of Aberdeen and in the burgh of barony of Oldmeldrum, near which he resided. Fordyce had been treasurer of Aberdeen in 1736, he was factor to Sir Alexander Gordon of Gight besides having a merchant's business in Bon-Accord, and he had recently married as his second wife Margaret, daughter of Walter Cochran, Town Clerk depute. He is usually styled "of Achorthies", or Auquhorties as we now spell it, which lies to the eastwards of Meldrum House.

Peter Williamson (right) in conversation with James Bruce "the Abyssinian", the famous traveller

Twenty years were to elapse, or nearly, before it transpired that this benevolent and prosperous gentleman, along with his father-in-law and several other business men and baillies in the city, had for years up to the end of the last Jacobite Rebellion been engaged in the most nefarious traffic that, at least to our modern way of thinking, can be imagined, the kidnapping of children and their transportation to what were then still the North American colonies of Great Britain. That this form of commerce was less reprobated by quite civilised persons in those days will transpire in the course of this article, although eventually the disclosures aroused a considerable amount of public indignation, apart from that which arose from the fact that the crime had been found out. But we have got to remember that in Scotland then and for half a century thereafter, miners were still unfree, and that ın England the Services were recruited mainly by kidnapping, and that the part author with the poet William Cowper of the devotional "Olney Hymns" was the evangelical slave-trading sea-captain, the Rev. John Newton.

No amount of blacks, however, can make a white, and the Aberdeen trade in children to the American plantations makes so disreputable an episode in our civic history that one would avoid allusion to it were it not the cause of the rise to fame of an Aberdonian who has more claims than most to be hailed as eminent, for amongst the 600 children of Aberdeen and its hinterland who were between 1740 and 1746 torn from their homes and consigned to slavery in North America was a lad from Hirnley, Aboyne, named Peter Williamson, described as "a rough, ragged, humle-headed, long, stowie, clever (by which is meant a growthie) boy". And Peter in the course of years which were roughly equivalent with those of the remainder of the eighteenth century, rose triumphantly above the tribulations and vicissitudes to which he was subjected and ended his career with a substantial fortune and with a reputation for resource, intelligence, and eccentricity not surpassed by any child of that Age of Reason.

It is probable that the practice of transporting children arose from a less criminal, though not less reprehensible, procedure. Very poor parents with overgrown families, rather than see their children starve, were prepared for a consideration to let them go to the colonies, where hands were wanted. There were cases of fathers selling their young sons for 1s. or 1s. 6d. for "listing" as it was called. The company of dealers who were in the market for the human merchandise kept accounts, and such transactions are recorded. Either Fordyce or the Town Clerk depute was the chief director; others included Alexander Mitchell of Colpna (now Orrok) who seems to have been the son of a minister, and one John Burnett, known as Bonny John, whose credit and influence stood so high that when in the early sixties an action was raised against him in the Court of Session for kidnapping a boy, no sheriff's officer could be found who would dare to serve him with the citation. In this particular case, the father found his son with others near a barn by the shore, and when he spoke to him and the boy said he wanted to come home, Burnett's overseer took a whip to him and drove him into a barn; and Burnett told the father that his son had engaged with him and would not be released.

The father, when the summons could not be served, interested the Earl of Aberdeen in the case and he and Burnett went to Haddo House, where Burnett was compelled to agree to return the boy within a twelve-month, under a £50 penalty. But Lord Aberdeen died very soon after, and the father, at the instance of the kidnapper, was himself trepanned into the army, and when after some years he succeeded in returning to Aberdeen, Burnett had gone bankrupt and left the country. The child was, of course, never heard of again. As the trade increased, the kidnappers became bolder, drove their victims in groups through the town, a man with a whip keeping them together, and housed them even in public workhouses and some in the burgh tolbooth until the ship came in that was to take them to America. It should perhaps be remembered that Aberdeen, not Glasgow, was then the principal port in Scotland for trade with the Western World.

It was in such circumstances that the redoubtable Peter was launched in life. But Peter was heard of again, and in no uncertain terms. His father was a tenant of Lord Aboyne, and Peter had been sent to stay with an aunt in Aberdeen when he was picked up. After about a month he was put aboard the ship *Kenilworth,* escaped shipwreck off the Delaware coast, reached Philadelphia and was sold for £16 to Hugh Wilson, a Scotsman who had in his youth been kidnapped from Perth. (This would seem to indicate that Aberdeen was late in taking up this form of commerce.) Wilson was a decent man who took care of the boy and sent him to school in winter, and on his death, which occurred when Peter was seventeen, left him £150, a horse, saddles and clothes. He bought a small property and won himself a wife, but one night in 1754, while she was at her father's, Peter was surprised by a band of Indians, carried off and tortured. By great good luck his life was spared, he escaped, and on returning to his home found that his wife had died. For the next two years he led an adventurous life with the British forces on the border and the Great Lakes, being taken prisoner with the garrison of Fort Oswego by the French under Montcalm and finally sent home. On account of a wound he was disbanded on reaching Plymouth, and sent off with a gratuity of 6s. to make his way back to Aberdeen.

When he reached York his money had, not surprisingly, run out, but he was able to interest some gentlemen there in his history and condition, he had written out a very vivacious and indeed valuable account of his adventures, and this he got printed, and sold, reserving a number of copies to fortify his purse when he should at long last reach Aberdeen. This tract, which is not the least notable and proved to be one of the most popular of all the literary productions of the sons of Bon-Accord, was entitled *French and Indian Cruelty exemplified in the Life and various Vicissitudes of Fortune of Peter Williamson, who was carried off from Aberdeen, in his Infancy, and sold as a Slave in Pensylvania.* The second edition was printed in Glasgow in 1758, another with a portrait of the author in Edinburgh in 1787; I rather think it was known to the famous Principal Robertson of Edinburgh, the celebrated historian of America who flourished in Williamson's day, because many of his observations on the manners of the American Indians almost word for word reproduce the descriptions set down by Peter. There was a 30th edition published in Aberdeen in 1839.

Peter certainly hit the high spots in the town. He was an ingenious and original fellow, very quick in the uptake, and he had laid to heart quite a number of the things he had seen when he was a prisoner of the Indians. No rock 'n roll exponent was more adept in carrying the groundlings off their feet. And so, when he proceeded, dressed and armed like a savage of the American forests, to whoop and dance in the Castlegate, he drew applauding crowds and his pamphlet sold like hot cakes. But it also got him into hot water with the authorities. The baillies could hardly be expected to take his aspersions on the Aberdeen magistrates of his youth lying down, for though Fordyce was still alive and no doubt a few others of the fifteen original baby-snatchers, the baillies of 1758 had not been personally involved in the kidnapping. So, most ill-advisedly, they had him up in the local court, convicted him of having promulgated "a scurrilous and infamous libel on the corporation of the city of Aberdeen and whole members thereof", ordained that the offending pages be torn out of all the available copies of the tract, and burnt by the common hangman at the Market Cross, fined him 10s., imprisoned him until he signed a statement denying the truth of his allegations, and finally kicked him out of the burgh.

Bitterly were the City Fathers to regret their punitive zeal. Peter was not the man to be intimidated. He had given in once, when the Indians got him, and that was a lesson to him. He had survived actual tortures at the stake, he had watched tomahawks circling around his scalp-lock, he had been wounded in that most unnerving of combats, the fight against Indian shadows in primeval forest; Aberdeen baillies were small beer after that. He went to Edinburgh, where he interested powerful persons in his case, and on February 1762, the Court of Session awarded him damages against the magistrates who had imprisoned him of £100 plus £80 expenses, "for which the Lords declared the defenders to be personally liable, and that the same shall be no burden upon the town of Aberdeen". The baillies were resourceful, however, and succeeded in evading the spirit of the decree. They prevailed upon the Earl of Findlater, to whom the town was due certain sums, to allow these monies to lie in the Common Good, whence the baillies drew out the amounts that had to be paid to Peter.

But Peter was not yet done with them. The Crown officers were so impressed by the evidence Peter had produced that they desired to institute criminal proceedings against the kidnappers, but there were insuperable legal difficulties, and Peter therefore had to proceed against Messrs. Fordyce and company on his own responsibility. He accordingly raised an action for damages against his kidnappers, which they rather adroitly sidetracked by offering to submit the question to arbitration by the Sheriff-Substitute in Aberdeen, and having gained that point, they proceeded to fill the Sheriff-Substitute so full that he pronounced his interlocutor (of course, favourable to them), just before he sank into a stupor. His potations on this historic occasion are not unworthy to be recorded.

On the day before he gave his decision "he was busy at hot punch about 11 o'clock forenoon" and became "very drunk". Then after dinner at 2 o'clock he "sate close drinking, as is the phrase in that part of the country, helter-skelter, that is copiously and alternately, of different liquors, till 11 o'clock at night", when his two maids carried him home dead drunk. Next morning soon after 9 o'clock, he had "a large doze of spirits, white wine, and punch" administered to him, "with cooling draughts of porter from time to time". After dinner with two others he sat down to a game of cards "drinking at the same time helter-skelter a bottle and a half of Malaga, a mug of porter, two bottles of claret, a mutchkin and a half of rum made into punch". He then delivered judgment in the arbitration and was taken home to bed, where he lay all next day which fortunately was the Sabbath "dead drunk and speechless".

Again the Court of Session had to step in. On 27 February 1768, Peter got judgment against Fordyce and others to the tune of £200 with expenses modified to £100. Whether he ever got the money is another matter. There is a queer story that at this time, one stormy night, a muffled horseman rode up to the house of Auquhorthies, handed in a letter, and disappeared again in the darkness. The letter was from the Provost of Aberdeen warning Fordyce that he was in a mess. The latter, so the tale goes, tried to escape by sea, was caught and imprisoned in Aberdeen, but, of course, got out on bail, and returned home. In a few days it was given out that he had died suddenly. *But*—and in Aberdeen they could anticipate Eichmann and Bormann—a few years later, when the grave was opened to receive the remains of his widow, it was found that the baillie's coffin contained nothing but some blocks of granite.

Peter Williamson settled down in Edinburgh. His original essay in literature had sold 1,000 copies in York and 750 in Newcastle, and in these two places he is thought to have netted some £30, which was good going for those days and might be even better going today. He set up in a tavern next to St. Giles' and Parliament House and came to be very well-spoken of especially by the legal fraternity. In 1769 appeared *A Nominal Economium on the City and Council of Edinburgh, by Peter Williamson, the Indian chief. Parliament House: Printed by Peter Williamson on one of his new portable printing presses.* Another of his works was *A Curious Collection of Moral Maxims and Wise Sayings, printed by Peter Williamson, Vintner in the head of Forrester's Wynd, Lawn Market, Edinburgh.* He also published an Edinburgh street directory in 1772, and he was responsible for a tract relating to the French Revolution, with the title of *Royal Abdication of Peter Williamson, King of the Mohawks.* He was also pleased to describe himself over his shop door as "From the Other World".

His most constructive effort was to establish a penny post in the Edinburgh area for which he received a handsome sum when the General Post Office took it over. But although it was not until 1837 that Rowland Hill suggested a penny post to the then Prime Minister, Lord Melbourne, it is he and not poor old Peter who has obtained the credit for the idea. Indeed, setting Peter aside altogether, it may be that Mr. Wallace of Kelly, M.P. for Greenock, a relation of the Forbeses of Craigievar, was before Hill with the suggestion, for which he received the Freedom of Aberdeen.

Peter died on 19 January 1799, at the age of sixty-nine, and left quite a tidy fortune. He certainly lived a full life and was as much in the news as most men. It is recorded that a relation with his name did very well as a merchant (not the kind Peter knew!) in Aberdeen, was police commissioner, baillie, dean of guild, chairman of the city parochial board, and representative elder to the General Assembly. In another incarnation Peter may have repeated his revenge!

Sir George Reid

Bon-Accord's artist par excellence

IT has long been accepted, by a sufficiency of the public to make it a theorem of universal application, that man does not live by bread alone. He has longings and aspirations that cannot be satisfied by pâté de foie gras or la Veuve Clicquot, and which lead him, or at least an appreciable number of him, to take pleasure in and pay hard cash for works of literature, of music, pictorial art, sculpture, and various other products of individual human genius ranging from Gobelins tapestry and Meissen china to Chippendale furniture and jewellery by Benvenuto Cellini. Fabulous sums have been and are still being paid by industrial tycoons and merchant princes, out of their abounding material resources, for works in these above-mentioned arts; and that the benefactions of the classical Maecenas were no mere flash in the pan is substantiated in our own time by, among others, the patronage of Henry Ford to John Burroughs.

Sir George Reid, P.R.S.A.
(Aberdeen Art Gallery)

In recognition of this alliance between the arts and industry, this series has already incorporated an article upon one of the half-dozen or so of men, not primarily connected with commerce, who have portrayed and by their art perpetuated the peculiar character of the people of the area which Aberdeen Chamber of Commerce serves, and the ethos of the territory itself. Of these perhaps the first to be mentioned and celebrated should be one whose dates of birth and death, whose activities and achievements are unknown, but who somehow stamped upon the indigenous population of the area a distinct set of characteristics and who indicated his prudence and prevision by taking with him to his grave the utensil then as now used for liquid nourishment and inspiration which gave him his nickname of the Beaker-man.

But it was not until the nineteenth century and the Victorian Age that there was born in Aberdeen and Aberdeenshire the four men who transcendantly interpreted their country and their countrymen by means of certain of the arts to which we have referred. William Alexander, whose "Johnny Gibb" is the North-East's prose classic, has already had his article. The other three were Gavin Greig (music), Charles Murray (poetry), and George Reid (art), and it is with the last, the only one of the quartet to be born in Aberdeen, that this essay is concerned. Aberdeen has for centuries been productive of talented artists. It is always invidious to single out any particular painter or group of painters as superior to their fellows, but George Jamesone (1586-1644) "father" of

Scottish painting; Sir John Steell (1804-91), the sculptor of the Walter Scott statue in the Scott Memorial in Edinburgh; William Dyce (1806-64), who was responsible for much of the fresco work that caused the House of Lords to be known as "the Painted Chamber" and John Phillip (1817-67) "the Scottish Velasquez" are outstanding; and in our own day—leaving pictorial artists out altogether—Douglas Strachan, with his work in stained glass, and J. Cromar Watt, the cunning artificer in metals, deserve to be ranked high.

But however eminent these men may have been, whenever those who have a knowledge of real art seek for a typical protagonist it is George Reid whose name and work spring to their mind, just as in architecture, without any disrespect to other great Aberdeen practitioners, it is Archibald Simpson of whom we think. But between architect and artist, between Simpson and Reid, a gulf is fixed by the very canons of their respective callings. The architect, by and large, must be dominated in any given work by the surroundings and the purposes of that work. He draws, as the artist does, upon the reservoir of past achievements when he decides the style and character of each project, but although he may prefer one style to all the others and use it whenever possible he himself gets little opportunity to demonstrate a style of his own. The artist is more subjective. Even when he is executing a commission, it is what *he* sees, it is *his* conception of the subject that becomes the finished article. Moreover, much of his work is chosen by himself. He has no circumstances, economic or social, to inhibit him. As nearly as it is possible in human life he can do as he pleases, hence he cannot but develop a style of his own, which may change with the years, but is still in its several manifestations recognisable. We say, therefore, of the East and Belmont Churches or the Old Infirmary, "That is by Archibald Simpson" but of the portrait of Sir Alexander Anderson or of the "Roses" in Aberdeen Chamber of Commerce Board Room, "That is *a* George Reid".

George Reid was born in 1841, son of the manager of the Aberdeen Copper Company. Two younger brothers also became artists, Samuel Reid R.S.W., and Archibald D. Reid, A.R.S.A. It is rather shocking that the only mention of the greatest of the trio in the Dictionary of National Biography should be in the notice of Archibald, where it is stated incidentally that the subject's brother was Sir George Reid, P.R.S.A. Young George attended Aberdeen Trades School and then the Grammar, but at the age of twelve he was apprenticed to Messrs. Keith and Gibb, lithographers, whose successors down to the recollection of older members of the Chamber were Messrs. Hay and Lyall, whose shop in Union Street was just round the corner from the Western Arcade at the top of Market Street. Lithography not often proved a stepping-stone to art, and George Reid soon disclosed how serious was his passion despite lack of means by attaching himself to a wandering portrait painter called Willie Niddrie, who gave him lessons once a week.

Before he left Keith and Gibb in 1860, Reid made his first known essay in a branch of pictorial art in which he came to be an acknowledged and unquestioned master, the pen-and-ink drawing. It has hitherto been understood that his first published portraits in this medium were in the 1881 de luxe edition of William Alexander's "Johnny Gibb". But the 'prentice hand was tried over twenty years before that, and the present writer feels considerable satisfaction in being the possessor of a copy of George Reid's first published work, not merely in pen-and-ink, but of any kind. Early in the last war William Kelly, the architect came across a copy of "Ye Nobell Cheese-monger" which had been bought at a sale and had been the property of John Black, tea merchant. This pamphlet was drawn and written in lithography by George Reid during his apprenticeship. It consisted of an illustrated skit, of a kind that became very popular in subsequent decades, on the raising of the Volunteers in 1860, and in particular on the adventures, real or imagined, in them of William Stevenson who had a grocery warehouse at 5 Belmont Street and lived at Burnieboozle, his house being known as Viewfield.

The sketches in the skit were of course Reid's,

and probably part if not all of the doggerel rhymes that accompanied them could be attributed to him also. This particular copy is called second edition and dated 1861, and Dr. Kelly believed it to be the sole surviving example of the pamphlet, the only other relics having been a page or two in possession of Lady Reid. There appears on the inside of its front cover a pen-and-ink sketch of the head of Stevenson, and it is this sketch which Dr. Kelly pointed out as the first extant example of George Reid's genius. The illustrations in the pamphlet itself being lithographs are not of course in the category of "originals". Eventually Dr. Kelly presented the booklet to the present writer with some other rarities of Aberdoniana. His covering letter is written in pencil, for he had fallen and broken his thigh, and in fact was never to rise again.

In 1860 Reid went to Edinburgh and for nine months, until his funds were exhausted, studied at the art school of the Board of Trustees there, at which such famous artists as Orchardson, Pettie and McWhirter also attended. On returning to Aberdeen he set to painting portraits at 50s. a time, frame included. In 1862, he had a landscape accepted by the Royal Scottish Academy, "A Border Tower" for which he asked £5 and got half. In 1863 he was back in Edinburgh again, and on a better footing for the Association for the Promotion of Fine Arts bought two landscapes from him, one the famous "Cawdor Castle" for £35. This set him on the way to realising his ambition of a course of study abroad and for several years he sat at the feet of A. Mollinger in Utrecht, of Yvon in Paris and of Josef Israels at The Hague. When he returned home he was equipped to paint landscapes, historical pictures, flowers, genre subjects, and portraits. Amongst his exhibits at the Royal Scottish Academy in the sixties were "The Orphan" and "Spynie Palace" and "Durham" which is in Aberdeen Art Gallery; whilst amongst his portraits was that of George MacDonald the novelist which hangs (I hope still) in the Mitchell Hall at Marischal College.

In 1820 he was elected an Associate and in 1877 a Member of the Royal Scottish Academy, becoming its President in 1891 and occupying the chair until he resigned in 1902 through ill-health. In 1891 also he was knighted, and laureated LL.D. by St. Andrews University, Aberdeen following in 1894 and Edinburgh still later. He made his regular residence in Edinburgh in 1882 but retained his home in Aberdeen, St. Luke's, now the Gordon Highlanders Club. That same year he married a daughter of Thomas Best, Aberdeen. He died in 1913 at his home in Somerset which he had set up when his health

Johnny Gibb

made residence in a supposedly more genial climate advisable.

As a young and struggling artist Reid kept soul and body together by painting portraits. We have seen some of them at auction sales, and while they bear evidence that Reid had already begun to develop that extraordinary flair for character study which made his later work of that kind so memorable, quite a number were not worth intrinsically much more that the few shillings they fetched. But by the time he painted the George MacDonald portrait, he had found himself and there was a succession of impressive studies such as these of Sir Alexander Anderson, George Thompson of Pitmedden (another of Aberdeen's Lord Provosts and M.P. for the city), Sir William Henderson; Peter Esslemont (yet another Lord Provost and M.P.); John Angus the Town Clerk; William Carnie ("We a' ken Willie Carnie, The craitur's fu' o' blarney"); Colonel Innes of Learney and A. M. Gordon of Newton; and from the wide world the great Tom Morris and Sir John Millais (who has another connection with the North East in that his boy blowing bubbles had his links with Hatton Castle). Reid could make a reasonably good job of any portrait, but give him a sitter with character, and the result was far above the common run of personal representations. In historical work he was hardly so successful, his "Savonarola's Last Sleep" being probably his best. With flowers he could be entrancing. His "Roses" and "Rhododendrons" are the finest things he did in this line, but there were others.

The North-Eastern patriot will, however, opt on all occasions for his pen-and-inks of landscapes, of buildings, and of personalities. Here George Reid was in a class by himself. No one has excelled, no one has equalled him in the faculty of evoking the soul of the area and its people. Apart from the skit we alluded to earlier we think the first of his pen-and-inks appeared in Samuel Smiles's "Life of a Scotch Naturalist" in 1876 (Thomas Edward of Banff). But the small field of the pages in that book detracted seriously from the effect of the drawings. To get the best effects from such landscape work there must be room and scope enough for the artist's idea to be developed, and in this respect the "Spynie Palace" in the Thomas Edward volume, when compared with the same subject as treated by Reid in Charles St. John's "Natural History and Sport in Moray" 1882, and in "Twelve Sketches of Scenery and Antiquities on the Line of the Great North of Scotland Railway", 1883, illustrates the contrast. On the other hand, there is a sketch of the Brig o' Balgownie in the earlier book which defies the limitations imposed upon it by the restricted page and is almost as good as anything Reid ever did.

The St. John classic has several times attracted the attention of illustrators, but the edition which contains Reid's landscapes and the animal studies of J. Wycliffe Taylor is the gem of the lot and is much sought after by collectors. It contains ten Reid sketches, of which the seascape "Covesea", the landscape "Kinloss", and the

Jamesone's House, Schoolhill, Aberdeen

"Elgin Cathedral", where the effect is heightened, as Reid often did, by presenting the scene in winter, are the best. But none is quite so good as the best of the twelve sketches in the North of Scotland Railway Guide, in which the running commentary is by Colonel Ferguson of Kinmundy, who was Chairman of the G.N.S.R. Board at that time. The writer and the printer in the de luxe issue of the guide have both been occasionally at fault in their facts or their spelling, but Reid was magnificent. His early "coach", Willie Niddrie, had been a pupil of James Giles, who did for the Premier Earl of Aberdeen that remarkable series of paintings of Aberdeenshire castles many of which appeared before the war in the most handsome of all the volumes published by the Third Spalding Club. Reid seems to have caught at secondhand as it were, something of the entrancing Giles flair for making a castle live with an individuality of its own. In the G.N.S.R. dozen Fyvie, Huntly, Drum, Balquhain, Barra, Crathes, King's College, St. Machar's Cathedral seen from the loveliest reach of the Don, a quite different interpretation of Elgin Cathedral from that in the St. John book, and above all Inverugie are sheer delight; and Huntly with a bar from "There's cauld kail in Aberdeen", Balquhain with one from "O gin I were whaur Gadie rins", and Inverugie with a phrase from the Jacobite ditty "When the King comes owre the water" linger most persistently in the memory partly through the musical association. Ever the much more pretentious "River Clyde" and "River Tweed" folios which Reid illustrated are not so successful as his Aberdeenshire scenes, despite the romantic glories of Neidpath and Norham on the Tweed and although the studies of the Broomielaw and Glasgow Cathedral are full of character particularly the former, with its cunning suggestion of hustle in the crowd awaiting the steamer on the pier.

The edition de luxe of "Johnny Gibb" published in 1880, contains some of George Reid's most finished work. There are several landscapes, including a magnificent "Bennachie" presenting the Mither Tap in a snowstorm, the "Walls" of Tarlair are vividly reproduced, while the vignette of Gushetneuk itself shows that Reid was as much at home with a "ferm toun" as with a "big hoose". The interior of the West Kirk of Aberdeen from the gallery here makes a companion to the superb "Collison's Aisle" which he contributed to Dr. Cooper's New Spalding Club edition of the Chartulary of the Church of St. Nicholas. It may here be interpolated that nothing is more astonishing in Reid's genius than the almost supernatural exactness of his eye. Even when well beyond what was in his day regarded as middle age he could draw freehand a gothic arch with every line distinct and clear although separated by a minute interval from its neighbours. His eye obviously was endowed with one of the qualities of the microscope.

The character sketches in "Johnny Gibb" deserve to come last as being the high summit of their creator's achievement. They were not imaginary countenances, although probably the artist blended features from more than one face to get what he regarded as the nearest possible approximation to the character he was delineating. Thus "Johnny Gibb" himself is believed to be derived partly at least from a man named Wallace who lived in Banff, while the original of Meg Raffan the hen-wife was Maggie Marr, who sold "plunky" in Boyndie Street, Macduff. The vital feature of the portraits is the verisimilitude, their faithfulness in reproducing what we would naturally expect to see in the lineaments of a Johnny Gibb, a Peter or a Mrs. Birse, a Jonathan Tawse, a David Webster, a Roderick M'Aul. It may perhaps nowadays be a truism to say that education, whatever it puts into a man's intelligence, tends to level down character until individuality is not easily recognisable. It is indeed difficult to escape the suspicion that the interesting people are not the distinguished, the eminent or the intellectual, but those who have contrived to be their own masters early in life and whose energies are devoted to the pursuit of their often humble calling. Certainly the faces round a market ring or on "the bob side" (if it's not now half-a-crown) at a football match, will display a greater and more animated variety of expression than a graduation ceremony. It is clear that George Reid, even in an age when it was possible to leave school at twelve and still be successful in life, had come to realise in which social strata the mind's construction could best be read in the face.

To these gifts through his art to his native city and community, Sir George Reid added other services that deserve to be recorded. He was actively associated with John Forbes White and Dean of Guild Walker in their building up of Aberdeen Art Gallery. The friend of Alexander Macdonald of Kepplestone, he was to a considerable extent responsible for the making of the Macdonald Collection and its assignment to the Gallery. Sir James Murray, another benefactor of the Gallery, was also advised by Sir George in many matters. It was Sir George who in 1905 opened the extended Art Gallery Buildings giving on that occasion a memorable address upon Sculpture. Aberdeen has always been lucky in the possession of sons able and willing to be worthy of her and not the least of them was this poor laddie of genius who fought his way single-handed to the top yet never forgot the rock from which he was hewn.

James Perry
first of the great London editors

TWICE before in this series the subject has been a journalist—James Chalmers, a newspaper proprietor who barked for himself, and William Alexander, who perhaps owed his inclusion more to his status as a novelist than to his merit as a newspaperman. For this third time the Fourth Estate claims our attention in one James Perry, little known and remembered in the town of his birth, who nevertheless was greater as a newspaper proprietor and as editor than either Chalmers or Alexander, and who indeed challenges comparison with the Northcliffes and Beaverbrooks of our own times and with the Delanes and Marlowes of the editorial sanctum.

James Perry

James Perry's real patronymic was Pirie, but London air is hard upon Scottish names, and just as the Angus lad, James Milne, father of John Stuart Mill, the inventor of the Utilitarian philosophy, had to change the spelling to Mill to fit in with the barbarous English insistence on giving voice to the silent "n" in his name, and just as a century before the poet Malloch became Mallet because they could not pronounce the "ch", and just as today Forbes is Forbs (so that Innes will soon be reduced to Inns and Fiddes to Fids), so Pirie had to become Perry to meet the demand of metropolitan articulation.

His father was a builder and contractor of some importance in Aberdeen, who appears to have had family associations with "the fit o' Bennachie", because when James, who was born on 30 October 1756 was old enough to travel, he was dispatched to Chapel of Garioch, where the Reverend W. Tait, schoolmaster, seems to have had something of a reputation in rearing the young into hopefuls. Eventually James, however, departed from the school which, by a coincidence, was to be the first alma mater, two generations later, of William Alexander, and was put to Aberdeen Grammar School, whence he proceeded to Marischal College, where he held the Guild Bursary for 1769-71.

His studies were terminated by the failure of his father's business in the Denburn, and James sought refuge and a livelihood in the law, entering the office of Arthur Dingwall Fordyce, an Aberdeen advocate who deserves a second glance here. Dingwall Fordyce had what we will hope was the felicity of receiving his main legal training in the Edinburgh chambers of Alexander Keith of Ravelston, among whose assistants in Fordyce's day was Walter Scott, destined to be the father of a greater Walter, and who, perhaps through his friendship with Fordyce, was to be appointed Edinburgh agent to the good town of Aberdeen, as a result of which association the Burgess Roll of Bon-accord is honoured by the inclusion of the name of the Author of *Waverley*. Arthur Dingwall Fordyce had a substantial practice, and resided at the mansion of Arthur Seat, a country house on Ferryhill which we now know as the Duthie Park, and where his nearest neighbour was the ingenious watchmaker John Ewen, author of *The Boatie Rows*. In the latter part of the eighteenth century Dingwall Fordyce acquired the estate of Eigie and Balmedie, of which his grand-uncle the great Aberdeen provost, George Fordyce, had been tacksman fifty years before; and at the beginning of the nineteenth century the lands of Brucklay came into the lawyer's family.

Perry put up with the law, or the law put up with him, for only one year, after which he became assistant to an Aberdeen draper—like Donald Smith (Lord Mountstephen) half a century later. He did not stay behind the counter long either, but John Payne Collier, the celebrated Shakespearian forger, who was inindebted to Perry for some early opportunities in authorship, declares of him that "he never quite lost the retail manner acquired in the draper's shop in Aberdeen". Collier's remark seems to have been typical intellectual snobbery. He probably found that Perry had a better brain than his own.

The next we hear of Perry he is in a company of actors. Amongst his associates was Thomas Holcroft, then a low comedian, who later acquired a reputation as a novelist and dramatist, in the latter character being the author of *The Road to Ruin*. The stage might have been the road to ruin for James Perry, had not the English actor-manager of the Theatre Royal in Edinburgh, West Digges, who took the part of Norval in the first performance of John Home's famous tragedy of "Douglas", told him that his Aberdeen brogue unfitted him for the stage. So James flitted again, this time to Manchester where he became clerk to a manufacturer named Dinwiddie. Then in 1777 Perry took his courage in his hands and the road to London and his true destiny.

In Manchester he had begun to write as a member of a debating society, but on reaching London he made little progress as a free-lance journalist until an article he stuck in the letter-box of the *General Advertiser* newspaper was inserted as an anonymous contribution. Some Manchester business men had given him letters of introduction, one of which he presented to a person who happened to be part proprietor of this newspaper. On Perry's asking, not very hopefully, if there was a place for him on the paper he was told there was not, unless—as an afterthought—he could write an article such as one that had appeared in that day's issue. It happened to be Perry's own. So he was taken on the staff at the remuneration of a guinea a week, plus half a guinea for helping with the *Evening Post*, published from the same office. As a reporter he made his name by turning in, unaided, eight solid columns a day—and they were solid then—on the trial at Portsmouth of Admirals Keppel and Palliser, a disagreement between whom had robbed the Navy of a victory over the French off Ushant in 1778. This feat of reporting of a cause célèbre put up the paper's circulation by several thousand. In 1781-82 Perry planned and became the first editor of the *European Magazine*. Then he was appointed editor of the *Gazetteer*, a newspaper run in the interests of Charles James Fox, the great Whig leader and antagonist of the younger Pitt. Fox became one of Perry's greatest friends, happily without infecting the Aberdonian with his own gambling propensities.

While with the *Gazetteer* Perry, who had himself experienced the difficulties of parliamentary reporting in those days, was the author of an innovation which really laid the foundation of the modern system of teamwork. He arranged relays of reporters to cover the debates, the men all being expert shorthand writers, and while so many took the notes, the others transcribed them, with the result that Perry's newspaper came out every morning with the full report of the overnight debates which no other newspaper could get through in time. What reporting must have been then is demonstrated by the case of "Memory" Woodfull, a journalist who had been known to sit for ten or twelve hours writing out from memory the speeches to which he had listened during the previous sixteen hours.

When the *Gazetteer* was taken over by the Tories, Perry became associated with another Whig daily paper, *The Morning Chronicle*. After acting as editor there for several years, he and another Scot in 1789 purchased the paper between them for £150. His partner dying shortly afterwards, Perry became owner-editor and in a short time the leading power in the newspaper world of London. He raised the circulation to some 7,000 a day, which was twice as much as that of its nearest rival, *The Times*, and, to take a long jump forward, when he died in 1821 the paper was sold for £42,000. We in our own day and burgh have had an instance of fabulous increment in the value of a newspaper, but nothing to equal the amazing rise in value of the *Morning Chronicle* under James Perry's inspired direction.

For, inspired it was. He investigated personally every branch of newspaper activity. We have seen how he revolutionised the technique of parliamentary reporting. He took a personal interest in his foreign correspondence, and actually spent a year in Paris during the French Revolution to improve his paper's connections there. Being a Scot as well as a Whig, he found it easy to get on terms with the leaders of the Revolution, and with that clever dog Talleyrand he struck up something like a friendship.

Perry's Paris visit, however, was rather too early to enable him to become acquainted with the lady who became Talleyrand's wife, the so-called Madame Grand, who had a connection with Aberdeen that she no doubt would have preferred to forget. There was an inscription in St. Nicholas Kirkyard on a stone now below the level of the sward, marking the resting-place of the body of Charles Jeffreyes Symes, Lieutenant and Adjutant of the Seventh Regiment of Foot, who died in Aberdeen on 26 December 1786, and upon whose grave "his most disconsolate widow" erected the stone. Whether she was his widow is a moot point, for she was the mistress of Sir Philip Francis, the reputed author of the *Lettres of Junius*, before the Aberdeen episode in her life, and ten years before she met the unfrocked bishop Talleyrand and eventually acquired the title of Princess.

One historian of the metropolitan press says of Perry, "he raised the moral, social, and intellectual character of the *Morning Chronicle* to an elevation to which no newspaper, whether English or foreign, had ever before attained". He used to stroll in Pall Mall and St. James's Street chatting with the great people and fashionable crowds there, and from his conversation he wrote talk of the town which was the original of modern gossip-writing. He introduced literary features such as no other newspaper had attempted, and in consequence commanded a stream of publishers' advertisements, Messrs. Longmans on one occasion sending sixty notices of the books issued by their house.

By another commentator described as "volatile and varied", Perry was frequently in hot water with the authorities, for the editor of a Whig organ such as his was, in those revolutionary days, was liable to have his slightest criticism of the Establishment construed into something approaching high treason. In 1898, although defended by Thomas Erskine, later a Lord Chancellor, and the most successful defence pleader of his day, he was fined £50 and gaoled in Newgate for three months for suggesting in his newspaper that "the dresses of the opera dancers are regulated in the House of Lords". His incarceration turned into a holiday and a triumph at His Majesty's expense, for levees were held in his honour in his Newgate cell, his table was loaded with presents of game and other good things, and to celebrate his release an entertainment was held at the London Tavern when a silver vase commemorative of his happy martyrdom was presented to him.

The next time he was faced with a big prosecution, in 1810, for having said that George III's successor would have "the finest opportunity of becoming nobly popular", which read dubiously when applied to "The First Gentleman in Europe" eventually George IV and the biggest rake of his time. Perry decided to trust to his own advocacy for his defence, and actually got himself off. He never appears to have run the risk that ended the life of another Aberdonian London editor, who was slain in a duel the year of Perry's death. John Scott, son of Alexander Scott, upholsterer in Aberdeen, and editor of the *London Magazine*, was shot by Jonathan Christie, a native of Fyvie, who was the second of Walter Scott's son-in-law, John Gibson Lockhart in a quarrel with John Scott which came to the stage of a challenge. Lockhart withdrew and Christie took the quarrel upon himself with the lamentable result mentioned.

In making the *Morning Chronicle* the great organ of opinion it became, Perry gathered round him a remarkable staff, permanent and occasional. Ricardo the economist; Sir James Mackintosh, the great Whig lawyer and publicist; Thomas Campbell the poet whose "Ye Mariners of England" was first published in its columns; Charles Lamb, still the most loved of all essayists; William Hazlitt, who was first a parliamentary reporter on the staff, and later its theatrical critic; Samuel Taylor Coleridge; Thomas Moore, later the biographer of Byron; Richard Brinsley Sheridan, the dramatist, who told his tailor he would pay his bill the day after the Day of Judgment; and John Campbell one day to be Lord Chancellor and author of *Lives of the Lord Chancellors*—all served under the orders of James Perry. Few newspapers, then or since, have been able to boast such a team of stars, and even after James Perry's death, and when his paper was going down the hill, the magic of his memory attracted both Dickens and Thackeray to its staff.

The profits of the paper the year before Perry's death amounted to £12,000. Of course, it was easier then. Taxes, despite the stamp duty of 4d. per copy (less 20 per cent), were comparatively light. In 1821 the total weekly cost of editing, reporting, printing and publishing was only £80. Newspapers of the standard of Perry's actually showed a profit on circulation alone, and the price of the advertisements was, therefore, "jam". The *Chronicle's* advertisement revenue would probably have run out at about £240 a week. But after Perry's death, things went wrong. In 1834, the circulation having fallen to less than a third of his figure, the paper was resold for £16,500 only. The *Morning Chronicle* disappeared in mid-Victorian times, despite Dr. Watson's assertion that the Red-headed League, in one of Sherlock Holmes's most ingenious cases, was advertised in the *Morning Chronicle* of 27 April 1890.

Perry's town house was Tavistock House, in Tavistock Square, where Dickens afterwards lived, and to which the author of this article was directed by mistake on a bleak winter morning on his first visit to London nearly fifty years ago, instead of the Tavistock Hotel, Covent Garden. At Tavistock House he was wont to hold literary parties which were regarded as taking the place of the old coffee-house gatherings of Augustan days, and of Dr. Johnson's Literary Club. At his country house he set up machinery for the multiplying of pictures—"the polygraphic art" as it was called; but the attempt was premature and failed.

He married in 1798 and had a family of eight, one of whom became so just a judge in India that when he retired from the Bench in 1847 the natives collected £5,000 as a testimonial to him. Mrs. Perry in 1814 on a health cruise was captured by Algerine pirates and suffered so severely that on being rescued she died on the voyage home. Perry's widowed sister, Mrs. Lunan, married Richard Porson, the distinguished scholar who is at one and the same time England's classical, and almost solitary, example of the poor lad of parts making his way in our Scots fashion to eminence. Porson was the son of a weaver. He spent his last years, until his death in 1808, with Perry, who must have been a tolerant "gweed brither" to put up with his slovenly habits and habitual drunkenness. Probably because Perry was, as a lady friend of his said, "a scholar and a gentleman", he contrived to find compensations in the immense erudition and cynical and witty conversation of his erratic brother-in-law.

Perry of all Aberdonians was the greatest book collector. In that respect John Morgan the granite merchant probably came the nearest to him. After his death it took twenty-seven days to disperse his library, and the 5,907 lots, covering 223 pages of catalogue, fetched £7,401 9s. Besides copies of all four Shakespeare Folios—the First Folio of 1623 went for only £28 10s.—he possessed the finest of all the specimens of the Gothenburg Bible, the first book printed from moveable metal types. Perry's copy, known as the Mazarin Bible, because it once belonged to Cardinal Mazarin, fetched £186, and has several times been sold since, always at ascending prices, the last occasion having been in 1923 when Dr. Rosenberg of New York purchased it for £9,500. A Kilmarnock edition of Burns made only 19s.; it would make more than a thousand times that now. A copy of Forbes's "Cantus", the famous Aberdeen song-book of 1662, made £10. His total estate was valued at £130,000.

Perhaps it should be remarked as a sort of appendix, that, in the discreet phrase of one who knew him well, "he not unwillingly turned his eyes upon the ladies". In these two interests, books and the fair sex, he apparently resembled that Roman Emperor Gordianus, whose twin hobbies furnished material for one of the more memorable of Gibbon's celebrated footnotes to *The Decline and Fall*. But these recondite subjects are not for a Chamber of Commerce, which would be more interested in the contrast of Perry's career with that of another famous Aberdeenshire newspaper proprietor, Robert Garden, the farmer of Tolquhon, who at the beginning of the present century owned the *Morning Leader*, another London daily newspaper whose politics, like that of the *Morning Chronicle*, were somewhat Left of Centre. But that is another story.

William Walker
last of the Victorians

THE choice of William Walker, author of *The Bards of Bon-Accord* to represent in this series the remarkable company of eminent Aberdonians who flourished during the latter half of the Great Queen's reign is based upon two factors. He represents those of his contemporaries who, while remaining in their native city, earned a high reputation for their business acumen and administrative capacity; and he excelled also, as so many of them did, in other and quite different walks of life, in his case the study of literature. It may be added—and it was a trait characteristic of several of the group—that he was a first-rate musician also. He left to Aberdeen University the flute that belonged to the celebrated weaver-poet William Thom, and he himself possessed, and loved to play upon, a Ruddiman fiddle that was known as "The Queen of the North".

Will Walker

The whole atmosphere in which William Walker in his prime, and his friends and associates moved was so utterly different from that which we know nowadays, that it is hard to believe he, the last of them, passed away only some thirty years ago. Even for the writer of these notes, who for many years was intimate with him and heard him live the great days over again, it is difficult to recreate both the background and the attitude to life of those times. Take for instance John Ramsay, M.A., one of the cleverest of a generation of Aberdonians that included David Masson, the editor of John Milton; Joseph Robertson and John Hill Burton the historians; Alexander Bain, the real begetter of the science (if it is a science) of psychology; the Blaikies and Sir Alexander Anderson, famous Lord Provosts; and a score of others distinguished in all sorts of walks of life. Ramsay was Editor of the *Aberdeen Journal* and an exceptionally erudite person.

Yet one of the most piquant anecdotes William Walker used to relate described an extraordinary incident that occurred in Union Street in front of Moir the grocer's shop, where the National Commercial Bank building now stands. He and John Angus the Town Clerk had got into some public difference of opinion which Angus at least was taking rather to heart. They met one morning at the spot mentioned and Ramsay as he passed "cocked a snook" or "made a long nose" at the Town Clerk. The later danced into the street waving his umbrella above his head and venting maledictions on the impudent journalist. Not that Ramsay would have cared.

At the end of his life, confined to bed by a painful and, as it proved, mortal malady, Ramsay was called upon one day by a tract-bearing female—the approach of moral rearmament was somewhat different then—and informed that his sufferings were the result of a misspent life. "Wifie", said the inextinguishable Ramsay, "the Scriptures say it's whom the Lord *loveth* that he chasteneth." Will Walker had the same faculty of barbed repartee. To a celebrated bookman who invited himself to look through Walker's library and take away anything he did not know to examine, Walker remarked with emphasis—"I've mony frien's that have the run o' my books. You are *not* in that category."

Anyone today who looks around and bethinks himself of the careers of Aberdonians who in the last thirty or forty years have made good is bound to be struck by the proportion of self-made men among them. It has been, happily, always so. Alexander Bain the weaver's son, may be the most memorable of the puir laddies who were Aberdeen's lads o' pairts, but many of the group now about to be described were poor men's sons. William Walker's father was the last handloom weaver in Aberdeen and in his day Secretary of the local Chartists. What a millenium away that removes him! The father hailed from an Old Deer family, as did, incidentally, on a different rung of the social and industrial ladder, the Crombies who in the middle of last century moved from Cothal into the Grandholm Mills of the once splendid linen firm of Leys, Masson & Co. Will Walker's mother as a child was carried by her parents from Kildonan in Sutherland when the clearances there were at their height.

He was born in 1840. Like many a son of a radical parent, he was himself a very decided Tory, except that his recollections of the Hungry Forties, when his mother had to turn away her head to escape the aroma of the "foostit" meal that was all that could be got to make their porridge, kept him a Free Trader. He went to a dame's school in Blackfriars Street till he was eight, when he became a message boy. He never had a day's illness he could remember, except once a headache, till he was close on 90. While still little more than a child he got a job in the office of the Equitable Loan Company, of which William Brebner was the manager. Brebner was an enthusiastic educationist and in the evenings taught French in the Mechanics Institution in Market Street, which then purveyed all the evening school and further education available in the city. Will Walker went to classes there for several years. A fellow student with him was that strange character Douglas Alexander Spalding, who was to become the tutor of, amongst other celebrities, the present Earl Russell the philosopher, better known perhaps as Bertrand Russell. Eventually Will Walker succeeded Brebner in the Equitable and retired as managing director.

He was still in his twenties when he got linked up with a whole galaxy of Williams—William Forsyth, Editor of the *Aberdeen Journal,* William Anderson, lieutenant in the police, William Carnie, later Clerk to the Royal Infirmary, William Alexander, creator of "Johnny Gibb", and William Cadenhead, who, born a poor boy like all of them, and after several vicissitudes including some years as an overseer at Broadford, had gone to the wine and spirit business of George Duncan, whose daughter he married, finally changing the firm's name to his own, and it still flourishes. Associated with these more or less closely were a number of booksellers, such as Lewis Smith, Archibald Courage, George Middleton and others. George Walker, of Brown's Bookstall, author of *Aberdeen Awa',* Alexander Walker, Dean of Guild, author of innumerable fascicles of local history, from whose chair these words are being written, James Rettie, another local historian and antiquary, all circulated in the animated constellation.

Will Walker's first literary effort, I think, arose from the proposals to alter the layout of the West Kirk of St. Nicholas, following on the great fire of 1874 which burnt the East Kirk and consumed the ancient wooden steeple of both churches and the old bells. The citizens, by the way, loved to try their arms at bell-ringing, and there was one picture in Carnie's reminiscences of John Ramsay, short and stout, having cast coat and waistcoat and slackened his gallowses, "tilting the towie" as hard as he could. The gallery of the West Kirk apparently was a harbourage of dust, in which the preacher could be heard but not seen. The renovators, with the Dean of Guild at their head, proposed to leave the gallery as an ancient monument while modernising the rest. Will Walker in reply wrote "Groans from the Believers' Gallery" in octosyllabic couplets and with a mordant wit, the occupants of the gallery being described as necessarily believers since they only heard and never saw.

As a result of the reputation thus gained he was credited with another squib on a different subject in which James Tulloch, who died at nearly a hundred only a year or two before Will Walker, was obliquely satirised. The remark to which Tulloch took exception was something to the effect that you needn't be an archangel to buy Archangel tar, Tulloch, a builder's merchant, having purchased a quantity of that commodity. But the author of the pasquil was William Cadenhead, whose fecundity in verses of locality and society was inexhaustible. He and Anderson, who was a much better poet, were friends and rivals in that respect and conducted a rhyming correspondence purporting to be from the various wells of the town, the Spa, the Corbie, and others. Cadenhead died at the beginning of this century at the age of 85—very young for a Cadenhead, for three of his brothers and sisters lived beyond 90 and one was almost a centenarian.

William Forsyth, who belonged to Turriff but lived in Aberdeen most of his life, and wrote "The Silver City by the Sea", "Bonaillie", "Kinreen o' the Dee", and "The Midnight Meeting" on the union of the two colleges, was a frequent contributor to *Punch* and to the *Cornhill* magazine which W. M. Thackeray the novelist edited. When Forsyth was editor of the *Journal* and James Adam of the *Aberdeen Herald* both then being weeklies, the one Tory and the other Radical, they used to meet in a howff in the Guestrow the night before their respective publishing days, and write one another's leading articles! One wonders if C. E. Montague of the *Manchester Guardian* had ever heard of their tricks when he wrote that best of all newspaper novels, *A Hind Let Loose*.

William Cadenhead (left) and William Carnie

William Walker and William Carnie and some of the others were enthusiastic playgoers. Mrs. Corbet Ryder (later Pollock) ran the theatre in Marischal Street mostly with her own repertory company, but she from time to time attracted many of the famous actors and some of the best known actresses of the middle Victorian years. Carnie and Cadenhead used to write prologues and epilogues to the plays, quite in the classical fashion, and the whole fascinating story of Aberdeen's dramatic faring then can be read in Carnie's *Reporting Reminiscences.* Will Walker as a boy used to do odd jobs about the theatre to secure a seat in the gods at night, and his knowledge of Elizabethan, Jacobean, eighteenth century and Victorian drama was encyclopaedic. It is not without interest that John Forbes Robertson, one of the leading London dramatic critics, was an Aberdonian who served his apprenticeship in the Aberdeen theatre audiences. He became the father of the great actor-manager, Sir Johnston Forbes-Robertson, who may have been seen on the stage here, though he retired in 1917, but who gave after the first war a memorable Shakespearean recital in the Y.M.C.A. Hall. His daughter again was a famous Peter Pan.

Another member of the coterie was Dr. Maitland Moir, son of the grocer outside whose shop the scene between John Ramsay and John Angus occurred, and a very much loved medical practitioner in the city. At the Riding of the Marches in 1889 he was one of those selected for "douping" and being a big heavy man he came down out of control. He complained of pain while speaking at the subsequent luncheon. He died a week or two later of a fractured pelvis. He was a versatile person. On one social occasion, when William Carnie was rather suggesting that no one could imitate the style of his very popular song, "There's aye some water whaur the stirkie droons", Maitland Moir rolled off the following impromptu:

> We a' ken Willie Carnie, the mannie's fu' o' blarney,
> He mebbe has a conscience but I doot it has nae boun's;
> I say na, gin ye please, that the craitur's tellin' lees,
> But—ye ken there's aye some water whaur the stirkie droons.

Carnie, the greatest exponent of psalmody in Victorian Scotland, once raised and conducted in the Music Hall a choir of one thousand voices. In another field of activity, when he announced he was opening a class for the teaching of shorthand, he had one hundred applicants. Our modern efforts pale into insignificance beside such examples.

But we have wandered far from the central subject of this sketch. While he took only the slightest part in local politics and administration, Will Walker spent the leisure of his best years in providing for Aberdonians a legacy which, so long as pride in their city remains in them, will never lose its value to them. Charles Murray, author of *Hamewith,* in his busy office in South Africa for thirty years, and in his wanderings about the world for other twenty, had near him on his desk or in his luggage one indispensable article, Will Walker's *Bards of Bon-Accord.* We are reminded of General de Gaulle, in the opinion of quite a lot of people the greatest man in the western world today, who always has at his elbow a volume of poetry. But whereas his fancy changes, Charles Murray's was always the same. And Charles Murray could not be described as a bookish man.

His habit, however, explains in part why Will Walker became the subject of this article. There have been some delightful books about Aberdeen. John Spalding's *History of the Troubles,* William Kennedy's *Annals of Aberdeen,* Joseph Robertson's *Book of Bon-Accord,* George Walker's *Aberdeen Awa',* but none of them so faithfully embodies the Aberdonian tradition, is so steeped (without being soaked) in its history, so radiates the charm that a wise, genial and cultivated mind commands as its birthright. It should be on the bookshelf (however restricted that may be) of every true Aberdonian. The present writer has three copies; one his own working copy; one of the four presentation copies on handmade paper which Will Walker gave to his brother James; and one, Will Walker's own proof copy with corrections and alterations, and indicating the help that James Walker gave in the writing of the book. That help covered the writing of the sections on about half-a-dozen authors. James Walker had received a longer formal education than William, he became a journalist in Glasgow, and he by a good many years predeceased his brother. Several of the articles would have been, on the whole, better done by William.

John Forbes Robertson

In later years Will Walker became deeply interested in ballads, folk-song and traditional music. He himself amassed a considerable collection, two of his chief correspondents being John Walker, of Moss-side, Portlethen and George Davie who in 1888 with W. W. Gorrod founded the firm of Gorrod, Davie, Kemp, Walker & Co. The collection has never been published. When Professor Francis J. Child of Harvard University was compiling his great edition of British Ballads, Will Walker was his principal collaborator in this country, his assistance on the music side being specially valuable. Of Gavin Greig, whose vast collection, made in the North East of Scotland, is the largest of any in this country, he was the friend and helper. In 1915 he put much of his knowledge of the subject into permanent form in his *Peter Buchan and other Papers,* and shortly before his death in 1930 he published Child's letters, some fifty in number, to himself. He did a great deal of the work in local history which appeared in small volumes and pamphlets.

He built up a library of many thousand volumes which took eight days to disperse. It covered many subjects but was especially rich in local literature, ballads and folk-song, Burns editions and Shakespeariana. His diligence in the making of notes and cuttings, all carefully arranged and the latter pasted up in separate volumes, was frightening. The capacity for such concentrated application has disappeared in modern generations. His young friends he adjured to have always at least two strings to their bow—their bread-and-butter business and a hobby to refresh, as Walter Scott used to say, the machine. He was full of that kind of homely wisdom and a sort of gay ironic tolerance of the riddle of the universe. A favourite quotation of his in latter years was Wordsworth's

> . . . the good die young;
> But those whose hearts are dry as summer's dust
> Burn to the socket.

He was 91 when on Boxing Day 1931 he died, and with him so far as Aberdeen was concerned, the Victorian Age may be said to have expired.

George Thompson, Jun.
and the clipper ships

ONE of the problems that have to be solved or evaded in a series of biographical sketches such as this, is created by the fact that in many cases the personality of the subject has not been projected on the screen of history as visibly as his achievements. Particularly is this the difficulty with men who have been immersed in business, either private or public, to the virtual exclusion of other interests. Artists of all kinds seem to have more time and inclination to devote to self cultivation, and so very often their characters are much more easily recaptured by the recorder.

George Thompson, Jun.

This is especially the case of a public servant and prominent business man like George Thompson, Jun., whose suffix "Jun." clung to him like a tail to a monkey to the very end of his exceptionally long life in 1895. He was not quite an Aberdonian, to be sure, having been born at Woolwich in 1804, but his mother was the daughter of a small farmer at Rubislaw, named Andrew Stephen, and he himself was deposited in his grandfather's Aberdeen home when he was two years old. His father was a stores superintendent at Madras for the East India Company and died young. The "p" in the patronymic rather argues for an English origin, but the young George's removal to the Granite City soon after he could walk and talk ensured that the influence of our community would prevail in him. Actually, apart from short spells he never left the city and its environs.

Fifty or sixty years ago passengers on the main Great North of Scotland Railway line may have wondered idly why their trains should stop at a halt which had a platform, a cabin, a waiting shed, and, of course, a name-board, but no habitations save the agent's cottage, a couple of cottar houses down the road, and a mansion among the trees. They *may* have wondered at that, although in those days before the policy of nationalization and the philosophy of Dr. Beeching had introduced some element of topsy-turvydom into life, a railway station was accepted as a place where trains stopped, not upon which the angel of destruction swooped. It was far more likely in those remote days that the passengers wondered why, in the sylvan policies of this mansion at Pitmedden, Dyce, in Aberdeenshire, there should be seen a pair of emus or cassowaries from far Australia. And it was but right and proper that they should wonder, for those sedate and dignified birds embodied part of the romance of Aberdeen's commerce—and a part, alas, that today, like the emus themselves, has mouldered and gone.

The Grammar School supplied George Thompson's academic education, and the office of the London Shipping Company, later merged in the Aberdeen Steam Navigation Company, his business training. Then he set up for himself about 1825 as a ship and insurance broker, adding shipowning and a timber business, all conducted from headquarters in Marischal Street. Although by that time Aberdeen's preeminence as the principal seaport of Scotland had disappeared, it was still a power in the land and on the ocean, and when George Thompson appeared upon the scene one of its most splendid epochs was about to open. None contributed more to the stoking of this blaze of glory than his famous Aberdeen White Star Line of ships and the vessels both in sail and steam that he commissioned for it.

Those were great days for the port of Aberdeen. Apart from several firms prosecuting the coasting trade, there were two shipping lines whose flags were familiar all over the world and more particularly under the Southern Cross and in the China Seas. One was George Thompson's Aberdeen White Star Line, often known simply as the Aberdeen Line, and the other was also named the Aberdeen Line, owned by John T. Rennie and Sons, but usually called the Rennie Line. It was started rather later than Thompson's.

The latter company was conducted with foresight and courage. In 1850 George Thompson was joined by William Henderson, a native of New Aberdour, who later was president of Aberdeen Chamber of Commerce, a Lord Provost of Aberdeen, and a knight, and who in 1852 married one of Thompson's daughters. George Thompson had taken to wife a daughter of the Rev. and celebrated Dr. Kidd, who was the central figure and at the receiving end of one of the best of all Aberdeen anecdotes, related in his little book of stories by A. M. Williams, at one time English master at the Girls' High School, and father of the late Rev. J. H. Williams, who was Provost of Fraserburgh. Dr. Kidd and Priest Gordon, a popular Roman Catholic padre, were great friends whose intimacy was, as is so often the case, founded on argument. One day Kidd remarked, "Can you tell me what difference there was between The Virgin Mary and my mother?" "No", rejoined Gordon, "but there is a mighty difference between their sons." That, however, is rather away from shipping lines.

William Henderson in 1854 went up to London to open a London office for the Aberdeen Line, which eventually was running boats out by the Cape to Australia once a month. The Aberdeen Line probably did not pioneer this service, for Aberdeen boats were coasting Australia when Sydney and Melbourne were tiny places, and it seems to have been William Duthie, of the Aberdeen firm of J. Duthie, Sons, and Co., who first opened up a service between London and Australia. His firm built such boats as the *Australia* and the *Ballarat,* which made the record run of sixty-four days to Sydney. But Thompson and Henderson greatly expanded and improved the service. Although we are anticipating, it may be recalled that when the famous historian of England and biographer of Thomas Carlyle, James Anthony Froude, made the voyage to the Antipodes that he chronicled in *Oceana,* it was in the Aberdeen Line's 4,000-ton packet *Australasian* that he made the trip in the winter 1884-85. He never lived higher in his life.

> We had a cow on board, and new milk every morning; bread every day fresh from the oven, and porridge such as only Scotch cooks and a Scotch company can produce. In respect of vessel, officers, attendance, provisions—of all things, great and small, upon which we depend for our daily comforts, it had been a happy accident that led me to the choice of the "Australasian".

Lots of people have found fault with Froude, but an Englishman who can so cordially appreciate real porridge is bound to raise a sympathetic response in any Scottish heart!

So well was the Line run, and so efficiently was it manned, that the casualties on it were by official figures six or seven times below the British average, which meant immeasurably better than anywhere else in the world. It was amongst the first shipping companies to have in its service large ocean-going vessels fitted with triple expansion engines. It specially catered for trade between South Africa and Australia. Hence the emus at Pitmedden, and hence, also the feeling of being not far from home in the heart of the present writer, when looking out at his hotel bedroom window on his first morning in Melbourne, he saw across Collins Street the magic words "Aberdeen Line".

But it was with its clippers that the Line reached its true immortality. Of all Aberdeen's achievements—artistic, literary, architectural, industrial, commercial—none has shed such lustre upon Bon-Accord and its people as the laurels won by the burgh's shipyards with their clippers. He must be a poor-spirited creature indeed who cannot feel his heart beat a little faster at the thought, though in our prosaic day it is no more than a dream of the imagination, of those glorious snowy ships gliding into Aberdeen bay and floating rather than sailing into the southern distance beyond Girdleness, the *Scottish Maid,* the first of them, the *Stornoway,* the *Chrysolite,* the great *Cairngorm* that beat the Yankees at the tea-carrying trade. These and many others issued from the yard of A. Hall & Co.

Although Hall & Co. were the leading yard, it was another company that captured the supreme chaplet. Of Walter Hood and Co., the principal partner was George Thompson, and when he entered the Australian trade in 1848 he began to use the yard to provide him with his ships. The *Phoenician* was the pioneer both of the White Star clippers and of the Line's Australian run. In the next ten years Hood & Co. turned out about one clipper a year for Thompson, but it was in the following decade that perfection was reached. *Jerusalem, Thyatira, Miltiades, Pericles, Salamis* and the peerless *Thermopylae* represented, with a few others, the flower of the White Star flock. The historian of the clippers, Basil Lubbock, says of them, "Their green sides, white figure-heads, white blocks, white lower masts, bowsprits and yardarms, gold stripe and gold scroll work were the admiration of sailors wherever they went".

Photo from a model of the Thermopylae *in the Art Gallery*

The *Thermopylae* was the fastest sailing ship in the world, not merely in her time but of all time. Her record day's run was 380 statute miles. Of 947 tons burthen, she was 210 feet long, 36 broad, 21 deep, and she was launched in 1868. During the next twelve years, although she was often beaten in the China tea races by

Clyde-built boats, her over-all performance surpassed that of any other, and only the Clyde-built *Cutty Sark* of the eighties was her equal. By that time the *Thermopylae* was out of the tea trade, but she flew the White Star flag till 1890, when she was bought by a Canadian firm that used her in the rice trade between Burma and Vancouver. Later she was sold to the Government of Portugal as a training ship, and in 1912 was towed from the Tagus out to sea and sunk—let us hope with her flag flying.

In 1840 George Thompson was persuaded—he was always a retiring person and required a good deal of solicitation to undertake public office—to allow himself to be elected Dean of Guild, which, of course, brought him into the Town Council. In 1842 he became an elected Councillor, and served his triennium. He refused to stand again then, but in 1847 he came forward and on re-entering the Council was made Lord Provost. He proved to be one of the most popular of Provosts, although he lacked—who for that matter had?—the panache of Alexander Anderson. But his three years' tenure of the Chair was almost as fruitful as that of his immediate predecessor Sir Thomas Blaikie.

During his long life he saw alterations and improvements at the harbour that were in almost continuous operation and which were thoroughly in keeping with Aberdeen's importance as a seaport in the middle of the century. And so it came about when, a day before schedule, Queen Victoria and the Prince Consort arrived in the harbour in the Royal yacht in September 1848, and tied up in the Victoria Dock, there was actually—according to Dr. John Milne—no other dock in the British Empire where the yacht could have been moored alongside a quay and where the Queen could land without recourse to a boat.

The Lord Provost presented Her Majesty, on the 7th, when she landed, with the silver keys of the City, and the previous day he conferred the Freedom of the City on the Prince Consort when the latter came ashore to see round the town. The Royal party were on their way to Balmoral for the first time, and it was also the first time in almost two hundred years that a reigning monarch had been in the burgh—and at that Charles II was only accepted in Scotland—and the first time in nearly three hundred years that a reigning Queen had set foot in Aberdeen, Mary Queen of Scots having made her not very happy visit in 1562. That visit may be taken as marking the commencement of Mary's decline and fall: legend has it that her half-brother, the Earl of Moray, forced her to watch, from the window of Marischal Hall, the execution in the Castlegate of Sir John Gordon, whom she knew and liked. Charles II's residence in the neighbouring house belonging to Menzies of Pitfodels, in 1650, was rather different: he had Lucy Walters with him, the mother of the ill-fated Monmouth, and he was requested to draw the curtains when he was in her company.

George Thompson was not a man with a single-track mind. He was closely associated in the formative Aberdeen days with Alexander Anderson as a director of the North of Scotland Bank, and he was much interested in the extension of railways to and from the city. He was Provost at the opening of the Northern section of what was then called the Aberdeen Railway, later the Caledonian, in 1848 for goods to Portlethen, and in 1850 for both goods and passengers to Ferryhill, where the terminal buildings were erected. He was also a director of the Great North of Scotland Railway (which partly explains the halt at Pitmedden), but the first section of it, from Huntly to Kittybrewster, was not opened until 1854.

Amongst other notable events of his Provostship were the opening of the East Poor house, consequent upon the new legislative dispensation of the Scottish Poor Law; the conferring of the Freedom upon Sir Robert Peel in 1849, the riding of the outer marches in 1848, and the celebration of the centenary of Gordon's College in 1850. He refused to serve as Provost for a further term, but sat in the Council till 1852, when, with his usual reluctance, he consented to contest Aberdeen as a Liberal in the election of that year, and beat his Tory opponent by 682 to 204 votes. He made no name for himself in Parliament, though he served his constituency well, and he retired in 1857. That year he bought the estate of Pitmedden of Dyce, and in 1864 that of Rainnieshill, Newmachar. He gave up the management of his firm in 1866. In 1880 the citizens of Aberdeen presented him with his portrait by George Reid.

In the haughs of Pitmedden there still stands a monument to the great Aberdeen medico who died early in the seventeenth century, Duncan Liddell, the owner then of the estate. Whether his ghost visited George Thompson, or whether there is a special influence in the neighbourhood of the Don, we know not, but in his retirement the laird of Pitmedden became Aberdeen's most generous contemporary benefactor. In 1882 he gave £4,000 to various Aberdeen institutions besides £1,000 towards the extension of the Royal Infirmary. Later he bestowed £6,000 on the University to provide bursaries in medicine, and in 1886 other £3,000 for a travelling fellowship in medicine. These, comparing money values and the opportunities of making money then and now, were exceptionally munificent.

'Alexander the Corrector'
immortal author of the Concordance

Alexander Cruden

HARD-HEADED Aberdonians may reflect, if not with profit certainly with interest, on the incontrovertible fact that the only one of their number, since their illustrious community appeared in history 900 years ago, who has attained to the wider immortality was mentally deranged. Nay more, the only other person intimately connected with Aberdeen who has acquired a like celebrity was also, to put the case at its mildest, eccentric. Alexander Cruden, with whom this essay is about to deal, was on at least three separate occasions in bedlam, yet his Concordance to the Bible has not only survived almost intact the assaults of several learned Editors but also remains, serene and unapproachable, as the indispensable aid in the English language to the study of the Scriptures. Cruden's sole rival amongst Aberdonians on the higher seats of Valhalla, is Sir Thomas Urquhart of Cromartie, alumnus of King's College and author of the translation of Rabelais that will never be superseded—and Sir Thomas, although he never wore a strait-jacket, was Sir Thomas!

All the piety and wit—and they have been considerable; all the business acumen—which has met with world-wide and centuries-old recognition; all the learning and the artistic sense—both of which have been various and profound: all these qualities, bestowed by nature liberally and from generation to generation, have failed to produce a single Aberdonian besides Alexander Cruden whose name has become and bids fair to remain a household word. We have had our "Chicago" Smiths and our "Silent" Smiths, our John Farquhars, our Strathconas and Mountstephens, our Forbeses and MacRoberts, all in the millionaire class; but their fame was enjoyed in their lifetime, whereas poor Cruden, to whom £100 was a fortune, laid up his treasure for the eternity after his death.

Alexander Cruden became a citizen of Aberdeen, and of the world (though he knew it not) on 31 May 1699, when he was born in a room over Cruden's Court, off Broad Street, to Baillie William Cruden, a merchant, and Isabel Pyper his wife. He was the second child, of a brood that ultimately extended to eleven. The Crudens a generation or so before had come to Aberdeen from Strichen—or Mormond village as at that time it would probably have been called. They were Presbyterians and no doubt—for in those tumultuary days all was black and white in religion—prettv strict. They were in easy circumstances. The Broadgate was a fashionable street. The rooms were reasonably spacious. When the last biographer of Alexander Cruden, Miss Edith Olivier, called upon the writer of these notes some thirty years ago, he was able to tell her she was in, if not assuredly the room where the Corrector was born, at least one of the apartments of the house of his nativity.

Of course he went to the Grammar School, then a single storey rambling building on the Schoolhill—there was no Gordon's College there yet—and later to the town's College, Marischal. We know very little of his young life, but his student days covered a period of tribulation at Marischal, which, owing to the part taken in the Jacobite Rebellion by its patron and Chancellor, the last Earl Marischal, found itself suspended for a couple of sessions. Cruden never seemed to have been impressed by this interruption of his studies. But interrupted they were, for he appears on the list of students from 1713 to 1716, and then when the classes were renewed in 1717 and 1718. He graduated M.A. in 1721.

Somewhere about that time, and probably explaining the lateness of his graduation, he encountered the first big cataclysm of his life. He fell in love with the daughter of a minister. Whether his courting was normal, we have no means of knowing. His subsequent courtships were anything but normal. At all events, and through no fault of Cruden's the association was rudely broken off in a manner best left unspecified. Poor Alexander took the matter so much to heart that it went to his head, and he had to be confined for a space. Years later, so the story goes, James Chalmers the founder of the *Aberdeen Journal* being in London, thought he would take the rather solitary Alexander to a house whose Aberdeen chatelaine would help to dispel Cruden's loneliness. The door was opened—by the long-lost first love, and poor Cruden turned away in a state of mind that can be imagined. . . .

After receiving his degree Cruden went by sea to London. Then for a decade or more our knowledge of his experience is rather thin. One account states that he acted as a tutor in a Hertfordshire family and in the Isle of Man. Miss Olivier says his first engagement was as tutor to the only son of a Middlesex squire of the name of Coltman. One wonders vaguely if there could be any connection with the Coltmans who were at Blelack House in the early years of the present century. Then she tells a sad story of Cruden being recommended to the Earl of Derby as a French reader. Cruden knew French but his pronunciation had no recognisable relation to the language, and when the Earl asked him to demonstrate his proficiency he spelt out each word!

Happily at both the Grammar School and Marischal a sound training in the Classics was given, and from time to time he was employed by Watts the printer as a proof reader. Whether he saved something from what would have been very scanty remuneration, or whether his people helped him, he was able to open a bookseller's shop under the Royal Exchange. In this strategic spot he had many opportunities of meeting the important people in the city. Small, slim and shy, he seems nevertheless to have had a way with him that won the goodwill of men, if not of women. The upshot was that when the bookseller to Queen Caroline died, he brought sufficient influence to bear to get the appointment. Not only did he engage the Lord Mayor of London to support his application, but he even had a word with the great Sir Robert Walpole himself, who professed himself satisfied with his character; and who knows but that the greatest of English Prime Ministers and most corrupt of party managers may not have lent a helping word in the Queen's closet, where his advice was paramount?

The Queen's Bookseller was a considerable personage. Not merely would his possession of the Royal Warrant bring snobbish customers to his shop, but the Queen herself was a genuine patroness of the arts, and a very good creature to boot, as we know from Lord Hervey's memoirs. Perhaps it was because he realised she would help him as an author that the bookseller now set himself seriously to the task that was to make him for ever famous. He may have been working at a concordance of Scripture sporadically for some time, but the general belief is that he compiled it in a year. Anyone who has occasion to consult Cruden's Concordance should require no instruction in assessing, however roughly, the amount of work it entailed. Actually its only predecessor with which it can be compared was that prepared for the Vulgate by a Dominican who became a Cardinal and who is said to have been assisted by 500 monks of the Order. Cruden had no one to help him, his system is far more complete than any of the others, and when his editorial work was done, he experimented with paper, print and general format until he was satisfied that his book was a dainty enough dish to set before a Queen. To her it was dedicated and she promised to remember him—and in a few days she was dead. In his dealings with the Queen, Cruden's luck was assuredly out, both then and before and after.

He called his magnum opus a "Complete Concordance of the Old and New Testaments". Such veritably it is. Subsequent editors have failed to glean any considerable omissions. Yet he himself protested that "though it be called *A Complete Concordance,* poor sinful man can do nothing absolutely perfectly and complete, and therefore the word *complete* is only to be taken in a comparative sense". He described a concordance as "a Dictionary, or an Index, to the Bible, wherein all the words used through the inspired writings are arranged alphabetically, and the various places where they occur are referred to, to assist in finding out passages, and comparing the several significations of the same word". The mind that is capable of speedily coping with such verbal drudgery is not perhaps so uncommon as might be imagined, but all such toil pales into utter insignificance when compared with the extent of Cruden's and the swiftness with which he discharged it.

No doubt in compiling his Concordance he had neglected his shop and his other sources of income. In 1737 it was published and the then essential patroness was dead, and the charges he had been put to were considerable. Not only so, but with the Queen's death his Royal Warrant lapsed. He was a Presbyterian in an England when only members of the Church of England could exercise full citizenship and when the frowns of the Establishment could light upon Dissenters. So very few bought his book. Anglican clergymen could hardly be expected to do so. Dissenting ministers in those days had their bibles, or at least the Old Testament, by heart, and scarcely needed a concordance. To make ends meet he had to sell all his stock of books, and have recourse once more to the uninspiring slavery of proof-reading.

And then there opened upon his slightly distorted imagination another prospect of financial independence. For a long time he had been in the habit of spending his Sunday evenings with a Mr. and Mrs. Bryan Pain, the husband having a chandler's shop in Piccadilly. They called Cruden their Chaplain for he was in the habit of leading their household in prayer. Pain died and Alexander took it in his head that he might hang up his hat. He approached the widow with what he describes himself as a "piece of love gallantry", whatever that may mean. Despite their previous friendship, which appears to have existed since he arrived in London, Mrs. Pain would have nothing to do with him as a husband. Eventually, after some hair-raising experiences which he describes with what may be exaggeration, he was carriel off and thrown into a private mad house in Bethnal Green by a man named Wightman, a rival bookseller, who possibly became the widow's second husband. Wightman at all events took control of the bookshop, but as he had failed to have Cruden properly certified, he was himself in a rather awkward position.

Alexander himself tells the whole story of his incarceration. He was chained to the leg of his bed, encased in a strait waistcoat so that he had to eat his food like an animal, and "Oh, what difficulties he had to perform the necessities of nature in a becoming manner!" Somehow he contrived to get a little money from home—his pockets had been rifled by his keepers—and to have a barber occasionally to tend his wig, who carried out letters to his friends. Wightman and his associates tried to get him to sign a paper that would legitimise their proceedings, but he refused. At last, after ten weeks of dreadful martyrdom he succeeded in escaping, with his chain and the bed-leg. He was apprehended by the watch, demanded to be led before the Lord Mayor, and the latter, despite the efforts of Wightman, declared him to be sane and released him. Cruden went off to the Coltmans with whom his career in England had begun, and took a rest cure.

Like our old friend Peter Williamson, Cruden raised actions against the people who had trepanned him. But although he had been in the City for a decade and a half at least, he was still a stranger in a strange land, he made the mistake of conducting his own case, which prejudiced the judge against him, and some of his opponents were substantial people, which prejudiced the judge in their favour. Worst of all, the defence produced a letter from Cruden's father (who in the meantime had died) referring to his mental disorder of twenty years before. Unlike Peter Williamson, he had his trouble for nothing.

For the next dozen years or so we have little news of Cruden. A sister came to live with him whom he married off on a "warm" husband. He himself gradually took to brooding over the shortcomings of the age, and from being a proof-corrector he transmogrified himself into "Alexander the Corrector of the People". He was profoundly disturbed by the godlessness of the English, their walking about on the Sabbath day, their "polluting Playhouses, monstrous Masquerades, and pernicious Card playing". On his belabouring in the street a young man who was using obscene language, his brother-in-law and sister put him in a strait waistcoat again and he was kept, though much less strictly than before, in a private asylum near the Three Jolly Butchers in Little Chelsea. He was soon out again, promising to forgive his sister if she would go to a madhouse for two days. The day of his release, in 1753, we are glad to feel that he was "able to linger a little in Mr. Keith's bookshop in Gracechurch Street".

But he was getting further off the rails than ever. He hung about the Court trying to get one of the Lords-in-waiting to present him for a knighthood, a £100 note in his pocket to pay the fee. He had himself nominated for election as a Member of Parliament for the City of London, only withdrawing at the last moment. He unsuccessfully sued some people who had taken part in his last committal to a madhouse for £10,000, but he was not so daft, when in reply to plea that he had been twice restrained already, he remarked, "Oh! Rare Logicians and Cloudy-headed Philosophers! If a person has been injured twice, is that a reason for injuring him a third time?" He pursued an heiress, a Miss Abney, with love letters and prayer bullets and fantastic threats, although he never spoke to her in his life.

Having tried in vain to persuade Parliament to pass an act appointing him Corrector of the People, he interviewed the Lord Mayor and got the Lady Mayoress to bestow her patronage on his plan before he set out on a progress as Alexander the Corrector. He spent a month at both Oxford and Cambridge, where he was knighted in each place by the ladies, and received by the authorities with the deference due to the author of the Concordance. He went to Eton and Windsor and Tunbridge Wells, but found the task of turning Society from its evil ways an uphill and unrewarding employment. He undertook something more to the point when, acting on information gathered at the universities that another edition of his masterpiece was overdue, he revised it and dedicated the second edition to George III, who gave him £100. The booksellers gave him £500, and a third edition earned him £300. He was now a wealthy man, with a housekeeper and a boy servant.

Perhaps his greatest moment was when he was presented to the King. George held his hand for a bit and congratulated him on what he had done for religion. His Majesty concentrated upon the Corrector, paying no attention to the other individual presented at the same time, the Rev. Lawrence Sterne no less, author of *Tristram Shandy*. Annoyed at being disposed of with a mere bow, Sterne asked his sponsor to have his name announced again. "My lord," said the King, "you have told me already."

Alexander revisited Aberdeen in 1769. He found traces of ungodliness in his native city but, we should imagine, little else save the houses that would be familiar to him. He went back to London, and one morning in 1770, on his failing to come down to breakfast, his woman servant went to his bedroom and found him on his knees by a chair, in an attitude of prayer, and dead. He wanted to lie in St. Nicholas Kirkyard, but they buried him in a dissenters' cemetery in Southwark which later became the site of a brewery, owned, curiously enough, by a family whose last representative in the business was a friend of the writer.

Cruden left enough to endow a small bursary in Marischal College, and some other benefactions to Aberdeen. The bursary and the memorial plaque recently erected near some of his old haunts in London are not likely to hold him so perennially in the world's memory as his Concordance.

John Forbes White

flour miller, classical scholar, art lover, starting the Art Gallery

John Forbes White

ONE of the engaging characteristics of the Aberdonian is that when he is good enough to be considered eminent he is frequently far from being in Charles Murray's phrase, "a' in a breist like the wife's ae coo". In a community which, in the opinion of the lesser breeds, finds the most tonic atmosphere in the environs of the shrine of Mammon, the number of successful business men whose thoughts in their spare moments turn to what are generally termed cultural subjects must be considerably above the average. There may be cited as examples, more or less in our own day, and with the necessary qualification of being dead, A. R. Gray solacing his last illness with the Greek classics in the original; Will Walker whiling away sleepless hours at ninety by repeating passages from Shakespeare; James Murray and Thomas Jaffray surrounding themselves and endowing their fellow-citizens with works of art; John Morgan the builder lecturing to the Philosophical Society on Omar Khayyam, and corresponding with Ruskin and Carlyle; and not merely art and letters but music has benefited in our city over a long series of generations by the interest in those matters of men who, despite their preoccupation with the Muses and Graces, were not likely to have been overreached in the market-place. It can hardly be without significance that Aberdeen's Town Council, in burghal days perhaps more spacious than the present, was in the habit of bestowing gifts or "propines" to burgesses who in prose or verse showed interest in music or letters.

Perhaps the Eminent Aberdonian whose life is about to be sketched will serve as an object lesson to clear, should they require clearing, our minds of cant —the cant of the academe who despises trade and commerce, and the cant of the business man who regards the Classics and the Arts as "Kids' stuff". For centuries the Aberdeen tradition has been that all the world's the oyster of the man with his head screwed on the right way, and that everything in the world is capable of repaying study and attention and practice, preferably more than one thing in a life-time. Which brings us without more ado to the subject of the present exercise, John Forbes White, grain merchant and flour miller, lover of the arts, classical scholar, who flourished in Aberdeen during the Victorian era, having been born half-a-dozen years before the great queen's accession and dying in 1904.

His father, William White, was a prosperous but apparently otherwise undistinguished flour miller and corn merchant, with his mill at

Kettock's Mills on the Don and his store in King Street at the corner of Mealmarket Street. He sent his son to the Grammar School where, under "grim Pluto", the great rector Dr. James Melvin, foremost humanist in Scotland, he grew to be dux and to emerge in 1844 ready to enter Marischal College as First Bursar at the mature age of thirteen. (No I.Q., eleven plus, primary departments, directors of education, in those days; only education!) At college no rival could ever catch the skirts of his coat, and he graduated M.A., the most brilliant student of his year, in that famous year of revolutions, 1848. He had ambitions to be a doctor, and in fact put in a year at Medicine, when he was prizeman in Anatomy. But a brother, who seems to have been intended for the business, decided to become a missionary, went to India and died there early, and John F. White had to take to the trade of the miller.

For this line of country the critics of the classical education might have us believe that his academic training would not have been likely to fit him. Actually, his father dying rather unexpectedly, he found himself in full control at the age of twenty-one and made a resounding success of the business, which he built up to be the largest of its kind in the North of Scotland. Far from impairing his commercial efficiency or disinclining him for progressive methods, White's more than usually thorough classical education, in the old Scots fashion of making the pupil capable of thinking, provided him with a capacity for invention and adaptability that stood him in good stead. His first administrative problem was how to improve the haulage to and from Kettock's Mills. He decided to substitute a traction engine for horses—let us not forget this was 110 years ago; and when on its first trip the engine stuck on the steep brae above the Bridge of Don, he built a new stretch of road (there was no county council then to negotiate with), procured a more powerful engine, and the job was done. Next, in 1854, he set off to the Baltic and made a tour of the German grain-shipping ports to study their methods of handling grain; and incidentally enjoyed himself in a bus (then called a diligence) between Danzig and Stettin talking Latin to a professor of Mathematics from Cracow. Then he went down to Hungary and the great wheatfields of the Banat and Transylvania, and the fruit of that trip was the Hungarian roller system of milling which he installed in the very modern mill he built at Dundee. In 1888, when his lease of Kettock's Mills expired, he closed down in Aberdeen and transferred his whole business to Dundee. He, however, retained one of his houses and spent a large part of the year in Aberdeen after migration.

During his Aberdeen period he played quite a prominent and varied part in the life of the city. He was on the Harbour Board from 1868 to 1879. He was for two terms until 1888 one of the General Council's assessors on Aberdeen University Court. He was a director of the North of Scotland Bank and the Aberdeen Jute Company, a promoter and director of the Canadian Mortgage Company, an extraordinary director of the Scottish Widows' Fund. He was a prominent member of this Chamber. In his own trade he was President of the National Association of British and Irish Millers in 1888. For quarter of a century he was a Vice-Consul for Sweden and Norway, and he was consular agent in Aberdeen for France. As a Liberal he persuaded James Bryce to stand for South Aberdeen at the 1885 election, but when Gladstone committed the party to Home Rule for Ireland he became a Liberal Unionist. When the British Association held its conference in Aberdeen in 1859 he was one of the local secretaries. He was a leading member of Aberdeen Philosophical Society and a Fellow of the Society of Antiquaries of Scotland. Aberdeen University laureated him LL.D. in 1886. This catalogue of his activities, which is not by any means complete, gives some idea of the range of his interests and the energy he infused into his life.

So far, nothing has been said of his principal interest. In June 1889 when George Reid's portrait of him was presented, it was said that "for the greater part of his life love of art in every form had been to him only a passion". With that passion it now falls upon us to deal. How it began there is no precise means of knowing. He was, however, one of the pioneers of amateur photography in the city where George

Washington Wilson did so much for the development of that near-art. To be a competent photographer in the middle of last century demanded an infinity of patience in the taking and endless labour in the developing of the negative. Perhaps his daily journey to his mill had something to do with the birth of his love for the sublime and beautiful. Aberdeen must be unique amongst the towns of Scotland in possessing within its bounds that last stretch of the lower Don from the Cruives to the sea than which, despite great industrial buildings and their inevitable concomitants, no lovelier river scene could be imagined—except perhaps Paradise itself at Monymusk. And there White had his country house, Seaton Cottage, which he would not give up even when he deserted Aberdeen for Dundee.

He married in 1859, and about that time, having seen a friend's house decorated by Daniel Cottier, he commissioned that artist to do both the cottage and his town house, at the corner of Union Street and Bon-Accord Street, and also, in memory of his brother, the stained glass window in St. Machar's Cathedral representing the missionaries John the Baptist and St. Paul. Cottier did another window there, in memory of George Jameson, John Phillip and William Dyce, as well as the famous West Window in St Giles'. These commissions were among White's first exercises in patronage of the arts. Early on also Professor Brown, who had been his professor of Greek at Marischal, was having his portrait painted by John Phillip. Probably because he could talk Greek or about Greek to the old man, White was asked to keep him company during the operation in order to ensure a genial expression on the face of the sitter. No doubt this intimate insight into the practical work of the greatest of all Aberdeen's artist sons helped to whet White's appetite for more knowledge of painting and painters.

But the experience which he himself regarded as the culminating point of his conversion occurred in 1862 when he visited the International Exhibition in London. There White was tremendously attracted by a landscape by an unknown young Dutch artist from Utrecht named Alexander Mollinger. Before he set eyes on that picture he had the attitude to art that might be expected in a normally well educated man. From that day forward he was not merely an art enthusiast but a critic of intense sincerity and of creative quality in so far as his keenness, insight and knowledge inspired and encouraged to higher flights many an artist who otherwise might not have realised the latent potentialities of his talent. In his town house he had a special gallery built to accommodate his pictures, which included a leavening of Aberdeen work along with a judicious selection of paintings by celebrated European artists.

The Sixties, it is well to remember, constituted a wonderful decade in Aberdeen's history—not merely on the commercial side but also in aesthetic and cultural respects. While John Phillip was fully and securely established as "the Scottish Velazquez", William Dyce—Aberdeen's other R.A.—had long completed his frescoes for the House of Lords and had turned his attention to church music. Both these great painters died during the decade. George Reid was in process of emerging from the chrysalis stage, and it was White who put him in touch with Mollinger and so greatly assisted in his development. William Robertson Smith was still the student, but soon to take the chair at Bawbie Law from which bigotry was to cast him out—into eminence. That other very fastidious Aberdeen artist, George Paul Chalmers, was at the height of his powers and about to be elected an R.S.A.

A little later there grew up a select coterie by the banks of another Aberdeenshire stream, the Ugie, when the Rev. James Peter, an Angus man who was Minister of Deer, gathered about him a group of extraordinarily gifted men whose meetings in his manse earned them the nickname of the Deer Academy, or sometimes, since all but Peter were Aberdonians, the Aberdeen Academy. Until the days of the Sit Siccar Club half a century later, the North-East produced nothing quite so impressive, and the Deer sodality had a rather more varied equipment than the later body. Probably the most distinguished member was William Robertson Smith, whose mother belonged to Crichie, in Old Deer parish.

George Reid was a member and it was owing to his friendship with Peter that he became the designer of the tower which now adorns the parish church. His brother Archibald D. Reid was also a member, though not I think the third brother Sam Reid, R.S.W., who began life as a clerk in White's counting-house. George Paul Chalmers was also of the group: he was found dying in an Edinburgh street after a dinner from which he had walked home with White. David Gill, later a knight and a celebrated astronomer at the Cape of Good Hope; John Kerr, an Inspector of Schools whose reminiscences may still be read with pleasure and profit; and John Forbes White himself completed the little club. The Rev. James Peter was the second founder of the Club of Deir, another club which goes back to the time of the French Revolution and may even antedate that grim event by some years. It is still vigorous and meets regularly.

The Aberdeen institution with which White's name and memory are most closely associated is the Art Gallery. To whom the idea of its inception was due is not certain, but White and his friend Alexander Macdonald of Kepplestone were the most prominent among its sponsors, and it is highly probable that White's was the original suggestion. His business technique, his intense belief in the social importance of art, and his very real local patriotism all point to his having been, if not the leader of the movement, at least first among equals. The Art Gallery was formally opened in 1884, the year of Alexander Macdonald's death. He was the son of the Alexander Macdonald whose adaptation of early Egyptian methods of stone polishing led to the great expansion of the Aberdeen monumental granite trade. His yard was the Constitution Street works until 1853 of the firm of Macdonald and Leslie, but in that year Leslie went off to devote himself to architecture—he eventually became Lord Provost—while Macdonald greatly developed both the quarrying and manufacturing sides of the business. On the old man's death in 1860 the younger Alexander took over.

Like White, an enthusiast for art, he not only built up a remarkable collection, but at Kepplestone he entertained all kinds of literary and aesthetic "lions" and many of his artist guests would repay his hospitality by a painting. It was not until his wife's death that his will, bequeathing his magnificent array of pictures to the city, became operative, and until 1900 the Art Gallery had to be content with a not very pretentious assemblage of canvases. White, however, did not lose interest when the project took shape. To him is due the Sculpture Section. He had always been an ardent Greek student and after his removal to Dundee he was responsible for the revival of the Homeric Society. His scholarship was acute and constructive and he suggested several valuable amended readings of obscure classical passages. In 1894 he made an extended tour of Greece, from which he returned as keen upon Greek art as he already was on Greek letters. The Sculpture Section, the campaign for which he launched with a lecture in the Art Gallery on "The Sculptural Monuments of the Greeks", but which he did not live to see completed, was the direct outcome of the tour of 1894. James Murray carried White's scheme through.

It is exceedingly unfortunate that a projected volume of White's critical essays and lectures never materialised. For the *Encyclopedia Britannica,* when his friend Robertson Smith was editor, he wrote articles on such artists as Poole, Vermeer, Rembrandt and Velazquez. Perhaps the best thing he ever did was an essay on Rembrandt and Velazquez in *The Quarterly Review*. These, with Corot, of whose work he owned a fine specimen, were his favourites. He lectured on them to the Edinburgh Philosophical Society. For the *Aurora Borealis Academica* he wrote upon William Robertson Smith, and elsewhere he wrote an obituary of that other great Aberdeen scholar, Robert A. Neil. He appended a critical account of George Paul Chalmers's work to a memoir of that artist. Besides these things White was a promoter of the Aberdeen Artists Society, initiated the Aberdeen Pen and Pencil Club in 1891, and was president of the Aberdeen Philharmonic Society.

Of few Aberdonians, or of business men anywhere, could it be so truly said as of John Forbes White, "He had fun".

A medley of
Scientific gentlemen

THE contributions of Aberdonians to the advancement of the Sciences have been many and varied. Yet when viewed in the mass they tend to leave an impression of disappointment. They present, for instance, nothing so spectacular as the achievements of Aberdonians in the art and practice of war, or in commerce, or in the scholarship which is described as "pure" presumably because it has nothing to do with any science save perhaps philology. That, then, is the impression. But perhaps it will be less emphatic when this article is completed . . . always provided the article is read!

Sir Arthur Keith

Aberdonians have, in respect of the sciences, laboured under three disadvantages. First of all, being the superlative of the three ascending grades of Scots—Scotsmen, damned Scotsmen, and Aberdonians—they are incurable metaphysicians. And—as one of the greatest Aberdonians demonstrated in connection with one of the most recently recognised sciences—metaphysics simply will not do in the scientific connection. The second handicap is that in Aberdeen's greatest age—roughly from the Reformation to the Restoration—medicine was the dominant branch of science, and nearly but not quite all the eminent Aberdonians were M.D.'s at least by degree. And the third factor was, and is, that Aberdeen University, beyond all the universities in Scotland, to go no further afield, always insisted on general culture as a background to its own teaching, even until days within living memory; and was equally urgent, until the very recent educational revolution that has contrived to put secondary considerations first, that in a university teaching had clear priority over research. That Aberdonian graduates were more successful in research under the old dispensation than they appear to be now is an ironic circumstance that need not be laboured here.

It is not possible in a short essay on so extensive a subject to be other than eclectic. We shall seek the bright lights—the outstanding men and the principal trends. Of the latter one of the earliest and most interesting, as it has been one of the most enduring, is the Aberdonian's fondness for botany. William Davidson (1593-1670), an M.A. of Marischal College, combined expertise in botany with the other favourite Aberdeen pursuits of medicine and wandering. He became physician to Louis XIII of France, and professor of chemistry at the Jardin des Plantes in Paris. In 1651 he was appointed physician to John Casimir, King of Poland, and keeper of the royal gardens at Warsaw. Somewhat similar was the career of Robert Morison (1620-83), another Marischal graduate, who was first the keeper of the French royal gardens at Blois and physician to the Duke of Orleans, and later senior physician to Charles II (for whose death he was not responsible, having predeceased his master), superintendent of the royal gardens, and from 1669 professor of botany at Oxford. It may be worth noting that he was killed in a street accident. Within the last century or so four Aberdonians have preserved the tradition —William Macgillivray, whose posthumous *Natural History of Deeside and Braemar* was published by special order of Queen Victoria; George Dickie, professor of botany from 1860 to 1877; his successor James William Helenus Trail, from 1877 to 1919—and to these two is due the widespread interest in botany which is still found amongst the educated middle-aged and old men of this area; and Macgregor Skene, emeritus professor of botany at Bristol, a pupil of Trail's.

Astronomy is another branch of natural science in which Aberdonians have been fond of specialising. Sir David Gill (1843-1914) whose principal work was done in the Southern Hemisphere at the Capetown Observatory, and John Lamont of Braemar, *alias* Johann von Lamont (1805-79) who attained eminence in Bavaria are the two most notable figures among the moderns. In earlier days James Cheyne of Arnage (died 1602), professor at and rector of the Scots College at Douai; Duncan Liddel (1561-1613), professor of mathematics at Helmstadt and one of Aberdeen University's principal benefactors; and (but only to be mentioned as proof of impartiality) Alexander Ross (1591-1654) chaplain to Charles I, which appointment may make his animadversions against Galileo and Copernicus less astonishing, made some noise in the world.

It was work in connection with astronomy, and with the telescope, such as it then was, and with optics that gave his right to immortality to the first and perhaps the greatest of Aberdeen's physicists, James Gregory (1638-75). He invented the reflecting telescope and had scarcely time to do more when he died. In passing, the extraordinary intellectual precocity of these people of three and four hundred years ago deserves a glance. They entered the university at twelve, graduated at an age when boys today have not yet left school, and were making their name of their way, at home or abroad, before they were twenty-one. To say that the area of knowledge was far smaller then does not explain why they were adults so early. Gregory was a son of the Presbyterian manse, like his much later-born relative Thomas Reid (1710-96) the inventor of the philosophy of Common Sense in contradistinction to the Rationalism of David Hume. That the latter system is today paramount is hard lines on a very sagacious and competent thinker such as Thomas Reid was. He held the Chair of Philosophy at King's College, until he succeeded Adam Smith as professor of moral philosophy in Glasgow. Adam Smith is one of Aberdeen's near misses in science, for the founder of the modern science of political economy was the son of a member of a well-known Aberdeenshire family who was born within sound of King's College class-bell. Another near-miss was the inventor James Watt, whose collaterals have been resident in Aberdeenshire for centuries, and whose last male representative was intelligence officer on the staff of Field Marshal Montgomery in North Africa, Italy and the West.

James Gregory had an elder brother David who, in addition to his remarkable fecundity—he is credited with at least twenty-nine children begotten under benefit of clergy—was an inventor in his own right. But while James's thoughts were applied to the usages of peace, David turned his attention to machines of war, and devised an improved cannon which shocked Sir Isaac Newton, when the specifications were shown to him, to such an extent that he successfully argued for the destruction of the plans as being too lethal for a civilised man to contemplate. We can do much better than that nowadays. Indeed, the modern rifle owes much of its efficiency to a son of an Aberdeenshire laird who invented the rifled barrel and to an Aberdeenshire minister who invented the percussion lock and cap. The former was humane enough, when testing his new small-arm the night before the battle of Brandywine Creek, to refrain from using it to shoot George Washington, with whom he had served in the Colonial wars; and the latter (like several Aberdeenshire parish ministers at the turn of last century) was a scientist and scientific observer of no mean ability.

No name is more closely associated with the emergence of the science of psychology in the modern world than that of Alexander Bain (1818-1903), who began life running errands for a weaving shop in which his father was employed, and who from 1860 to 1880 filled the Chair of Logic and Rhetoric in Aberdeen University. He it was who led the way in applying to psychological problems and phenomena the exact methods that had become the rule in other sciences. He founded the magazine *Mind*, which incidentally is still printed in Aberdeen. Its first editor was one of his pupils George Croom Robertson, Grote Professor of Philosophy of Mind and Logic in University College, London, and an exponent of Bain's ideas whom only a premature death prevented from making a name for himself as illustrious as that of his master.

Bain's chair in those expansive days included the professing of English Language and Literature, and his contribution to the former of these subjects is not today fully appreciated. Books upon several aspects of English grammar and composition and his treatise, *Education as a Science*, thoroughly fulfilled what has always been the Aberdeen concept of the educative function of a university. His work on language links up with a much earlier manifestation of Aberdonian enthusiasm for the lordship of words. One of the first of the Aberdonians whose books have been preserved was John Vaus (1490?-1538?), professor of humanity at King's College after a spell in Paris; he specialised in the study of grammar. A century later came George Dalgarno (1626-87) who ran a school in Oxford, invented a deaf-and-dumb alphabet, devised a form of shorthand, and finished up with (in the words of the *Dictionary of National Biography*) a "classification of all possible ideas and their representation each by a specific character without reference to the words of any language".

A far greater personage than Dalgarno, and one of the world's lords of language, was Sir Thomas Urquhart of Cromarty (1611-60), King's College's most distinguished alumnus, and best known as the translator of Rabelais. He may be said—unfortunately the story is too long to be given here—to have started the Great Civil War. At King's his hobbies were (he tells us) "optical secrets, mysteries of natural philosophie, reasons for the variety of colours, the finding out of the longitude, the squaring of the circle, and ways to accomplish all trigonometrical calculations by signes without tangents with the same comprehensiveness of computation". When he reached Worcester in 1652 with Charles II's Scots army, he had four large portmanteaux full of clothes and three trunks with a hundred manuscripts of his own amounting to 642 quinternions of five sheets each. One manuscript on a universal language was rescued. He wrote a treatise on trigonometry which is entitled *Trissotetras*, and upon his favourite conception of a universal language he wrote *Escubalauron* (the Worcester one) and *Logopandecteision*, which introduces (in six books) this celebrated language, "contrived and published both for his own utilitie and that of all pregnant and ingenious spirits". Urquhart's own diction and style were extravagant and euphuistic; but their extraordinary vitality and ingenuity could even now be applied as a tonic to our speech.

In mathematics and applied science Aberdeen's most spectacular contribution is probably the Niven family of Peterhead. Charles Niven (Senior Wrangler, 1887) become professor of natural philosophy at Aberdeen. William Davidson Niven (Third Wrangler, 1866) was director of studies at the Royal Naval College, Greenwich. James Niven (Eighth Wrangler, 1874) and George Niven (Fifteenth Wrangler, 1881) both diverged into medicine. The University's most eminent natural philosophers have, however, been immigrants—George Paget Thomson in recent times and James Clerk Maxwell a century ago. It must have been to the latter that an inconspicuous paragraph in a local newspaper referred some time in the late fifties of last century (the present writer saw it but failed to make a note of it). This paragraph mentioned that an Aberdeen professor (no name mentioned) had commenced experiments with a farmer in the neighbourhood of the city with the use of "galvanism" for the improvement of crops.

This little mystery at least has the merit of linking up a great name with a great industry. For two centuries and a half the north-east of Scotland has been prominent and pioneering in agriculture. These words are being written in the farmhouse built by Provost George Fordyce of Aberdeen, the father of the real founder of the North of Scotland College of Agriculture, Sir William Fordyce, and grandfather of Dr. George Fordyce, whose somewhat primitive speculations in agricultural theory won him a fellowship of the Royal Society, to which in 1774 he added the rather different distinction of membership of Dr. Johnson's Literary Club. In the second and third quarters of the eighteenth century, Aberdeen town and county in common with the whole of the United Kingdom became impressed by the potentialities of wealth latent in the soil. Several landowners, of whom the most prominent was Sir Archibald Grant, Bt., of Monymusk, and at least two provosts of Aberdeen, one of them George Fordyce, took the lead in suggesting ways and means of improving agriculture. Sir Archibald Grant's work still endures in the lovely woods of Paradise on the estate which his descendants have kept in the forefront of agricultural progress in the North-East. Grant and a son of Fordyce were probably the two most practical members of the Gordon's Mills Farming Club formed in 1758 and the first of a host of such societies in the area. Later, when stock-breeding came to be appreciated as a major branch of the industry, it was in Aberdeenshire that the two great beef breeds of cattle were developed—the Scotch Shorthorn by Amos Cruickshank at Sittyton and the Aberdeen-Angus by William McCombie at Tillyfour. In our own day James Cruickshank of Port Erroll with his little notebook and critical comments was an essential juryman in determining the practical value of all kinds of agricultural experiments, until his death during the last war.

Of mathematicians, Aberdeen or its University has always been prolific, from Alexander Anderson (died 1620) who occupied a chair in Paris and was the subject of a florid eulogy by Sir Thomas Urquhart, to Hector Munro Macdonald (died 1935) professor of mathematics at Aberdeen, whose academic distinctions were legion yet were equalled by his prowess as an Alpinist and his skill in wines and cooking. His caustic accuracy was a legend amongst his colleagues and his students. Walking one lovely spring morning with him on Deeside, H. M. to all appearance blind to the natural glories about him, the present writer drew his attention to the purple sheen of the budding birches. "You ought to know your spectrum better than that. That's not purple. There's no such thing as purple. That's voilet [*sic*]" was the response, growled out with an expression of satanic ferocity that might have daunted anyone who knew him not well.

If the proper study of mankind is man, Aberdeen's modern anthropologists, Arthur Keith, R. W. Reid, and Alexander Low (confining ourselves to the dead) have not let the land of their nativity down. And away back in the golden age Marischal College's first graduate, Robert Gordon of Straloch, who supervised the Scots section of Blaeu's atlas, the first of its kind to make a serious attempt at achieving accuracy, and his son James Gordon, parson of Rothiemay, the first person known to have preserved views and plans of the cities and buildings of Scotland, deserve mention. Aberdeen Town Council gave the parson a silver cup, a silk hat, and a silk gown for his wife in appreciation of his work for the burgh. He gave similar services to Edinburgh, but we have no record of any acknowledgement.

John Morgan
builder, businessman and local planner

WHILE Aberdeen has for nearly three centuries been fortunate in her architects, that very fact may have tended to obscure the equally important fact that architects cannot function to the best of their ability without the co-operation of the builders. Going back to the city's earliest buildings that have survived, we know that Bishop Elphinstone, who inspired the founding and construction of King's College, the Old Bridge of Dee and Greyfriars Church, and pushed on the work of erecting St. Machar's Cathedral, employed a master mason named Thomas Franche or French, and was advised on the architectural side by Alexander Galloway, the parson of Kinkell. Franche was a Linlithgow man, and it is conjectured that the Crown of King's owes its origin in part to Franche's knowledge of the similar tower of St. Michael's Church, Linlithgow, which was demolished in 1820.

50 *Queen's Road, Aberdeen —John Morgan's house*

Of all Aberdeen's master masons none is more deserving of our respectful remembrance than John Morgan, who died in the summer of 1907. If Aberdonians with a taste for beautiful building are proud of the city's many striking examples of Archibald Simpson's genius, they ought likewise to bear in mind with some pride the public buildings and streets, by whomsoever designed which were put together by John Morgan. We have had first-class builders besides Morgan, just as Archibald Simpson is by no means Aberdeen's sole architect of distinction; but both builders and architects who know the worth of those two will acknowledge that none are better exemplars than they of their respective lines of life in the history of the city.

John Morgan belonged to Kennethmont, where his father was a farmer. He was born in 1844, and being the first of a large family he was thrown on the world early, leaving school before he was fourteen. His mother had a brother in the building trade in Aberdeen, named Adam Mitchell, and to this uncle John Morgan came in his late teens and took a job as a working mason. No doubt his relationship to the boss gave him a better chance of advancement than most, but Mitchell was a very hard-headed Aberdonian, and we may be sure that when, in a short time, the young mason was taken into the office, his translation was as much due to his brains as to his blood.

He had, in fact, evinced at that early stage in his career an aptitude for the preparation of plans and specifications which, as he grew older, made him such a formidable competitor in tendering for public works. Mitchell, who built and later owned Heathcot, in 1865 won the contract for the construction of the Denburn Valley railway which became necessary to link Kittybrewster with the new city terminus of the Great North of Scotland Railway when the Joint Station was decided upon. It was altogether fitting that many years afterwards when he was in the Town Council John Morgan should have taken a prominent part in the laying out of Union Terrace Gardens and the widening of Union Terrace.

It should perhaps here be mentioned that, like quite a number of his contemporaries in business whose early formal education had been short, John Morgan very soon proceeded to educate himself with the help of such friends as had had more opportunities in that line, but always with his own innate good taste and common sense as his best instructors. One result of this self-culture displayed itself in his capacity for seeing both the needs and the possibilities underlying the problems he set himself to solve, whether for the public good or in his own business. He would not have been the eminently successful builder he was had he not possessed a good deal of the artistic refinement and practical application of the architect. The structures that he built, indeed, show not merely constructional efficiency but a remarkable ability to enter into the spirit behind the instructions which he took from whatever architect employed him. The working plans of the Denburn Valley railway which had been in their way his first creative job he later presented to the Public Library.

Eventually John Morgan became his uncle's principal assistant and partner, and when in 1877 Adam Mitchell died, he conducted the business for many years on behalf of himself and his uncle's heirs under the firm name of Adam Mitchell and Company. Long before he died, however, he was operating as builder, contractor and licensed valuator under his own name. Regrettably there was no son to carry on the business at his own death.

The last quarter of the century was a period of intense activity in the building industry. The city was expanding. The granite industry was in the full tide of its vigour. A series of able provosts were diligently improving the amenities of the city. The various religious denominations were in active competition with one another, and churches were being built in considerable numbers to cope with the intenser religious fervour that that competition inspired.

For all these developments John Morgan's firm was well prepared, and into them all its principal entered with buoyant enthusiasm and really outstanding local statesmanship. He was the builder of the new Marischal College—the Mitchell Hall and Tower, the former Students' Union in the gully felicitously known as the Drain, and the magnificent frontage, which has evoked so much adverse criticism in circles which held as a cardinal principle of architecture that granite was not a medium for elegant or decorative construction. And if Marischal College represents John Morgan's claim to be regarded as a great mason, so Aberdeen Fish Market is the chief of his monuments in local statesmanship. In the *History of a Great Industry* recounting the development of Aberdeen as a white fish port, William Pyper, who more than any other single individual was responsible for the real establishment of trawling at the port, tells how a deputation went south in 1888 to see how English towns managed their fishing. Daniel Mearns and James Walker, both Lord Provosts later on, William Pyper, and John Morgan were the members, Morgan the only one not directly interested in the fishing industry.

'A better deputation never left the city.' 'They were the most frugal four that ever went from good old Bon-Accord at the call of civic duty.' 'They travelled third class and always at night, and worked all day.' 'The City Chamberlain was a bit staggered when the bill of bare outlays was presented to him' (how the shades of the four just men must shudder today!) 'The deputation owed much to John Morgan.... To him may justly belong the credit of being the guiding spirit in the foundation of the present Fish Market.' At this distance of time, may one salute a great-hearted man who could so generously, and gratuitously, recognise the worth of another?

The list of buildings built by John Morgan's firm in the city is a long one. A few of them may be mentioned. The Northern Assurance buildings; Canada House; the railway offices in Guild Street; part of the Art Gallery; Nazareth House; Murray's Central Meat Market; The Caledonian (originally the Grand) Hotel; parts of the Palace and Imperial Hotels; a lot of churches, St. James's and St. Margaret's for the Scottish Episcopal Church, St. Peter's for the Roman Catholic Church and Carden Place, St. Ninian's and Queen's Cross for the (eventually) United Free Church, of which he was himself a member.

Here we may be permitted a moment's relaxation. Perhaps not so relaxing, for it throws a harsh light upon certain modern tendencies. My grandfather, who lived in the seventies and early eighties of last century, when he was in town, in Albyn Cottage, believed in God and Auld Zion to the complete exclusion of all other deities and communions. But on St. George's Day, and Shakespeare's, 23 April 1882, the newly built Queen's Cross Church heard its first sermon from its new young minister George Adam Smith. For some unexplained reason, my grandfather, who had laid a strict embargo on his family prohibiting them from crossing the threshold of those profane churches, relaxed his objection so far as it concerned Queen's Cross Free Church. In consequence, his half-dozen extremely presentable daughters, who included my mother, were permitted, having been fortified by attendance at the North Parish Church in the morning (the previous family residence having been in what was then the socially salubrious Wales Street), to make part of the Queen's Cross congregation that heard George Adam Smith at night. And every Sunday, to accommodate the audience, which included a high proportion of young people, forms had to be brought in and set in the aisles. In those days Church union and Christian unity was not mentioned probably because there was no need to mention it.

Back to our Morgans. King Street and Kittybrewster Schools were of his making, and the Wallace Statue. As a speculative builder he laid out much of Thomson Street and Belvidere Street, where he built twenty-six houses; Argyll Place, Crescent and Westburn Drive, forty-five; Hamilton Place and Fountainhall Road, twenty-eight; in the two Dens, seventeen, six in Forest Road and twenty in Queen's Road. As a Town Councillor from 1885 to 1892, as Convener of the Improvements Committee, Master of Shoreworks, member of the Public Library Committee, and finally Treasurer, he did a great deal of the expert practical and planning work in connection with the completion of Rosemount Viaduct, the building of Schoolhill Viaduct, improvements in Justice Street, Hutcheon Street, and Ferryhill, and in 1891 the extension of the city boundaries to include Torry and Woodside and the burgh of Old Aberdeen. He it was who was principally responsible for the building of the Public Library, being convener of the special Town Council Committee on the subject. Also, as a Governor of Robert Gordon's College until his death, and for some years convener of its education committee, he led the way in developing the technical side of the institution.

Morgan activities in Aberdeenshire and beyond included alterations at Balmoral; Culter Paper Works, Murtle Hydropathic, Craigmyle House, Blackhall Castle, Kincardine Lodge, Dalmunzie, Whitehaugh, Tyrie Parish Church, the Royal Bank Buildings at Inverness, the old Peterhead Academy; Chicago Smith's monument at Elgin; the Queen Victoria Memorial at Balmoral. In London he supplied granite dressings for banks and offices, in Liverpool for shipping and insurance offices, and for banks in towns as far apart as Sunderland, Leicester, Torquay, and Douglas, Isle of Man. Nor did Great Britain mark the limits of his business. He supplied materials for buildings in New York, Toronto, and Sydney.

John Morgan built a house for himself on the site where Rubislaw House, the mansion of the Skenes of Rubislaw, had stood. There he built up a library that was outstanding in the city in an age when there were several very ardent book-collectors in Aberdeen He specialised in Ruskin, Thomas Carlyle and Edward Fitzgerald (with particular emphasis on 'Omar Khayyam' upon which an essay, most tastefully printed by Aberdeen University Press, of which hc was a director, and inscribed by the author, lies before me as I write). He also possessed a full set of the publications of the Kelmscott Press of William Morris, which must have been worth a small fortune in itself. He was, however, one of the select band who were swindled by the eminent bibliographer Thomas J. Wise, when he sold as genuine first editions a score or so of short works by Victorian authors such as Mrs. E. B. Browning and Matthew Arnold. These little books purporting to have been published before their contents were included in bigger collections from their authors' pens, were shown by two young book-lovers in the thirties to be forgeries. Chemical analysis of the ink and of the paper used demonstrated conclusively that the much-revered and venerable bookman, Dr. Wise, had in his youth perpetrated a gross but profitable trick on a wealthy but not usually very gullible section of the public.

John Morgan was ony 63 when he died, and he had been an invalid from a painful disease for long before that. His achievement was therefore all the more remarkable and meritorious. That he should have been practically self-educated was probably one of the basic causes of his success. He had the natural intelligence, and it was not conventionalised by formal training. It should perhaps be added as an epilogue that the *Daily Journal* which carried his obituary notice also contained a memorial sonnet upon him, perhaps the only verse epitaph earned by an Aberdeen businessman!

John Farquhar of Fonthill

the fantastic millionaire

Fonthill Abbey

Of all the extraordinary creatures who have had, or earned the title of Aberdonian, none is more fantastic than John Farquhar of Fonthill. That the number of present-day Aberdonians who have heard of him is minute, and that a large percentage of those who have will probably associate Fonthill with the Ferryhill ward are evidence of how cavalierly we treat the memory of our great characters. Davie Do a'thing, Sir Thomas Urquhart, Alexander the Corrector, the Rev. Alexander Keith of Jermyn Street, " the Wandering Scholar ", Sir Alexander Anderson, all have uncommon and unconventional claims upon our remembrance, if not always our respectful remembrance. But John Farquhar, in the richness of his schizophrenia, cows them a! Like truth, he is a jewel with many facets.

Bilbo, in the parish of Crimond, south-west of the road to Old Rattray, once a royal burgh and now nothing but a gable-end, was the birthplace of John Farquhar. Bilbo is probably the combination of two Norse words meaning a sheltered place. It was certainly at John Farquhar's birth nothing much to speak of, nor were his people far up in the world. In fact little is known of them save that they were in modest circumstances, although they may have been related to the family of which Sir Walter Farquhar, one of the eminent Scots physicians in London in John Farquhar's time, was an illustrious son. John was born in 1751, had the parish schooling of a Buchan laddie of those days, and when still in his teens left home to become a cadet in the service of the East India Company at Bombay. That he should have got a post like that seems to indicate that if he himself was not, some of his relations were " better come o' ", and in one account of him it is stated that he was friendly with a son of one of the leading officers at Bombay. One never knows with poor Buchan loons. For any one of them to be in the good graces of the lords of the earth is almost a commonplace. But none of them ever rubbed shoulders with such intellectual ermine as John Farquhar.

In the Bombay service in one of the innumerable wars which the English profess they never wanted to wage but which somehow in those days always brought them land and loot, Farquhar was wounded in the hip and lamed for life. It probably is further evidence of some obscure social pull that he should, being physically what he was, get such an appointment at all. For he was a little ablach of a mannie, short and slim, though not quite in the category of his parish's representative at "The Souters' Feast":

An ill-faur'd skyple cam fae Creemon',
A perfec' scunner ti the weemen.

John seems to have kept clear of the girls all his life. Perhaps that was why he became, and apparently became with comparative ease, a millionaire.

At all events, he left the service of John Company, either before or after migrating to Bengal. There he is said to have set up on his own account as an independent trader or merchant—it is not quite clear which, and there was a definite distinction, for, while a trader would do business with the natives and so be in competition with the Company, a merchant might merely supply certain of the needs of the Company's personnel. But which he was does not really matter, for it was not at his business that he made his fortune. Indeed, it might be deduced from his habits when he reached the affluent stage of his career, that he had had to live pretty bare in his independent business career in Bengal.

Having no social distractions, he seems to have devoted his spare time to study, and his capacious intelligence, as shall be seen, was not satisfied with one subject. But he became known in the British community because of his hobby of amusing himself with chemical experiments. At this point Farquhar began, and we watching him begin, to move in exalted circles. As his hobby became a subject of talk he attracted the attention of Warren Hastings, the greatest of the Company's servants, and when Hastings went home in 1785, he probably passed on to his successor his high opinion of Farquhar's abilities. Or, of course, those abilities may have been such as to commend Farquhar without any official testimonial.

The successor was Lord Cornwallis, whose surrender at Yorktown in 1781 really set the seal upon American independence. One wonders, when he met Farquhar, whether mention was made of another eminent Aberdonian, born the son of a laird a few miles from Bilbo, Major Patrick Ferguson of Pitfour, one of Cornwallis's subordinate commanders in the American War. Ferguson invented the breech-loading rifle, was one of the best trainers of men in the history of the British Army, is cherished even today by the well-informed in America as the man who didn't shoot George Washington, and fell at the battle of King's Mountain some time before the debacle that led to Yorktown.

At any rate, by a curious near-coincidence, this other Aberdonian, John Farquhar, who came into the life of Cornwallis, was also destined to improve the fortunes of the British army. When Cornwallis arrived to be Governor-General in Bengal in 1786, a struggle with various native potentates was looming which was to end temporarily in the capture of Seringapatam. Cornwallis, preparing for the campaign, found that the Company's gunpowder factory at Pultah was in a mess, and it was but natural that he should turn to his chemical-experimenting acquaintance John Farquhar for advice. He got it, and on the strength of it Farquhar took over as superintendent of the factory, reorganised it, and—being a cautious man and so having retained at least the fabric of his own concern—eventually emerged as sole contractor for quite a lot of things to the authorities. With his alert Buchan interest in all human activities, Farquhar cannot have failed to watch the methods of his friend Warren Hastings, who like Clive before him as representative of John Company enthusiastically skinned the natives. There is little doubt that John Farquhar with at least equal efficiency skinned John Company. Certainly after a few years he felt himself justified in retiring to England with a fortune of half a million pounds. That was a bigger fortune than any British tycoon can boast of today, so much has the value of money declined since then.

During his stay in Calcutta there was another person there for a time who was destined to have a queer connection with Aberdeen. But with her we may be sure John Farquhar never made acquaintance. When his friend Warren

Hastings's principal enemy, Sir Philip Francis, left for home he took with him a grass widow named Madame Grand. While Farquhar was making his fortune she turned up in Aberdeen with a young British officer who passed for her husband. Him and a child she buried in St. Nicholas Churchyard. And then, having almost become the wife of an Aberdeen professor, she disappeared. She came to the surface again in the Paris of the First Empire, where she entered a higher stratum of history as the Princess Talleyrand. Napoleon said she was a fool of a woman, which may be. But she succeeded in marrying the greatest of all French diplomatic strategists, the bishop turned atheist who did more to overthrow Napoleon than all the armies of the European Powers, and who was responsible, albeit the representative of a vanquished nation, for ensuring for the Continent a peace that more or less lasted for a hundred years.

To return to John Farquhar. Hame cam our gudeman, to Gravesend. For some years he had been investing his money, through Hoare's Bank, and it all went into the Funds, which owing to the rather amateurish finance of the Government were actually much more of a good thing than they were meant to be. To save his coach fare he walked from Gravesend to the City, and presented himself at his bankers in such shabby attire and with such an air of impecuniosity that the staff were for throwing him out when Hoare himself happened to come in and he was able to establish his identity. He got a pound or two of pocket money to keep him going until he procured a house. He bought one near Portman Square, where he installed himself with an old crone for a housekeeper. During all his years there the house was never painted or repaired, and neither brush nor broom was allowed in his own room. Down at heel and in ancient clothing, he was often taken in the streets for a beggar, and was offered alms, though whether he took them we do not know. He used to put a crust of loaf in his pocket to save him spend a penny on a pie. And all the while he was putting pound to pound. The interest on his investments went back partly into the Funds and partly into real estate, and he also became a partner in a great agency house in the City, called Basset, Farquhar and Co., and in Whitbread the brewers, which he came more or less to own.

Yet with all his saving and scraping he gave most generously to charity. He may have been slovenly in dress, and like Dr. Johnson disagreeable at meals, when he took them, but he studied hard all his life, in the classics, mathematics and mechanics, as well as chemistry. In the course of his exercises he developed what is said to have been a terse, concise and rather agreeable style of expression. On the religious side he showed himself, like many Scots before or since, actively interested in what the Sergeant-major would have called fancy religions. We have had Scots committed to Islam, Confucianism and other esoteric cults. Farquhar became intrigued by Brahminism. The result was that when he sketched out the scheme of what he intended to be his most splendid benefaction, a third university for Aberdeen, which was to cost £100,000, he inserted in the draft charter certain reservations on religion. At the beginning of last century Aberdeen might have been none the worse of a third university, but it has to be remembered that however slack her existing ones were she had already two, and as London University's birth—thanks mainly to Scotsmen—had still some years to go before being thought of, England had only as many universities as Aberdeen. That, let alone "religious reservations" in the days before Catholic emancipation, was enough to make Parliament turn the project down.

In 1822, at an age when he ought to have known a great deal better, Farquhar took the most spectacular step of his life. He bought Fonthill Abbey, in Wiltshire, from William Beckford. It is not too much to say that had he never made this purchase, he would never have figured in the Dictionary of National Biography or indeed in any other compendium of famous men, in all of which eminence in business is almost an inevitable disqualification. But because he bought Fonthill, and probably because Fonthill's previous owner was William Beckford, the *D.N.B.* and other dictionaries have investigated him a little, and labelled him " millionaire ". Even we, however, who have shown that John Farquhar had otherwise given good reasons for being remembered, must here pause a moment to survey the marvel that was Beckford. However fantastic John Farquhar was, he was very plain John beside the scintillating and grotesque William.

Beckford's father, also William, was an alderman, a member of Parliament, twice Lord Mayor of London. He was quite fabulously wealthy and—they don't always go together—quite incredibly courageous. He it was who inspired London Corporation to give active official support to John Wilkes, one of those clever rogues whom the English on second thoughts love to set upon the pedestals of virtue. John Wilkes and William Beckford together defied Parliament—and won; and William Beckford alone and in audience defied George III—and won. The words he spoke to the King when the latter attempted to infringe the liberties of the City are carved upon Beckford's tomb and pointed to with admiration by Lord Macaulay's biographer, the historian Sir George Otto Trevelyan.

William Beckford, senior, when he died in 1770 left a vast fortune, which his son and heir inherited in its entirety, there being no such thing as death duties then. He immediately began to spend it lavishly, but though he lived well over the allotted span, built two mighty mansions (one a castle in Portugal, if not in Spain), collected one of the classic libraries and a vast mass of antiques and curios, he never succeeded in getting through it. The Fonthill where he was born he more or less rebuilt in a style of oppressive magnificence, with amongst other elaborations a tower 260 feet high. It was this appalling place, with all its contents except for the books and a few other preciosities, that John Farquhar purchased. But besides this rococo palace Beckford wrote—and this was to his credit—the quite unique romance of *Vathek*, written according to himself in three days and two nights on end, but actually only recast and revised in that time. It is an Oriental romance, recounting the adventures of a Caliph with Eblis the devil, introducing many surprising and terrible situations, and a very delightful heroine, the whole atmosphere being indescribable both in its sombre beauty and its exotic magnificence. He wrote a lot of other things but *Vathek* is his one claim to immortality, unless we except the fact that on Gibbon's death he purchased the whole library of the greatest of historians, and shut himself up with it until he had read it all.

His great collection of books was not sold until many years after his own death but John Farquhar, on buying Fonthill, proceeded to get rid of the contents. Some stuff he may have kept, for he had himself been a collector of other people's unconsidered trifles for a long time, but Beckford's accumulations he sold in an auction which occupied thirty-seven days. Of it William Hazlitt, his pen dipped in vitriol, wrote: "an immense museum of all that is most curious and costly and at the same time the most worthless in the productions of art and nature. The only proof of taste he has shown in his collection is his getting rid of it."

Beckford spent quarter of a million on Fonthill. That may, or may not, be a clue to what Farquhar paid for it. In 1825 the great tower fell down. In 1826 John Farquhar himself went the way of all flesh. Careful in his investments, he forgot to make a will. He left a million and a half which was divided amongst his seven nephews and nieces. Some of them lived in Aberdeen. Some of his money may be fructifying in Aberdeen still.

A bunch of Bon-Accord's grandsons

In a previous article of this series passing reference was made to some of the sons and grandsons of Aberdonians who had played a more than commonly decisive part in the making of our world and civilisation as we know it. In this quatercentennial Shakespearean year when England is going to considerable lengths—not without justification—in pluming herself for having produced a genius who is still "out-topping knowledge", it may not be undesirable to restore the balance by some account of the still enduring achievements of a few of the grandsons of remote and septentrional Bon-Accord.

While quite logically we are entitled to regard these illustrious personages about to be passed forthwith under review, as eminent Aberdonians, one or two qualifications of that latter distinction must in fairness be mentioned. In the first place, not all of them, in fact a minority of them, hailed from the good burgh itself. They mostly derived from Aberdeen's hinterland and county. It has, however, always been accepted that a native of the county as well as the burgh is entitled to be termed an Aberdonian. In one or two cases the birthplace of their sires can be but vaguely identified. In one or two cases the Christian names of their sires are undetermined, the fathers being either of humble birth or, as is not uncommon even with modern Aberdonians, rather too prone to hide the light of their identity under a bushel of silence or reticence. But with the admission of these restrictions, we may go ahead.

The first of these grandsons, then, is—almost inevitably—a Gordon, and almost no less inevitably a man of blood. Those who can still find, in these days of thrillers and who-dun-its, a measure of excitement and interest in the reading of history, will call to mind the great Imperialist and Catholic general, Wallenstein, who in the Wars of Religion in the first third of the seventeenth century, was playing a spectacular part when in 1634 he was murdered. The man who contrived his murder—though it was another who delivered the fatal stroke—was Colonel John Gordon, son of John Gordon of Milton of Noth in Strathbogie, and grandson of Sir William Gordon, the first laird of Gight and brother or half-brother of that Catherine Gordon whom King James IV married in 1496 to Perkin Warbeck, the impostor who claimed the English Crown, and who visited Aberdeen in that year. Even then, it will be observed, Aberdonians (and especially Gordons) got around. In passing it may be observed that Warbeck or his retinue imported into Aberdeen a disease which has persisted ever since.

The Colonel John Gordon of our story was like his father, a soldier of fortune. He had been born abroad, and though a Calvinist (which was most unusual with a Gordon) he took service eventually with the Holy Roman Emperor. He and a Major Walter Leslie of the Balquhain family served together and in 1634, when Wallenstein, who was the Emperor's principal general against the Swedes whom Gustavus Adolphus had been leading so meteorically, became suspected of treachery and the Emperor issued a patent empowering his officers to slay him. Wallenstein, with a heavy bodyguard, took refuge in the town of Eger, of which Gordon was the commandant. Gordon and Leslie first held what we should call a cocktail party for the officers of Wallenstein's staff, and having filled them fou, cut their throats. Gordon then sent a couple of Irishmen to the General's lodging. Wallenstein had been having (most astonishing exercise for those days!) a bath and received his visitors in his shirt. They at once "liquidated" him. Leslie in reward was made a Count, and married an Austrian princess. A descendant was the Count Albert Mensdorff who was Austrian Ambassador in London before the first

World War. Gordon became a marquis and High Chamberlain to the Emperor. He died in 1649.

The next eminent grandson is a much more interesting and respectable chap—no less a personage than Admiral Martin Harpertzoon Tromp, who in the time of Cromwell sailed up the Channel with a broom at his masthead to indicate his ability to sweep the English fleet off the sea. He had already beaten the English, but after he mounted the broom his luck gradually deserted him. First Blake, with a whip at his masthead, and then Monk defeated him, and in battle with the latter in 1653 Tromp fell with a bullet in his heart. His son Cornelius Von Tromp was also an admiral in the Dutch service but hardly earned the distinction of his father.

Martin Harpertzoon Tromp was the son of a man Harper of Peterhead. In those days Dutch fishermen used to use Keithinch—one of Peterhead's early names—as a base for the ling and cod fishing, and there were many of them there every year during the season. Harper became so friendly with them that he went to Holland with them, married a Dutch wife, joined the Dutch naval service, and died in a sea-fight with the English off the coast of West Africa. His son, probably a cabin boy or the equivalent of a middy, was taken prisoner.

We now, following the years, enter into a period where the eminence of second and later generation Aberdonians presents us with a positive embarrassment of riches. Adam Smith, author of *The Wealth of Nations* and generally acknowledged "father" of Political Economy—though there were economists before his day—was born at Kirkcaldy in 1723, but his father, also Adam Smith, was born at Mains of Seaton, Old Aberdeen, where his father was tenant. Adam Smith's place is established beyond any peradventure with the top dozen of great Scotsmen that include John Knox, David Hume, James Boswell, Robert Burns, Walter Scott, James Watt, David Livingstone and James Clerk Maxwell. It is unnecessary here to do more than refer to *The Wealth of Nations* as the most enduring monument to Adam Smith's very fruitful life as a professor and philosopher. In the

Adam Smith

world of letters there have in our time been few more exciting incidents than the discovery in an Aberdeen auction room of the manuscript of a set of Adam Smith's lectures, which up to then were known only as it were by hearsay. Another curious thing to be noted about Smith is that he was a Scotch cousin at no great distance of Mill o' Tifty's Annie, the heroine of the celebrated ballad of that name, who died for love of the piper of Fyvie Castle, and whose tombstone is carefully preserved in Fyvie churchyard.

The year after Adam Smith's appearance saw the arrival of an even greater philosopher in the person of Immanuel Kant. He was born in

Immanuel Kant

Königsberg, in East Prussia and his grandfather, according to his own statement, was a Scot. He was, moreover, an Aberdeenshire Scot, probably a near relative of that eident Calvinist and perfervid supporter of the National Covenant, the Rev. Andrew Cant, minister of Old Pitsligo, and from 1641 to 1660 of the West Kirk of St. Nicholas.

From Dickson, Henderson and Cant,
Apostles of the Covenant,
Good Lord, deliver us!

So ran the stroud during The Troubles of the Civil War, but Cant was not afraid to suffer for his principles. His daughter Sarah was the wife of Provost Alexander Jaffray, one of the greatest of Aberdeen's civic heads. Of Kant's philosophy and his most famous work *The Critique of Pure Reason* this is not the place to write, and even if it were we would beg to be excused for reasons much more practically philosophical ("philosophy" being "the love of wisdom") than anything Kant ever produced. But he, with Plato, David Hume and perhaps Hegel constitute the four-square foundation of the history of philosophical inquiry.

The birthyear of James Watt, the man who watched the kettle steam as King Alfred did not watch the cakes smoke, was 1726. James Watt's grandfather hailed from Kintore, where a representative of the family still lives, and whose burghal history, a much prized and scarce work, was written by Alexander Watt, of cognate blood. Lord Montgomery's intelligence officer was another of the same line. James Watt's chief claim to fame is his bringing to a practical state the steam engine which had already been invented. Watt invented the separate condenser and a great many other devices that enabled the steam engine to be applied to a multitude of uses, instead of the single one which alone it could perform when he took it in hand. He eventually went to Birmingham from his native Clydeside. It is perhaps instructive to know that even 200 years ago there were demarcation difficulties in industry there, for James Watt could not get permission to work as an instrument-maker until the University took him on its staff.

James Watt

The last King of the unhappy country and kingdom of Poland must be included amongst these eminent Aberdonians. Stanislas Augustus Poniatowski, born in 1732, was the great-grandson of Lady Catherine Gordon, a daughter of the second Marquis of Huntly. He ascended the throne of Poland in 1764 and revealed a flair, not altogether uncommon in Scots, for living at a very high level of extravagance. On one occasion he gave a banquet on the Vistula. The male guests in barges launched an attack on an island in the river garrisoned by the female guests dressed as Amazons. When they surrendered, there was a grand ball. As Sir Winston Churchill might have said, "Some battle! Some party!" A contemporary description of the King mentions "his noble visage, his dignified manner, his gentle and melancholy gaze, his silvery hair, and his beautiful, slightly perfumed hand". As a young man at the Russian Court he was a particularly favoured lover of Catherine the Great before she came to the throne, yet when he was King she twice engineered partitions of Poland which reduced it to a third of its original size, and when he was deposed a year or two before his death in 1798, she completed the process of dismemberment by the third and last partition. Poor King Stanislas died in prison writing his memoirs.

We now cross the Atlantic. Some people in America are inclined to ascribe the success of the revolutionary movement that gave the American colonies independence to the energy and above all the oratory of Patrick Henry. Patrick, born in the same year of 1736, in Virginia, was a son of John Henry from Aberdeen, who himself attained considerable celebrity as a "well-educated" man. Patrick started life as keeper of a general store, which failed. Then his house was burned down. He tried another store, and failed again. So he went into law, and became a member of the Virginia Bar in 1760. Five years later in the House of Burgesses, the provincial parliament, he was leading the attack upon the Stamp Act. He was the leading personality in the Virginia Convention which, so far as Virginia was concerned, brought that State into the corporate resistance of the other States to the British Government's colonial policy. He dominated the first two Continental Congresses. "Caesar had his Brutus. Charles the First had his Cromwell. George the Third may profit by their example." "Give me liberty; or give me death!" "If this be treason, make the most of it!" These examples of his oratorical method are sufficient to indicate which was the ultimate fountain from which has welled in so many gushing streams the rhetoric of transatlantic politics.

At the outset of the troubles the Governor of Virginia outlawed him, but in 1776, when the colonists had taken up arms, with Henry a Colonel of Militia, he succeeded the governor who had outlawed him. Once the colonies had won clear, Henry, who was a strong Conservative, was one of the chief opponents of the Federal Constitution, rather curiously anticipating the snag upon which that constitution almost foundered in 1860 in the Civil War. Thomas Jefferson, another Virginian and ultimately a President of the United States, said of him—"His fame is his best epitaph. He appeared to speak as Homer wrote." Otherwise his character has been described as that of "a canny Scot, shrewd, courageous and headstrong". Without his compelling vivid oratory it is quite a possibility that the colonies would not have gone the whole hog.

If Patrick Henry led the American colonies towards independence, John Marshall was the real moulder of the American Constitution. Thanks in part to Henry's friendship and advocacy, Marshall became in rapid succession a member of the House of Representatives in 1799, Secretary of State in 1800, and Chief Justice of the United States Supreme Court in 1801. That supremely decisive appointment he held for thirty years until his death. When he took over as Chief Justice the Supreme Court was supine and a failure. In a series of great judgements Marshall put it at the apex of the constitutional framework. He it was who by his wisdom and remarkable juridical insight raised the court to the position of being the arbiter of constitutional causes and the interpreter and judge of congressional legislation. No man in American history save George Washington is so revered by Americans today, and it is a strange fact that almost invariably, at least when speaking of him to a Scotsman, they lay less stress on his English father Thomas Marshall than on his Scottish mother Mary Keith. Her father came from that part of Scotland which most Keiths see fit to leave!

From U.S.A. we switch across to U.S.S.R. It was in Russia that both Napoleon and Hitler met their fate. The former was a genius. Michael Andreas Barclay, created Prince Barclay de Tolly by Tsar Alexander in 1815, was German-born but the great-great-grandson of the Barclays

Field-Marshal Barclay de Tolly

of Towie-Barclay, Auchterless. He joined the Russian army as a cadet, lost an arm in the savage battle of Eylau, and by 1812, when Napoleon invaded Russia, he commanded the Russian army. He followed the old Scottish tactic of the scorched earth, which had been the rule in the wars with England, when the Scots had to withdraw before superior force and destroyed everything—which, if they left it, would have been destroyed in any case by the invaders. The subordinate Russian commanders, losing patience in the constant retreat and jealous of a non-Russian leader, forced Barclay to stand and fight at Smolensk, where the Russians were beaten. Barclay lost his command to Kutosov, who was thrashed at the Battle of the Berodino and had to revert to Barclay's tactics. Kutosov indeed was not much good, and had he been in charge from the start, Napoleon might have won the war. As it was, when the tide turned, Barclay was soon in favour again and Russian Commander-in-chief, and took part in the great Dresden and Leipsic campaigns that really broke Napoleon. After Waterloo, Towie-Barclay came on the market, but he turned down the suggestion that he should purchase it. He died in 1818.

There is a gravestone in Rathen kirkyard commemorating John Greig, farmer in Mosstown, Cairnbulg, and his wife Anna Milne. Greig died in 1774, and his son Alexander, born in 1739, crossed the North Sea to Bergen in 1760 and became British Consul there in 1771. It is said he used to come back to Rathen occasionally for Communion. He married a Norwegian, his son and grandson succeeded him as British Consul, and the latter had a son Edvard, the surname now spelt Grieg, born in 1843, who after musical training in Leipsic blossomed into Scandinavia's greatest composer. By something of a coincidence the grandfather of Scandinavia's greatest singer, Jenny Lind (1820-87), the Swedish nightingale, was domiciled in Fraserburgh. While Grieg's best-known work was his music to Ibsen's "Peer Gynt", he is nearly unique in his art because of his intense preoccupation with folk-music, which inspires much of his work and almost all of his exquisite lyrics.

Buchan, and the Fraserburgh area at that, has yet another distinguished grandson to add to the list in the person of William Lyon Mackenzie King, Prime Minister of Canada off and on from 1921 to 1948. His grandfather John King was born and baptised in 1814 at Ladysford, Tyrie. Mackenzie King himself received the Freedom of the City of Aberdeen in 1937.

There are others who might be listed such as the related Andersons and Geddeses, but they may yet warrant an article by themselves; and perhaps Field-Marshal Mackensen, if he was indeed a Mackenzie from Inverurie. Even Robert Burns might by a stretch of territory be included, for though his father hailed from Glenbervie the Burns family belonged as much to Aberdeenshire as to the Mearns, and Robbie's paternal grandmother was a Keith. And of course there was Byron. But as was said to begin with, we are a modest race, and enough is enough.

Charles Murray

engineer, pioneer, administrator and poet

ONE cold spring morning in 1933 the *Aberdeen Press and Journal* appeared with a set of verses printed in large type across the centre three columns of the leader page. Before noon there was not a copy of that issue to be had in town or country for love or money, although the presses had been started again to turn out a fresh printing. The verses were carried over into the *Aberdeen Weekly Journal*, published for once in greater quantity than was customary. Even that was not enough. A considerable number of proof pulls were taken before the type was broken up, but these in a very short time had all been disposed of. To this day, for these verses have never been published in book form, requests for copies are by no means uncommon.

Charles Murray

(From a bronze in the Aberdeen Art Gallery)

Only one poet could have won such unsolicited testimonial of the esteem in which the public held him, and only one community could have thus spontaneously produced such a tribute. Many of those who read these words will remember that the poet was Charles Murray. And it may be doubted, with all deference and humility, whether in our day any poem by any writer in the British Isles—for W. B. Yeats in Dublin and A. E. Housman in Cambridge were still alive then—could have evoked such a display of enthusiasm. As he writes these words the present writer has the manuscript of "There's Aye a Something" before him, and he can still vividly recall "the stoun at the hert" when, that long-past February morning, he opened a letter with the St. Jean-de-Luz postmark and read:

> Belcanny is foggin', wi' siller laid by,
> Wi' byres fu' o' feeders an' pedigree kye,

and realised that after many years of almost complete silence, the Old Master had done it again.

This year sees the centenary of Charles Murray's birth. He was born about a mile this side of Alford—a plaque on the house marks his birthplace—on 28 September 1864. His father Peter Murray was a vricht, a joiner, who eventually became ground officer on the Haughton estate. Peter was, like many a carpenter before and since, a personality and a philosopher, who practised the making of verses, had a decided artistic streak, and possessed a remarkable fund of Doric words. His wife, Margaret Robbie, who died two years after Charles was born, leaving him and a sister Sarah to be brought up by Peter and her sister, Mary Robbie, belonged to a Deeside family with character and ability. All these qualities in some degree descended to the two children. Sarah eventually came to study at Gray's School of Art and showed considerable talent in that time. Charles, after schooling in the village under a very good schoolmaster, in due course arrived in Aberdeen in a pair of new moleskin breeks, with a gravat round his neck and a Scotch bonnet on his pow to start as an apprentice with Walker and Beattie, the civil engineers. That was in 1881.

In 1888 he emigrated to South Africa. There to begin with he was a partner in a firm of civil engineers with two other Aberdonians. Then he was a surveyor for mining companies, and just before the Boer War manager of one at Krugersdorp. In 1900 he took a commission in the Railway Pioneer Regiment, but when the Boer War entered into its later phase of tip-and-run on the veldt, he became a Deputy Inspector of Mines for the Transvaal. In 1902 he was promoted to be Registrar of Crown Titles, in 1905 to Under-Secretary for Public Works, and in 1907 to Secretary for Public Works in the Transvaal. Even for an Oxford man this would have been good going. That Murray made it says much for Gallowhill School, Alford, Aberdeenshire and for Golden Square. And let us not forget that he was being selected in a crowd of what was probably the most brilliant congeries of civil servants in the history of the British Empire—Milner's young men. The Transvaal job was actually a key one, being concerned with all Government property in what was the most populous and difficult Province in South Africa—not yet, be it remembered, a "Union".

That union came about in 1910, and there could be only one Secretary for Public Works in the Dominion—Charles Murray. Already in 1905 he had had to move from Johannesburg, where he was at home, to Pretoria, where he had to establish himself. His headquarters remained at Pretoria after the union, but he had the terribly ticklish job of reconciling the independent systems and amalgamating the staffs of four different provinces. He did that in a very short time, and straightway his Department was seen according to the ideas and ideals of Charles Murray. On top of that, and in addition to the sufficiently onerous task of keeping an eye on the Union's property over an area of 472,000 square miles, he had to supervise the building of the principal administrative offices of the Union at Pretoria.

His struggles with the architect Sir Herbert Baker became almost a legend. Baker was a very great exponent of his profession; after Pretoria he did similar work at New Delhi, and he was responsible for the Bank of England building in London in 1921. But from Murray he probably learnt more about the financial side of his work than from any other associate. Murray had authority to spend £1,180,000 and no more on the project. He refused to authorise one extra penny. Baker came to him with all sorts of improvements and modifications of the original plan. Murray costed them and when Baker threatened, he called his bluff, and then proposed certain alterations which, without affecting the design, effected a sufficient saving on materials to enable the improvements to be incorporated. That tussle reflected what was his considered, unalterable, and permanent basic principle as a servant of the State, which was to look after the welfare of the taxpayer first, foremost, and all the time.

As a corollary to that, he had no great belief in direct labour. A certain nucleus he had to have, but he kept it as small as possible. To facilitate their negotiations with his Department, he encouraged the principal contractors to form what eventually became the Master Builders' Federation. While he did everything he could to assist them in their tendering for contracts, he saw to it that specifications and bills of quantities were very carefully drawn indeed, and at tennis and golf he kept an eye on the contractors when perhaps they did not realise he was sizing them up. When he retired in 1924 it was his way of building and his way of working that obtained in the Union.

All his life he was an individualist. He had used his brains to take advantage of the opportunities that came his way. His beliefs and his practice in departmental life, as outlined above, were a whole age and universe removed from those which obtain in the Civil and other public services today. In fact, when he became

Secretary for Public Works in 1910 he had to break down and do away with, in Cape Province and Natal, the system that dominates our extravagant public finance and administration in this country today. At the same time, the tax dodger was anathema to him. When Hitler's war came along he used to anticipate the due date for the paying of his income tax, and one of the last letters he wrote me shortly before his death, contained a few lines, commencing "It's ill to be auld", lamenting his inability to do anything to help win the war except to "ripe the moggan, rank oot the cash". Yet he had no use for free education or free libraries, and was wont to deprecate the example of millionaires like Andrew Carnegie devoting some of their surplus wealth to provide what people should acquire by their own efforts. He was prepared to help the underdog who had gone down after a fight. He was once described as a Tory with radical tendencies.

During the Kaiser's war he served as a Lieut-Colonel in the South African Defence Force. He was one of the founders of the Transvaal Scottish after the Boer War. That regiment was affiliated with the Gordon Highlanders until, I suppose, the Union left the Commonwealth. The association was appropriate. Johannesburg in those days was lousy with Aberdonians, mostly at the top. Alexander Aiken from Peterhead took the lead in establishing the University of the Witwatersrand. It was Murray who saw to it that the sites for both the University and (ironically) the Johannesburg Public Library were denied to the speculators in real estate. I believe one of Paul Kruger's ministers was born in the house in Victoria Street, Aberdeen, which I owned for nearly forty years. Patrick Duncan, a Buchan lover from Deveronside, ultimately became Governor-General of the Union, and there are still Aberdeen Mackenzies in Jo'burg.

In 1912 Murray was guest of honour at a public dinner in Aberdeen at which Ashley Mackintosh, First Bursar and Professor of Medicine (they liked their doctors to be educated in those days!), presided, and at which the list of those present is a cross-section of the life of the North-East, town and gown, business and professional, urban and rural. In 1920 Aberdeen University made him an LL.D. In 1922 his services to South Africa were (his friends thought, inadequately, but he never courted the mighty) recognised by a C.M.G. In 1925 before a gathering 500 strong he was presented with his portrait by Fiddes Watt, R.S.A., and Mrs. Murray with his bust by H. S. Gamley, R.S.A. (now in the Art Gallery). John Buchan (Lord Tweedsmuir to be), who had been with him in South Africa, made the presentation. After his retirement in 1924 he spent his summers for a good many years at the Brig of Alford, his winters in Rome or the South of France, with an occasional trip to South Africa and one triumphal jaunt round the world. He finally settled at Banchory, with many apologies to his friends for deserting his beloved Don for "the Dee"—he always insisted the latter river could not do without the definite article. His health for years had required constant care—actually he went originally to South Africa on account of chest trouble which the air of the high veldt was advertised to cure. He died on 12 April 1941, and as one London commentator wrote, "his death seems to dim the daylight, for his personality was part of it".

Charles Murray is remembered in our North-East today as a poet, as our poet par excellence and head and shoulders above all who went before him. That assessment, while fair so far as it goes, is too restricted, and one of the reasons for the space given in this essay to his administrative work in South Africa and his acute business sense is to show the wholeness of the man. It is also intended to indicate that one can be a great artist as well as a successful man of affairs, and that proficiency in any walk of life is not necessarily to be attained only—as the new generation seems to believe—by concentrating upon one thing. And in fact, as well as being good in business and in poetry, Murray was a competent soldier, a very expert angler, a quite clever artist in pen-and-ink, and probably without peer in the telling of stories, whether Scots or English. One would like to have seen his personality projected into literature with the same memorable picturesqueness with which he immortalised the Packman and the Antiquary, the Braw Lass and Skeely Kirsty:

> She cured for pleasure, nae for fees;
> Healed man an' beast wi equal ease;
> She gae a lotion for the grease
> To Spence the carrier,
> That cured his mear, when the disease
> Gaed ower the farrier.

Charles Murray began, like most clever loons, to write verses early. His old dominie said the first attempt he saw was that of the teenage Charles welcoming the first down upon his upper lip:

> It's comin' noo
> Abune my moo'.

He was scribbling before he left Aberdeen, but once he got to South Africa the inevitable nostalgia, and as he himself put it, a desire to give pleasure to an old man in the Howe of Alford, caused him to set about the writing of verse in soberer earnest. In 1893 William Smith at the Bon-Accord Press published a very thin volume, *A Handful of Heather*, partly in Scots and dealing with things and people recollected from Donside, and partly in English on characters on the Rand. Twelve copies were printed for circulation and a few more were done, as was customary then, and handed out by the printer. Murray in later years called in and destroyed every copy he could find, and only one, which appears to have eluded his vigilance, survives, and it is understood to have vanished from its owner's shelves.

In 1900 Wyllies published *Hamewith*, containing the best of the previous booklet, but thoroughly revised, with a frontispiece by Douglas Strachan, the Aberdeen artist (who curiously enough in later years adopted Murray's policy of calling in and destroying his early work). Some of the *Hamewith* poems had appeared in *Chamber's Journal*, *Black and White*, and other publications and their author was becoming slowly known to a public that knew neither Aberdeen nor Bennachie. But later on when some of his friends insisted upon finding a more national platform for him, it was only after repeated refusals from literary agents and publishers (all of whom, if they lived a few more years, were to regret bitterly their rejection) that Messrs. Constable almost by accident undertook to publish a new, still further revised, and extended *Hamewith*. Andrew Lang, then doyen of literary Scots in London, wrote the preface, and the first London edition appeared, with a second illustration by Douglas Strachan, in 1909. Murray was never disposed to say much about the success of his writing—he was very like Walter Scott in that respect—but he did confess that right up to his death he never had less than a pound a week in royalties. Recently a letter in the *Scotsman* deplored the almost impossibility of selling Scottish verse. I myself a couple of years ago purchased copies of two volumes of verse by one who is regarded as the major Scottish poet since Burns—and although they have been in print for nearly forty years, they were remaindered copies. Against such a background the broad and lasting appeal of *Hamewith* is eloquent.

In 1917 an illustrated edition in quarto with fifty-six drawings by A. S. Boyd, was published and although later reprinted it is now almost as rare to come by as the Wyllie and Constable "firsts". In 1917 also appeared *A Sough o' War*, containing rather more than a dozen poems all about the struggle then in progress. In 1920 Constable issued *In the Country Places*, poems that had been written since 1909, many of them quite recent, and all of them showing an even more masterly command of the idiom than those that went before. In 1927 the first Collected Edition appeared, and many reprintings have since been taken up. Unfortunately more than a dozen poems which appeared subsequent to that date have not been incorporated in the collected edition by the publishers. Some of the lyrics have been set to music.

This is not the place in which to embark upon a criticism and appreciation of his poetry. Less than quarter of a century has elapsed since he died, and for some years before his death and ever since many wild and whirling words have been written by exponents of what has been called the Scots Literary Renascence, mainly suggesting that before the end of the Kaiser's war no verse worth reading had been written in Scotland for generations. Actually this so-called Renascence, if it contains anything more substantial than wind, was pioneered by Murray. Robert Louis Stevenson was writing Scots verse before him, but always one felt with his tongue in his cheek, and J. Logie Robertson ("Hugh Haliburton") had done some not unworthy translation but his verse was inclined to be academic. Murray wrote Scots as a Scotsman who knew and used the dialect. There were purists—including a couple of first-rate Doric exponents in the Byth district—who used to complain that Murray's was not the idiomatic dialect of everyday life. That criticism was just and no one would have agreed more heartily than Murray himself. A great deal of the Scots poetry written especially in Aberdeenshire and the city since Murray's day is couched in the Doric as spoken. It is idiomatic, it is full even to phonetic spelling of the dialect speech, it is verse, but it is neither artistic nor memorable, and we'll leave it at that.

Murray did for Aberdeenshire verse what William Alexander did for its prose, what George Reid did for its art, Archibald Simpson for its architecture, Gavin Greig for its music. They are in these respects the representative Aberdonians. All of them, it should be noted, had more than a single string to their bow. They were not exclusively professional or single-track specialists. That for Aberdonians is perhaps one part of the secret of their greatness. And of course also each one of them reflected that unassessable quality that is innate in every true Aberdonian. That is why we take such pleasure in the work they have bequeathed to us. We may know of verses, stories, pictures, songs, buildings, more worthy in an artistic sense, but none that more truly expresses what deep down within him every true Aberdonian feels, and likes, and thinks.

There's brawer mountains ower the sea.
An' fairer haughs I've kent, but still
The Vale o' Alford! Bennachie!
Yon is the Howe, an' this the Hill!

James Melvin

greatest of dominies

It is surely one of the paradoxes not merely of our own day and generation but of our history, that our schoolmasters have had so few tangible proofs of the community's recognition of its debt to their kind. None of the four so-called learned professions has been so parsimoniously treated as the schoolmasters. Yet it may be affirmed without fear of valid contradiction that without the education which, over half-a-dozen centuries, they (or the best of them) have imparted, we should never as a nation have so signally overcome the handicaps that comparative poverty and lack of power and population would have made insupportable.

In no part of Scotland has education, in various guises, been more assiduously cultivated than in the North-East. And while it would be invidious to attempt to distinguish between town and country as to the quality of their schools, Aberdeen by virtue of its size and prominence has for long and most widely been noted for its educational distinction. Of Aberdeen's seminaries, its Grammar School (not even forgetting rival academies in the Aulton which were temporarily more spectacular, and its younger rival, with which for well over a century it stood cheek by jowl in the Schoolhill) has the most impressive record. And of all the Grammar School's rectors there is none whose reputation has worn so well as James Melvin's, who guided its destinies during the second quarter of last century.

He was, of course, heir to a great tradition, built up over a long sequence of centuries. We must confess to a shocked surprise some years ago when the living scions of the school accepted without demur the assertion by a professional historian that their boast of being the products of an institution seven hundred years old was ill-founded. There is in fact in Scottish educational history at least one instance which seems to conflict flatly with the argument upon which the unfavourable verdict was based. That by the way.

The first head of the Grammar School who figures at all prominently in the annals of the town does so for a reason that has no obvious connection with education. John Marshall, the rector, was carpeted by the Town Council in March 1521 and November 1523 in connection with some obscure dispute, involving 'The Curt of Rowm', which has been interpreted to signify that he was a pioneer of Lutheran opinion in the burgh. The dates do not give Marshall much time to imbibe these doctrines, but he may of course have had knowledge of the earlier Huss and the still earlier Wyclif. On the other hand, the rumpus may have been due to a dispute between the Council and the Bishop as to who was superior of the School; but as popular Gavin Dunbar was then Bishop that seems improbable. It doesn't really matter.

The next outstanding rector was a Dundonian, David Wedderburn, who directed the school in the early part of the seventeenth century. He was a distinguished Latinist in an age when Scottish Humanists were legion. He wrote a great deal, and almost always in Latin. In 1617 when James VI was on a visit to Scotland and had promised to call at Aberdeen but failed to appear, perhaps because he owed the town quite a lot of money, which incidentally the Crown has never repaid—Wedderburn wrote a couple of Latin odes in honour of the prospective occasion. The Magistrates recognised his effort in a gift of 50 merks, a merk being two-thirds of a pound Scots, which in turn was one-twelfth of a pound sterling. When James died in 1625 Wedderburn turned out a Latin elegy, for which the Council gave him nothing, being probably quite relieved to see the end of the wisest fool in Christendom, as Henri Quatre of France had called him. In 1630, however, the rector got £100 Scots from the magistrates for a Latin grammar. Such recognition reflects creditably upon the attitude of authority then to literary and pedagogic distinction.

William Meston, the Jacobite poet, was a master, if not perhaps an ornament of the School early in the eighteenth century, in the second half of which its rector was that James Dun whose chief claim to remembrance is that he was father-in-law to James Beattie, author of the Essay on Truth, and for a few months an usher at the Grammar. And by that time James Melvin had come on the scene.

He was an Aberdonian born 1794 and bred, son of poor parents, who entered Marischal College nevertheless as First Bursar. Until the advent of the Affluent Society, poverty was in Scotland the fountain of distinction, and the main incentive to ambition. On graduating Melvin became an usher or class teacher at the Udny Academy, a very remarkable country school developed in 1786 by George Bisset, the parochial schoolmaster, to eke out his income. He died in 1812, and was succeeded by his son James, a classfellow of Melvin's at Marischal, the son entering on his responsibilities at the advanced age of 17. Thus it came about that Melvin taught the future Sir James Outram, 'the Bayard of India', whose widowed mother being a sister of James Anderson, then the farmer at Monkshill, sent her boy to the parish academy. There's a wealth of romance, albeit of a very practical character, in the achievements of these small Aberdeenshire schools whose story deserves to be written before the memory of them is lost in the deluge of modern centralised education.

From Udny Melvin moved Aberdeen-wards to the Aulton, where he was appointed under-master at Old Aberdeen Grammar School under 'a Mr. McLaughlan', a seminary destined in a decade or two to become a very celebrated place indeed. And then in 1822 one of his old teachers at the Grammar brought him back to his old school to help him, and to him he succeeded as class master after public competition in which he signally distinguished himself. Four years later, after a like public trial and demonstration of his surpassing gifts, he was Rector at £250 a year, and so he remained until his death on 20 June 1853. The day before he had collapsed in class. In that quarter century he had not so much revolutionised as revitalised education in the North-East, at a time when such an intellectual tonic was sadly needed. And although he was no innovator, and his method (as will be seen) was not such as to inspire much enthusiasm in a sybaritic age, he accomplished his purpose to a marvel.

One example, from the county rather than the town, may be cited to show how enduring his power has been. Amongst his pupils was Alexander Anderson, who was indeed in later life to display a greater command of pungent vernacular than of cultured Latin, but who, old rascal though he was, knew a really good thing when he saw it. Of the innumerable benefits Aberdeen's greatest Lord Provost bestowed upon the county of his birth and the city of his adoption, not least was his arranging that one of Melvin's young men should become head of his own old parish school. In the sequel, Strichen, until the Act of 1918 pulled away the foundation of the

Scottish educational structure, had a roll of sons in industry, commerce, administration, and the higher culture wholly disproportionate to its size and population.

Nearly three-quarters of a century after Melvin's death the tradition of his teaching lived on in that rural outpost. The base may have been widened and the branches of learning may have spread abundantly, but the old Latin roots still remained the stay and source of the whole. With the Classics as the main theme, English, French, German, Mathematics, Physics and Chemistry, History and the reading of Italian were for the asking, and if the curriculum was an exacting one, those who groaned under it in their youth look back upon it with grateful complacency in the years of such discretion as has been vouchsafed to them.

Melvin was accepted, even south of the Dee, where Aberdonian pretensions are scrutinised with a hypercritical eye, as—to quote Professor David Masson, one of his pupils—'at the head of the Scottish Latinity of his day'. His great classical library went to the university, where in a special bay at King's it is commemoratively linked with a memorial window which depicts as a quartet of Scottish Humanists George Buchanan, the tutor of Montaigne and historian of the Reformation in Scotland; Arthur Johnston of Caskieben (now Keith Hall), physician to Charles I and translator like Buchanan of the Psalms into Latin verse; Thomas Ruddiman, the Banffshire laddie who was robbed on his way to classes at King's and who became Keeper of the Advocates' library in Edinburgh and whose 'Rudiments of the Latin Tongue' was a standard textbook in Scottish schools almost to within living memory; and Melvin, whose only production was a Latin Grammar that in the North East mostly supplanted Ruddiman. It is not without significance that three of these four eminent scholars were Aberdeen graduates. And were we to fill the gap between Melvin's death and the present time two of the most likely contenders would also be products of Aberdeen.

'Grim' or 'Grim Pluto' was the nickname applied to Melvin by his pupils whilst they sat under him, although the sentiments with which they looked back upon their years at the desks before him were far from partaking of that quality. We may be wrong, but we think no other schoolmaster in Aberdeen, or perhaps in Scotland, has been accorded the honour awarded to Melvin of having the centenary of his birth celebrated by a public dinner, at which his silver tea and coffee service was set in the midst of the company along with other relics more evocative of a dominie's memory. Sir William Geddes, 'Homer', Principal of the University, was in the chair, and the company was academically more splendid than any that ever fed under the lights of Aberdeen, save perhaps that heterogeneous multitude who attended the Strathcona Banquet at the Quatercentenary celebrations, few of whom, however, unlike the Melvin celebrants, were able to get home on their legs.

John Forbes White, who developed into more of a Grecian than a Latinist, has left a full length pen portrait of Grim Pluto. The great thing with Melvin was accuracy. The Latin version was the lynch-pin of the whole structure of his educational method. 'So earnest was he', says White, 'that it seemed to give him positive pain when a good pupil made some horrid maxie', or major error. 'On the other hand, it gave him pleasure to write "sine errore" and still more when he could add, in his beautiful penmanship "et elegantissime" at the bottom of a version. His jibes were severe and sarcastic, but the culprit felt that they were deserved.' White might have been sitting, not in the Schoolhill of Aberdeen in the 'Hungry Forties' but in the halcyon days before the First World War overlooking the market stance of Strichen. Only the penmanship of the later dominie might have been less elegant than the others! And maxies were perhaps even more to be deplored when for penance they had to be corrected, according to their gravity, from 300 to 1,000 times after the school-day ended at 4 o'clock on a winter's afternoon with a mile to walk and a byreful of stots to 'sort' before tea-time and the nightly five-hour round of homework.

Melvin's Grammar School in the Schoolhill

The impact of Melvin's personality must have been terrific. Boys are not as a rule easily disciplined. The teenager of today is not so exceptional a phenomenon as some publicists would have us believe; he is only more obvious because the line of development of our civilisation has presented him with rather more frustrations than his predecessors of early Victorian times. But all his pupils who have put on record their recollections of Melvin reveal their sense of awe in the presence of the great schoolmaster. White has a dramatic account of the Head's daily appearance at the school. 'Even the youngest are hushed to silence as he passes through the crowd. . . . We are all conscious that a strong man is by us. . . . His living influence was the dominant feature of his class. His personality was tremendous. To be under him was an education in itself, for he moulded the accurate habits of thousands of boys.' As a glance at the roll of his pupils will show, he was responsible on the human side for the modern Aberdeen, just as Alexander Anderson was responsible for its modern corporate character.

Indeed, his influence spread rather further afield. For a number of years he was Lecturer in Humanity at Marischal College, which then had no Latin Chair. His salary was £80 and he lectured only in the winter. At the school his daily hours were three in the morning and two in the afternoon. His Marischal lectureship was, in all but fact, superseded in 1839, when a Chair of Humanity was at long last founded and John Stuart Blackie was appointed to fill it. Eventually he did so with an unconventional zest which greatly advanced the study of humane letters, but at first he was at loggerheads with the authorities because he refused to sign the Confession of Faith, submission to which was then regarded as a much more important qualification in a professor than proficiency in his subject. Melvin, who was a licentiate of the Church of Scotland, had no difficulty in that respect, and he continued to conduct the Latin class until in 1841 the doctrinal dispute was settled. A very loyal Auld Kirker, in 1843, when every one of the city's ministers went out at the Disruption, Melvin played his part as pulpit supply.

'He was a Roman of the Romans, Ultimus Romanorum, I should say, and one can easily picture him in the company of Cicero and of Livy, of Virgil and of Horace, the authors whom he loved so well. He liked the old Scottish tongue and rolled out with gusto on rare occasions scraps of Scots poetry, with special attention to one of Allan Ramsay's passages of paraphrase from the Classics.' Thus did J. F. White describe him.

Geddes contributes something more to our knowledge of his appearance and character. 'More like an ideal Roman head than would have been found on any other shoulders in a whole Campus Martius of the Aberdonians.' White is more particular. 'A large-framed man with round shoulders, dressed in black . . . with head bent forward, and treading lightly on his toes.' Thus he appeared day after day at school, which then stood where Gray's School of Art is now. He lived in Belmont Street, a bachelor, with mother and sisters, infrequently stirring out of teaching hours from his cloistral house. We have a description of its book-lined walls, filled from floor to ceiling on shelves specially fitted to their places. His was reputed to be the finest

Classical library in Scotland, and he used to say he had an edition of Horace for every day of the year.

His teaching method in the higher stages of education aroused the admiration of such an inspired teacher as Geddes. 'It was really beautiful to hear him dissect a passage in Horace, and then put it together again thrillingly complete.' Evidently Melvin had something!

His name lives on. There is a Melvin House in the Grammar School today, that school which shortly after his death was built at the compulsive direction of Alexander Anderson, who for all his brusqueness cherished a pious affection for his native parish, his old school, his ain romantic toun, and the best of dominies.

Sir Thomas Urquhart

translator of Rabelais

In the sketch of Alexander Cruden, compiler of the Concordance to the Bible, it was remarked that the two Aberdonians most assured of immortality were the two maddest speciments of the breed that deserved the epithet of 'Eminent'. The other one was Thomas Urquhart of Cromartie, knight, who had probably the misfortune to be born outside the geographical bounds properly to be designated as Aberdonian, but who in his breeding both family and educational and in many of his exploits proved himself to be a worthy member of the circle of Bon-Accord.

Thomas's father was also named Thomas, and was hereditary sheriff of the county of Cromarty wherein lay the chief messuage of the family. Other Urquhart lands, however, gave them a substantial stake in the counties of Aberdeen and Banff—Craigston, Dunlugas, Balquholly (now Hatton), and other estates were theirs. Thomas the father married a daughter of the fourth Lord Elphinstone somewhere about 1600. She may have brought a bit of bad luck into the family, for the first Lord Elphinstone was slain at Flodden and the second at Pinkie, and Lord Balmerino who was executed in 1746 for his part in the Forty-five belonged to a cadet branch. Perhaps, however, the Urquharts had not to go far within their own ranks to find ill-fortune.

Our Thomas was born five years after his father's marriage, somewhere from 1604 to 1606. He seems to have spent some of his youth at Craigston, and came to King's College, Aberdeen, in due course. He apparently did not graduate but he was there in 1622 and he set on record his opinion of Aberdeen which in itself would earn for him the right of inclusion amongst Aberdonians. The good town, he says in one of his books, 'for honesty, good fashions, and learning, surpasseth as far all other cities and towns in Scotland, as London doth for greatness, wealth, and magnificence, the smallest hamlet or village in England'. No one could say fairer than that! Better still, although his people had but very recently ceased to be Papists and were now enthusiastic Episcopalians, he could write of the Presbyterian, Dr. William Guild, that he was of all divines in Scotland for a century 'the most charitable, and who bestowed most of his own to public uses'.

For quite a long time Urquhart was little heard of. He appears to have had family troubles, however. In one of his books he traces his pedigree from Adam, working down in Scriptural times to Japhet and thence to a gentleman named Holocleros who about 1565 B.C. married the daughter of a Spanish king. He then deduces the line into modern times, to a Thomas Urquhart who about A.D. 1476 married a daughter of Lord Saltoun and had by her twenty-five sons and eleven daughters all of whom married. Little wonder that the seed of the Urquharts was scattered over the face of the earth.

On leaving King's College, Urquhart set off on an extended tour of the Continent. There is a story that somewhere about 1628, when he would have been 23 years of age, he was laureated poet at Paris. But he himself ascribes the same distinction to Arthur Johnston of Caskieben, who was a poet, which Sir Thomas never was or claimed to be. But of his trip abroad, he says himself that he visited France, Spain and Italy, where 'for speaking some of those languages with the liveliness of the country accent, they would have had him pass for a native'. But he was a perfervid Scot, and insisted on his Scottish extraction. As he puts it in his robust way, 'I always endeavoured to employ the best of my brain and heart towards the furtherance of the honour of that country unto which I did owe my birth'. This resolution 'gave me the courage for adventuring in a forrain climat, thrice to enter the lists against men of 3 severall nations, to vindicate my native country from the calumnies wherewith they had aspersed it'. He implies that he 'disarmed them' but whether the duels were of the traditional kind with swords, or like those which Panurge engaged in while in Paris in the pages of Rabelais, is not quite clear.

Proud as he was to be a Scot, and an Urquhart, and for all his professions of filial piety, Thomas used pretty high-handed methods with his rather feckless father. The latter, who had been knighted by James VI and I during his visit to Edinburgh in 1617, and who in other people's business was 'surpassing dextrous in arbitraments', rather let his own estate slide, for 'hee thought it did derogate from the nobility of his house, and reputation of his person, to look to petty things in matter of his own affairs'. The result was that everyone took advantage of him, and by 1637 he had to get from Charles I a letter of protection against his creditors. That very year, indeed, our Thomas and his brother Alexander were put on trial for having in the previous winter locked him in an upper room of his own mansion of Cromarty. Noble friends engineered reconciliation and the case was abandoned. It is conjectured that the two sons had taken this very forcible method of getting their father restrained from 'his negociations with many cunning sharks, who knew with what profitable odds they could scrue themselves in upon the windings of so good a nature'. As will transpire, our Thomas's nature was very much on a par with his parent's.

The year after the unfortunate episode just mentioned, Urquhart stepped upon the stage of national history. The family had accepted episcopacy, but in common with most of their sect refused to sign the National Covenant of 1638. At that time Thomas was residing at Balquholly, now Hatton Castle. In the first week of May 1639, the politico-religious dissensions in Aberdeenshire as in the rest of Scotland having reached trouble point, the lairds of Delgaty and Towie-Barclay, who were Presbyterians and had signed the Covenant, hearing that Urquhart had some muskets and other weapons of war at Balquholly, made a surprise raid upon it and got off with the lot. The late laird of Hatton, Sir Garden B. Duff, who was the representative during his later life of the Urquhart family, used to point out the very room in the castle from which the arms were abstracted. It had been a cellar then; three centuries later it was part of the library.

This raid on Balquholly was the first overt act of hostilities in the whole of the British

Isles, of the Great Civil War. On 10 May 1639, Urquhart with some of his relations and Episcopalian friends assaulted the castle of Towie-Barclay, where the plundered arms were stored, in an attempt to get them back. But the Forbeses and Frasers, powerful Covenanting families, who had manned Towie-Barclay, repulsed the besiegers, and one man of Urquhart's party was killed by a shot from the house. This man's was the first blood shed in the Civil War. From this little affray there developed the skirmish, on 13 May, known as the Trot of Turriff, in which Lord Fraser was surprised by the Episcopal party, Urquhart and others, and put to ignominious flight. The victors moved on Aberdeen, and took possession of the town, but on 23 May, Urquhart and his friends had to fly by sea to England and Charles I.

The result of all Urquhart's endeavours and adventures in the King's service was that he received a knighthood at Whitehall on 7 April 1641. Despite the alarms and excursions in which he had been involved, he had already started to write, and in that year appeared the first-born of his genius, 'Epigrams, Divine and Moral, By Sir Thomas Vrchard, Knight'. It was published in London and Urquhart appears to have remained in the south for several years after the Trot of Turriff. His father died in his absence, in 1642, after a long illness and leaving his affairs, and consequently those of our Thomas, in a very embarrassed state. Not only were substantial debts to be liquidated, but some of the family estates had been sold, and five brothers and two sisters had to be provided for, all on a rental of about £1,000 a year, which was quite a large income in those days but not sufficient for the claims upon it nor perhaps for Thomas's ideas of how to live.

His own account of the situation in which he found himself and of his efforts to clear his feet may not convey a very clear picture, but it is too flamboyantly characteristic to be omitted. 'Notwithstanding the grievousness of such solicitudinary and luctiferous discouragements, able to appall the most undaunted spirits, and kill a very Paphlagonian partridge, that is said to have two hearts, I did nevertheless, without attristing my self a jot, undergoe the defraying of the debt, although not as a debtor, with as much alacrity and cheerfulnesse as if it had been of my own undertaking.' He alleges that by following the advice of his friends he adopted a course which resulted merely in exchanging new creditors for those of his father, 'my Egyptian bondage by such means remaining still the same, under task masters different only in name, and the rents neverthelesse taken up to the full, to my no small detriment, and prejudice of the house standing in my person'. In such circumstances he returned to the family mansion at Cromarty.

By this time the Civil War was in full blast in England, although it was not until 1644 that it warmed up in Scotland. But there is no sign of Sir Thomas, not even in the entourage of the Great Marquis of Montrose, when that gifted soldier flashed like a meteor through the North-Eastern and Highland counties. Montrose, indeed, like his master Charles at Naseby, was meeting his Waterloo at Philiphaugh when Sir Thomas's second book, *The Trissotetras,* appeared in London in 1645. While his sentiments were wholly on the Royalist side, he seems to have plunged himself into a life of seclusion and study at Cromarty, for he told a sporting gentleman who called upon him that 'I was employed in a diversion of another nature, such as optical secrets, mysteries of natural philosophie, reasons for the variety of colours, the finding out of the longitude, the squaring of a circle, and ways to accomplish all trigonometrical calculations by signes without tangents, with the same compendiousness of computation, which, in the estimation of learned men, would be accounted worth six hundred thousand partridges, and as many moor-fowles'.

The 'Trissotetras', whose lengthy and characteristic sub-title begins, 'or, a most exquisite Table for resolving all manner of Triangles, whether Plaine or Sphericall, Rectangular or Obliquangular, with greater facility than ever hitherto hath been practised', was obviously a fruit of those studies. But we must hasten on and away from a subject that may today allure the technically minded. Only we indulge one last loiter to admire Tom's tribute to his mother (to whom his book was dedicated). Amidst the neighbouring countesses and other great dames, he declares, 'as Cynthia amongst the obscurer planets your ladieship shines, and darteth the angelick rayes of your matchless example on the spirits of those who by their good genius have been brought into your favourable presence'. And he concludes his panegyric with the hope that she may live so long 'that the sonnes of those whom I have not as yet begot, may attaine to the happinesse of presenting unto your ladieship, a brain-babe of more sufficiencie and consequence'.

Urquhart's existence from about this time onwards was a most exciting and crowded one. Robert Lesley of Findrassie, a descendant of the Norman Lesley who took part in the assasination of Cardinal Beaton at St. Andrews, James Sutherland tutor of Duffus, and Sir James Fraser of Darkhouse pestered him, partly on pretexts of money owing and partly, apparently, on account of his known Royalist sympathies. A garrison was installed in his house, some of his tenants killed, and his library poinded and sold. After the execution of Charles I he was declared a rebel and traitor as one of a party that seized Inverness. Then, when Charles II came to Scotland, he served in his army and was at the battle of Worcester in 1651. Urquhart was taken prisoner and he lost his luggage containing manuscripts to the extent, so he says, of 128½ quires of paper. Some of his papers he recovered and in fact the next few years were his most prolific in point of publications. Moreover, he was allowed a great deal of liberty by his captors, who were much kinder to him than the creditors of the estate up north.

Another edition of *Trissotetras* appeared in 1650. In 1652 there came on the scene (we'll give them their English instead of their unwieldy Greek names) *The Jewel,* which he said he found in the gutters of Worcester the day after the fight, and which is a vindication of the Scottish nation with sketches of many of its eminent sons; and *The Peculiar Promptuary of Time,* in which he sets forth the pedigree of the Urquharts. In 1653 came the *Introduction to the Universal Language,* a subject which occupied the more sober intelligence of another Aberdonian, George Dalgarno, in Oxford about the same time. In Urquhart's invention, there are twelve parts of speech, the verbs have eleven tenses, seven moods and four voices, and, in short, besides having 'sixty and six advantages above all other languages', he claimed that 'for variety of diction in each part of speech, it surmounteth all the languages of the world', and that it was 'the most compendious in compliment, and consequently fittest for courtiers and ladies'.

Sufficient quotation has been made to give an idea of Sir Thomas Urquhart's literary style and method and the truly extraordinary range of his intellectual interests. It does not matter if many, perhaps all, of his conclusions and theories were fantastic or extravagant. It would be instructive could the scientists, philosophers and leaders of opinion today be transported now into the year 2265 and discover what their present cherished thought will look like then. As for Urquhart's style, there never has been anything quite like it. Compared with other unconventional concepts of expression, like the rather earlier Euphuism, with which his style is sometimes equated, Urquhart's manner of writing was virile, picturesque, and memorable, giving evidence of an originality of mind and mental inventiveness of an almost unique kind. He had too, obviously a keen sense of humour, a highly developed power of observation, and on the whole a lovable personality.

These were the very qualities that fitted him for the perfect accomplishment of the great task of his life, the work that has placed him amongst the immortals, his translation of the first three books of the Works of Francois Rabelais. The first two were published, separately, in 1653, the third long after Urquhart's death in 1693, and as the third was probably worked over by a prosaic reviser, Pierre Le Motteux, only the first two are authentic Urquhart. Outside the Authorised Version of the Bible, Urquhart's Rabelais is universally acknowledged to be the most brilliant of all translations into English. Of course, it is only loosely to be described as a translation. There is a great deal of Urquhart and of Scotland in it, fitting in with Rabelais' own thoughts and the genius of France like the pieces of a jig-saw puzzle. But never did any man so completely enter into the spirit of a classic as Sir Thomas into the amazing world of Gargantua and Pantagruel, of Panurge and Friar John. The whole thing is little short of a literary miracle.

It has been said that no one reads Rabelais now—none in the French and few in the English. That means that only the wise read him. For in French literature the two best loved authors throughout the world are Montaigne and Rabelais—and the former was tutored by a Scot and the latter translated by another. An English man of letters who ought to have known better committed himself to the observation that 'Sir Thomas Urquhart determined to show the world that a true Briton could not be outdone in his native treasures of obscene language by the most erudite of Frenchmen. It is enough to say he succeeded'. From a representative of a nation that holds the scurrilous Dean Swift and the sniggering Rev. Laurence Sterne in high honour, such an opinion must carry considerable weight.

Actually it is unfortunate that the crude perceptions of low fellows of the baser sort should have invented the term Rabelaisian. The French masterpiece is in fact one of the most genial, as it is one of the most cultured and penetrating satires ever penned—a satire, actually, not only upon the follies and abuses of the Church, State and people of its time, but also upon those who read it. To translate it adequately required a standard of intelligence and a sense of justice, as well as a sense of humour and knowledge of human nature not easily to be confined in a single skull, but Sir Thomas Urquhart possessed that cranium.

It seems that even Cromwell (who appreciated his Aberdonian contemporary Alexander Jaffrey) liked him. When confined in the Tower, Urquhart enjoyed many privileges. Although an enemy to the Government, he suffered none of the indignities that awaited yet another scientifically-minded Aberdonian, the Rev. Alexander J. Forsyth, who a century and three quarters later found himself in the same place, working for the Government. Eventually Thomas slipped away to the Continent. There, when he heard the English had asked Charles II to come back, he died of a fit of laughter. Truly he had a sense of humour.

William McCombie

cattle-breeding maestro

One of the principal sources of Aberdeen's enduring vitality is the reciprocity between its interests and those of its hinterland. All through the city's history there has been apparent this interplay between the produce, the pursuits and the people of the North-East and those of native urban Aberdonians. Seldom has the connection been better exemplified, seldom has it operated more signally to the greater glory of Bon-Accord than in the career and achievements of the eminent Aberdonian about to be described.

William McCombie 'the most renowned breeder, feeder and exhibitor of cattle in Europe', belonged to a Glenisla family, who about 300 years ago, for reasons best known to themselves and to what representatives there were in those days of law and order, fled to Donside and settled at Mains of Tonley in the parish of Tough. The great-grandson of this migrant, following his father's trade of cattle dealer, became the biggest practitioner in Scotland in this branch of agricultural activity. At a single Falkirk Tryst, the greatest of the Scottish cattle fairs around the beginning of the last century, he stanced no fewer than 1,500 cattle, bought in the counties from the Dee to Caithness and all of them driven from their farms of origin to the banks of the Forth, many of them shod with those thin half-moon slivers of shoes without whose protection their feet could not stand up to the friction of the hard and stony drove roads. This cattleman, Charles McCombie, was able from his dealings to purchase the estate of Tillyfour, in the small mansion-house of which his famous son William was to be born, to live and to die.

William McCombie was born in 1805, a second son. Their father regarded farming as 'a poor business', and endeavoured to divert his sons to more respectable callings. His elder boy Charles became parish minister of Lumphanan and an LL.D. of Aberdeen. William also was despatched to Marischal College, but 'They say—What say they?—Let them say' was interpreted by the Donside loon in a rather different sense from that intended by its noble coiners, and two sessions of academic existence convinced him that there were better ways of earning a living. How he contrived to evade his father's wishes has never transpired, but apparently while still a student he and one of his father's farm-servants clubbed their scanty means together, rented a small grass field and bought a few cattle. The old man declared that the animals 'had not the countenance of beasts', but a substantial profit accrued, and McCombie senior surrendered.

In 1821 William was driving cattle from the Highlands and Moray, and in 1824 he took over Tillyfour as his father's tenant. For a spell, both in partnership with his father and after the latter's death in 1830, on his own, he conducted an extensive business as a cattle-dealer. The golden age of this type of cattle business was drawing to a close. George, the best-known of the three 'stately Williamsons' of St. John's Wells, Fyvie, next to the McCombies the biggest dealers, had died in 1823. Of others Anderson of Pitcarry, Stoddart of Culter-cullen, Lumsden of Aquhorthies, the Martins, the Wiselys, and the Wisharts were all prominent. But it was McCombie who first deciphered the writing on the wall. The displacement of cattle by horses for farm work, the sowing of turnips in drills instead of broadcast, and the linking-up by rail in the mid-forties, thanks to Alexander Anderson, of Aberdeen with the south spelt the doom of the droving and pointed the way to the feeding of cattle on the farms of the North-east for Smithfield market, the most exacting centre for top quality beef in the world.

So McCombie switched over from droving and dealing to fattening and feeding. But he saw that even that was not enough to keep abreast of the times. In 1830 he bought his first Aberdeen-Angus cattle. They could hardly be said in those days to be pedigreed but the men he purchased from, the Williamsons of St. John's Wells and Walker of Wester Fintray, had always mated black poll with black poll. Moreover, in Angus a few farmers with Hugh Watson and the Earl of Southesk in the forefront, had been using polled black bulls on polled Buchan cows with excellent results. Intending to force his way into the select London meat market, McCombie found himself compelled to turn his attention to the quality of his stock, and to the mechanics of breeding and feeding them. He went to London and studied the type of carcases the market demanded. He tried out various feeding experiments until he was satisfied he had found the secret. He tested the breeds of cattle and came to the conclusion that the 'Buchan hummlie' was the best, with the smaller, horned Aberdeenshire black breed not to be despised. Its last representative died in 1883 on the farm of Pitbee, in Chapel of Garioch.

Before proceeding to consider the change he wrought in the agricultural fortunes of the North-East, and indeed of the whole world, we may pause for a moment to look at the man himself. His family have done very well by Aberdeen city and county. A cousin founded the *North of Scotland Gazette,* later known as the *Aberdeen Free Press,* and of this McCombie, also a William, Sir Henry Alexander, a Lord Provost of the city, was a grandson. A cousin once removed, H. D. McCombie, was Convener of the county. There are still McCombies in the parish of Tough, and the present bearer of the name, on the bothy ballad farm of the Guise of Tough, sticks to his famous relative's breed.

Here is a word-picture of the great William in his drover days. 'The stalwart figure, with weather-beaten face, clad in rough woollen garb, stout stick in hand, the breast well bulged with bank notes, speaking in gruff tones, and ratifying large transactions by simply "striking hands", presents a contrast to the polished man on "Change".' Prosperous as a dealer, he was progressive as a farmer. His father had neglected Tillyfour, preferring the adventitious profits of the market stance to the unrewarding labours of a tiller of the soil. The place was badly farmed, much of it in bog, moor, and marsh. When William died Tillyfour was a smiling land, as one commentator put it. Beside the three farms, which the estate comprised, he had his fat cattle at Bridgend (now occupied by an Aberdeen Angus herd) and he was tenant of Dorsell, situated between the Leochel burn and Badens hill.

He was no commonplace farmer either. He was one of the crack shots of his day, whose bags of grouse in his earlier years were mentioned in the same breath as those brought down, when he was old, by such noted shots as Lord Walsingham, Lord de Grey, Frederick Milbank and Archibald Stuart Wortley. He was a devotee of greyhound coursing and was the owner of a celebrated bitch named Amy which, he said, 'went from the slips like a shot out of a smooth-bore'. He bred fast trotting-shalts, driving with a pair, and making Aberdeen from Tillyfour in what was then an incredibly short time. He was a bachelor. He told one of his several French farming pupils that he never could find the time for courting. The sales of fat cattle for the season ended in January. The buying of stores and the mating in his pedigree herd began in March. That left him only February, which was not long enough to consider such a momentous project.

He was up every morning between five and six, reading his mail and dictating or writing letters clad in a long, light-coloured dressing-gown and slippers, with his silver snuff-box at his hand. After breakfast he was out and through his courts and byres and fields, inspecting the crops of turnips, oats and pasture that agriculturists came from 'a the airts to see. To local or county meetings, as to his outlying farms, he drove in his carriage, and often he was away for days at shows and sales in Scotland, England and France. Every night when he was at home, he led his servants in family worship, and on Sunday evenings he conducted a Bible class at Tillyfour.

In the early sixties the rinderpest broke out. The first case occurred at the Barnyards of Strichen. Local administration was very rudimentary in those days, public health organisation before Disraeli's great premiership was non-existent and there was no departmental animal health machinery to cope with such a disastrous epidemic. In a day or two McCombie had convened a meeting of lairds and substantial farmers, who proceeded to establish along the Dee a sanitary cordon which prevented all cattle imports till the danger was past. In 1868 he was returned unopposed as Liberal M.P. for West Aberdeenshire. In 1874, when the Liberal landslide occurred, he had eight votes for every one cast for his Tory opponent. In the Commons, where his strong doric accent was heard to effect, his most notable speech was one of a single sentence. He had been on his feet and speaking, and used the word 'water', pronouncing it with the emphasis on the 't'. A facetious Englishman asked the Speaker if 'water' was spelt with two t's in Scotland. 'No, Sir,' retorted McCombie, 'but we spell manners with two n's'.

In 1862, after one of his early international successes, of which more later, McCombie was entertained at a public dinner by the agricultural community. The Marquis of Huntly presided over a company of 400, who heard him tell in grim phrases how he came to establish his supremacy in the pedigree and fat stock shows. 'English agriculturists always maintained that no Scot would ever take a first place in competition with a Shorthorn, a Hereford, or a Devon; but I have lived to give them reasons for changing their opinion.' Terrible old man he became to the less systematic farmers with whom he competed, but he started many a youngster on the road to successful living, and his conduct towards the general community may be gathered from the dinner which several hundred small tradesmen, crofters and farm servants gave him in the Vale of Alford. Of that tribute he was prouder than of any success that came his way. He resigned his seat in 1876, after a slight stroke, and he died early in 1880. One London newspaper described him in Sir Walter's words, as 'a prince of the people'.

Two things of great and enduring importance McCombie accomplished. First of all, he established the primacy of Aberdeenshire-bred and Aberdeenshire-fed beef. This has brought untold millions of money not only to the farms, both large and small, of the North-east, but also to the trades and professions of Aberdeen itself. He achieved this by no accidental discovery, but by close and intelligent observation, by experiment based less upon theory than upon experience, and by the patient collation of results obtained over a series of years and from a wide variety of kinds of cattle. In order to fix his Aberdeen beef in the estimation of the public, he had not only to produce an article that repaid himself; it had also to be such as would commercially and financially satisfy the fleshing trade especially of London, and it had further to meet the taste of a public that enjoys nothing so well as a well-flavoured and sumptuous meal. To make his point McCombie had to show his cattle, and win consistently. His first essay in the showyard was in 1832. Strangely enough, his first major break-through with fat cattle was at a Paris International Exposition in 1856, when he had several first prizes with Aberdeen-Angus oxen but lost the championship by the casting vote of the chairman of the judging panel. In 1862, however, at the next international, he took all the first prizes for oxen, and the championship with a 2,750 lb. steer. There were 450 entries.

Similar triumphs had been in the meantime won at Birmingham Fat Stock Show and at the Smithfield Club's Show, where several first prizes for polled steers had been and were to be gained. But 1867 was the great year. The finest steer McCombie ever bred or showed, Black Prince, swept the boards at Birmingham, and went on to win what was in effect, though not then in name, the supreme championship at Smithfield. Since a supreme championship was instituted, the Aberdeen-Angus have secured by far the largest share of the honours, and since 1918 only thrice has the champion not been a pure-bred of the breed or one of its crosses. On the way to Smithfield, McCombie, who had had a visit from Queen Victoria and could have given a modern publicity agent a year's start and beaten him, sent Black Prince to Windsor for the Queen to see. When the champion was slaughtered, he had a baron of beef despatched to Windsor with his humble duty. The London butcher who bought the beast insisted on being paid for the baron, thus losing the chance of a lifetime.

McCombie paid, for he was looking ahead. The Queen came to Tillyfour again. McCombie, so the story goes, had a seat for her Majesty so sited that she could only see in front of her. He then marched his black polls round and round several times, till she cried 'Enough!' She started an Aberdeen-Angus herd some time later which during her reign and that of Edward VII produced some first-class cattle and indeed ranked high in the annals of the breed and of the showyard. In the year of his Smithfield triumph, there appeared his only essay in literary authorship, *Cattle and Cattle Breeders*, which despite the lapse of a century must still be regarded as the best classic of its kind. It went through three editions in his life-time, and a fourth appeared later.

McCombie's second great achievement was the establishment of the Aberdeen-Angus breed. He found it one of several competitors, he left it at his death the acknowledged quality breed of all breeds. Soon after he started his herd in 1830 the brothers Cruickshank got together the historic Scotch Shorthorn herd at Sittyton, Newmachar. They, or rather the practical farmer brother Amos, made it the great grading-up breed, and by so doing, in an area of cattle-breeding expansion, he made it the premier beef breed. But Cruickshank trusted to physical conformation rather than pedigree in his matings, whereas McCombie insisted that pedigree must always be paramount. The proof of the pudding is in the preein' o't. Today the Aberdeen-Angus commands the fabulous prices. In most of the cattle-raising countries of the world it is the most sought-after and in all but two the dominant breed.

To go into McCombie's formative work is not only impossible in a short article, it is out of place in this *Journal,* suffice it to say that there is hardly a family in the seventy-odd tribes of the breed in Britain today that does not owe its excellence as well as its existence to McCombie; and the same applies to the equal number of families to be found in North and South America and Australia and New Zealand. Some of his bulls, according to contemporary testimony, could have been better, but it was their breeding that mattered with him, and their sons made the herds that they went to and improved the families they touched. His heifers were peerless. When he contemplated Pride of Aberdeen as she paraded before judges on her first assignment, it is not fanciful to imagine in him the selfsame emotion that Leonardo de Vinci experienced when he caught on canvas that immortal glance from La Giaconda, or Shakespeare felt when he saw 'Macbeth' worked out on the stage, or that moved Beethoven when the titanic harmonies of the Ninth Symphony sounded behind his deaf ears. For Pride of Aberdeen, and her mother, Charlotte, and Jilt, and many another grande dame of Tillyfour were in their fashion just as epoch-making and have endured just as well as those cultural masterpieces throughout the vicissitudes of time. Perhaps, considering the hazards that occur in a century of breeding, their intrinsic worth has been more inviolate.

Andersons

versatile genius of descendants of an Anderson skipper

Several times in this series the eminence of the subject has applied as much to his family as to the individual. The Haddens, the Menzies, the Gibbs, the Jaffrays, the complicated pattern of relationships in the pedigree of Dr. William Guild and Davie Do a'thing all indicate that breeding can count as much in the production of human brains as of bovine beef. But two of the families in Aberdeen's history achieved such a wealth of corporate distinction as to merit inclusion as families—the Gregories and the Fordyces. The Gregories were famous academes over half a dozen generations and two centuries of time; the Fordyce greatness was almost exclusively apparent in one generation. The Fordyce notables were all men, whereas some of the Gregories who, under other names, got into the *Dictionary of National Biography* owed their brains to their mothers.

There is a third Aberdonian family whose record in some respects eclipses all others. It first came to notice almost 400 years ago; its members have been prominently in the public eye without a break for the last 250 years; its laurels have been carried forward as much by its daughters as by its sons; its honours have been won in science, politics, theology, war, education and commerce. Sir Alexander Anderson belonged to its fringes and Davie Do a'thing was probably a member of it. The tribal name of this third eminent Aberdonian family was Anderson.

The first historical glimpse of them shows a seaman, skipper and perhaps owner of the ship in which, in 1589, the fifth Earl Marischal, founder of Marischal College, went over to Denmark to wed by proxy for King James VI the Princess Anne of Denmark. After the ceremony the bride set sail in a Danish ship, escorted by a dozen vessels carrying her suite and guards. The Earl Marischal remained aboard the boat that took him over. Had the princess chosen to sail in the Anderson ship, she would have made Scotland soon and safely: it was the only boat of the convoy that weathered a heavy storm and reached its intended destination. Anne and her attendants were fortunate to find shelter in a Norwegian port, and thither went James himself a month or so later to claim his bride. One little sidelight on the first meeting of the young couple may be permitted. In a contemporary account we are informed that James was 'minded to give the queen a kiss, after the Scots fashion, at meeting, whilk she refused as not being the form of her country. After a few words privily spoken betwixt his majesty and her, there passed familiarity and kisses.'

To return to Skipper Anderson. He was an Aberdonian, but of his parentage we have no record. There were quite a few Andersons in the burgh 400 years ago who were prominent enough to earn mention in local annals, and even the redoubtable Davie's pedigree has never been clearly ascertained. The probability is that all the branches in Aberdeen then were fairly nearly related, and that the skipper, obviously a competent mariner, was cousin in some Scots degree to Davie, the greatest engineer of his time in Scotland. The Earl Marischal did pretty well out of the Danish affair, getting the lands of Deer as a recompense, but he was no skinflint and he repaid Anderson by making him his miller first at Ravenscraig and then at Inverugie. And to be a miller in those days was, next perhaps to the laird, the most lucrative of all jobs in the rural economy. There are descendants of his still in the Inverugie-St. Fergus district.

Confession is said to be good for the soul, wherefore it may here and now be admitted that the story of this family has confounded the writer of these notes, accustomed as he has become to the achievements, the adventures, the eccentricities, and the originality of Aberdonians. It is, in its entirety, so madly incredible as to border upon the fantastic. Within present limits it is not possible to present it in anything like its complete form.

Dr. A. G. B. Young, who is himself a member of the family, in a paper to the Buchan Club some years ago recorded the following tally of distinctions:

> A Chief of the Imperial General Staff; a First Lord of the Admiralty; an Ambassador to the United States; a President of the Royal Society of Water Colour Painters; a Chairman of the South Wales Coal Owners' Association; a principal woman Factory Inspector; a Master of Gonville and Caius; a Fellow and Tutor of Balliol; a Fellow of Trinity College, Cambridge; a Regius Professor of Botany; one of the earlier women M.P.s; a Director of the Bank of England; an M.P. for the City of London; a Colonel Commandant of Engineers. . . . There are two millionaires. On at least 35 occasions the King has honoured a descendant of the miller, and other countries have also recognised their services.

It will transpire in the following paragraphs that there's a lot more of that kind of thing to be said.

The family threw off several outstanding characters in the two centuries after 1589—outstanding both physically and mentally. But it really began to take over control of affairs in the middle of last century. From a branch that had gone to Sutherland about 1773 there sprang Joseph, who took to war and the Seaforth Highlanders, rose to be a lieutenant-colonel, and eventually owned an 85,000 acre estate in Australia and founded a dynasty there. Soldiering must have run in this branch's blood, for Joseph's sister became the mother of one of Aberdeen's most martial sons, Field-Marshal Lord Milne of Salonika and Rubislaw, who began to emerge from the common ruck when his battery hit the Mahdi's tomb at the Battle of Omdurman and who eventually commanded the British troops in Macedonia 1916-18 and the Near East 1918-20, and was Chief of the Imperial General Staff 1926-33. Montgomery excepts him from his castigation of all those who, until the Second World War, followed him in this office, and rather surprisingly (for one of his prejudices) claims that Milne should have been succeeded by another Aberdonian, General Sir John Theodosius Burnett-Stuart of Dens and Crichie. Another of Joseph's sisters, Elizabeth, marrying George Geddes of the Hudson Bay Company, had for her youngest son Auckland Campbell Geddes, of whom more anon.

George, another son of this Sutherland branch, was a naval surgeon, settled in Peterhead, and his youngest daughter became the mother of Charles Creighton, M.D., one of the burgh's most redoubtable sons. He was a leading researcher in anatomy and in cancer, wrote what is universally regarded in the profession as a medical classic, *The History of Epidemics in Britain*, and for versatility threw off a series of studies of Shakespeare's plays, on what he considered to be the allegories in *Othello* and *Lear* and the 'Second sense' in *Macbeth, Antony and Cleopatra, Cymbeline* and *The Winter's Tale*. These recreations of his may be too much expressed in fancy, but they may be quoted as pioneers of a long series of similar extravaganzas in literary criticism which are regarded as very modern and sophisticated today. But the *History of Epidemics* was Creighton's masterpiece: if we are not mistaken, an Aberdonian now in London, himself at the very head of the medical profession, is working upon a sort of parallel inquiry at this moment. Creighton died in 1957.

Creighton was an Aberdeen graduate, and a pupil at the Old Aberdeen Gymnasium in the Chanonry, started, owned and run by another Anderson, his Scots cousin. It is when we come to this representative of the family, Alexander Anderson, that we enter upon what we may be pardoned for imagining to be the realm of fantasy. Alexander Anderson (1808-1884) was the son of a Peterhead doctor, 6 foot 3 inches tall and weighing 23 stone, and known as 'Nosey' from his large proboscis; he in turn was the son of a Peterhead doctor who died in 1812. Alexander took Arts and Divinity at St. Andrews University, was presented to the church of Boyndie in Banffshire, in 1830, and in the following year married a daughter of Dr. Alexander Gavin of Strichen, who had been a surgeon on Nelson's flagship at the Battle of Copenhagen, and is credited with the authorship of that loveliest of all Aberdeenshire folk-songs, *Mormond Braes*. The Rev. Alexander Anderson—I am indebted to Dr. A. A. Cormack, who has done so much good work in the byways of local history, for many of my facts in this connection—was a most painstaking pastor. In one year he visited 208 families and held 28 catechisms. A friend of the great Dr. Chalmers, he 'went out' at the Disruption with all his elders but one, the factor, and in 1845 was called to be the first Free Church minister in Old Aberdeen, the church still to be seen in the High Street, where it accommodates various university classes today. In 1847 he came to the conclusion, after prolonged investigation of the authorities, that adult baptism was the right thing. The Free Church promptly slung him out. One who was baptised into it and regards it with respect may be permitted to say that in Alexander Anderson and William Robertson Smith it cast out two of its chief ornaments. Anderson proceeded to found the George Street Baptist Church that was later merged with the congregation in Crown Terrace. At the same time he bought a school building and four acres of ground (now the Cruickshank Botanic Garden) at the south-west corner of the Chanonry and launched the seminary that earned enormous renown as 'The Gym'. In 1858 he helped to found the Y.M.C.A. in Aberdeen.

On his staff were John Harrower, later Professor of Greek at King's, James Hastings, later editor of the monumental *History of the Bible*, and John Clarke, his son-in-law, prominent in Aberdeen educational circles. Pupils included his relative Lord Milne, Sir Herbert Grierson, Professor of English, Sir Alexander Ogston, Professor of Surgery, Sir William M. Ramsay, Professor of Humanity, Sir Robert Williams of Park, Col. Blair, who was secretary of the Unionist Party in Scotland, Thomas Gordon Walker, Lt.-Governor of the Punjab, and Harvey Adamson, another relative, who became Lt.-Governor of Burma. Anderson's aim, and he was almost the first educationist to realise the need for it, was to provide a step in the educational ladder just short of university level. It is a tricky climb and it looks as if, since the 1918 Education Act began to exercise its not wholly beneficent influence, we had lost our footing again at this elevation.

If Alexander Anderson's colleagues and pupils were to give distinctive service to the nation, his family were destined to play an even more varied and illustrious series of roles. His eldest son, Alexander Gavin, and his second and third sons, James and William, all went into shipping. Alexander besides being a shipowner was chairman of the Adelaide and New Zealand Bank, and of his family, Maxwell became chairman of the Adelaide Steamship Company, and his namesake Sir Alexander Gavin Anderson, was a member of Burma Executive Council and a chairman of the Burma Chamber of Commerce. William was chairman of the Australian Shipowners Association. James founded the Orient Line of steamships and by his marriage with Elizabeth Garrett gave two distinguished personalities to the Empire. Elizabeth Garrett Anderson herself deserves special mention. She studied medicine before 1860 but the Colleges both of Physicians and Surgeons refused to let her sit their examinations, so she approached the Society of Apothecaries, who were more progressive, admitted her to their examinations and gave her licence to practice in 1865. In 1870 she became an M.D. of Paris. Until 1890 she was senior physician to the New London Hospital for Women. She was a member of the first London School Board, and the first woman mayor (of Aldeburgh) in England. Her daughter Louisa Garrett Anderson who died in 1943, was in 1914 joint organiser and chief surgeon of the women's Hospital Corps Volunteer Unit, and from 1915 to 1918 chief surgeon at the military hospital in Endell Street, London, W.C. Her brother Sir Alan Garrett Anderson, who died in 1952, as well as being a director of the family shipping company, was in control of the railways for the greater part of the Second World War, and was a president of the Association of British Chambers of Commerce.

These were the Rev. Alexander's sons. His daughters were at least as distinguished as the sons. The eldest was one of the first women doctors. Another married John Clarke. Yet another became the wife of a Swedish architect who was trained in Aberdeen, by whom she had a son who became chairman of the Swedish Tobacco Monopoly and other organisations. The youngest daughter, Christina Helen Macleod, married her Scots cousin Elizabeth Anderson's son Auckland Campbell Geddes, and bore him three sons, Eric, Auckland and Irvine, and one daughter, Alexandra or Mona. Mona was the originator and Chief Controller of the W.A.A.C. in the 1914-18 War. Auckland's career had the diversification that frequently occurs in Anderson biography. He was Professor of Anatomy at Edinburgh, Dublin and Montreal consecutively, became Director of Recruiting in 1916, Minister of National Service in 1917, Minister of Reconstruction in 1919 and later the same year President of the Board of Trade, which he left in 1920 to become British Ambassador at Washington. On retiring in 1924 he became chairman of the Rio Tinto Company. He returned to national war work in 1939, became Lord Geddes in 1942, and died in 1954. His brother Irvine entered the family shipping company and became chairman of the Orient Line and president of the U.K. Chamber of Shipping. It was as recently as last Midsummer's Day that Sir Donald Anderson, a great-grandson of the Rev. Alexander Anderson, announced as chairman of the P. and O. Line the placing of orders for three cargo boats in Japan. Another great-grandson, Sir Colin Skelton Anderson, has been chairman of Council of the Royal College of Art and president of the International Chamber of Shipping.

The most romantic and adventurous of all the Anderson careers was that of Christina's eldest son Eric Campbell Geddes. Educated mostly in Edinburgh he went off to the U.S.A. in his teens, and for four years roughed it as a brakesman on freight trains, a lumberjack, and a labourer in a steel works. Then he got to India and found himself managing a forestry estate. This involved the running of a 50-mile light railway, and when it was merged in a bigger line he became the traffic superintendent. In 1906 he returned to this country, which still offered exceptional opportunities to men of his calibre and temperament. He joined the North-Eastern Railway of which in 1914 when war broke out he was deputy general manager. That autumn he raised a battalion of Northumberland Fusiliers; in 1915 he was deputy director-general of ammunition supplies; in 1916 director-general of transportation in France and later inspector-general, with the rank of major-general, of transportation in all theatres of war; in 1917 he was Controller of the Navy with the rank of Vice-Admiral—a 'giddy harumfrodite, soldier and sailor too'; the same year he entered Parliament to become First Lord of the Admiralty.

From 1919 to 1921 he was the first Minister of Transport, superintending the amalgamation of all the British railway companies into four groups. The complicated financial arrangements which these mergers involved prepared him for his next job as chairman of what came to be known as the Geddes Axe Committee, which was appointed to devise economies in national expenditure. This Sisyphean task he accomplished rather more efficiently than Sisyphus would have done, but with the inevitable frustrating revolt, for of the £86,000,000 economies he recommended, he complained that only £52,000,000 were effected, and they soon disappeared also. He shook the dust of the political desert off his feet, like a wise man, in 1922, and became chairman of Dunlop Rubber, which he greatly reorganised, and as first chairman of Imperial Airways he set British civil aviation on as strong a foundation as the inhibiting influence of nationalisation, later imposed on it, would permit. He died in 1937, perhaps the highlight of this remarkable Anderson family.

Sir Alexander Bannerman

the city's first reform M P

Aberdeen has not been so rich in what we might term swashbucklers as many a place in Scotland that had fewer opportunities for producing them than were presented to the sons of Bon-Accord. There were of course Gordons like Sir John of Haddo (who literally lost his head) and Lord Lewis (who skinned the Aberdeen lieges during the Forty-Five); but that sort of rhodomontade was endemic in a family whose name curiously enough, was not Gordon at all after the first two or three generations. There was Sir Alexander Stewart hero of Harlaw, who was not really an Aberdonian though Aberdeen had almost as much to do with him as with any of its own citizens. During last century several of the indwellers might have qualified, including Sir Alexander Anderson himself, and (on the academic side) that very inspiring professor John Stuart Blackie. While it must be to Aberdeen's eternal regret that the county, not the town, can claim what little credit is attached to possession of such a ratepayer as that Prince of Rakes, Abington Baird.

But coeval with these last mentioned three, preceding the eldest of them by almost a generation in birth, there pirouetted across the Aberdeen stage an artist in the tricks of vote-catching and in the manufacture of terminological inexactitudes, Alexander Bannerman. He belonged to a very old Aberdeen family indeed, whose surname was derived from their employment at the Scottish Court away back in the misty days before the Norman Conquest of England. Probably they, who bore the King's standard on the march and in procession, were not then inhabitants of Aberdeen. Somewhere perhaps in the eleventh century they lost the honour, although according to the historian nearest to that period John of Fordun, they were deprived for no fault of their own. The Scrymgeours—now represented by the Earl of Dundee—succeeded them, though the Stuarts of Inchbreck who also came to have a close connection with Aberdeen, also laid claim to the distinction.

After losing the job of carrying the royal standard, the next time the Bannermans came into the public eye was when one of them, Donald, was the King's doctor—the first, incidentally, of a long line of Aberdonians and Aberdeen graduates to fill that office. At Scone in 1366 David II granted 'delicto medico nostro'—to our dear doctor—lands in Clinterty, Auchronie, and a bit more of the country lying west of Bucksburn and Bankhead. The doctor's son got Sclattie a little later. This son, Alexander, was Provost of Aberdeen in 1382. Nothing of much importance occurred during his provostship but in 1387 he bought from Sir Alexander Fraser of Philorth and Cowie the estate of Elsick. A. M. Munro, who doesn't make many mistakes, fell in error in his *Memorials of the Aldermen, Provosts and Lord Provosts of Aberdeen* when he described this Alexander as of Waterton and Elsick, locating Waterton at Ellon. Actually the Provost's Waterton was part of the royal grant first mentioned, and we know it today as Stoneywood though Waterton House there perpetuates the old name. The Bannermans did own Waterton of Ellon eventually, but not until about 1452, when they acquired it and Balmacassie and Abbothill in Ellon parish.

In 1608 a girl of the family, Margaret, married George Gordon of Haddo and became the mother of the Sir John Gordon whose execution in Edinburgh in 1644 was lamented by those of his contemporaries who found it possible to overlook his considerable talent for bad behaviour. The same year Margaret's nephew Alexander fought Sir John Gordon 'for the first blood, whilk Haddoch lost and Elsick was victor'. In 1682 Charles II created the head of the family, again an Alexander, a baronet. His sister, marrying Sir Alexander Keith of Ludquharn, became grandmother of the Sir William Keith of Ludquharn who apparently first carried Bannerman blood to North America when he was appointed Governor of Pennsylvania. He was the friend, though apparently not a very sincere or dependable one, of Benjamin Franklin, who first visited this country on the strength of a recommendation by Sir William.

The second baronet, yet another Alexander, had a son Patrick, born 1678, a merchant in Aberdeen, who was a central figure in a rather lurid episode in the burgh's history. When the last Earl Marischal, on 20 September 1714, marched into Aberdeen and proclaimed the Old Pretender ('Old Mr. Melancholy') as King James VIII in the Castlegate, the Provost was a Hanoverian in sentiment with, apparently a good many of the Council, whereas the Incorporated Trades were Jacobites almost to a man. Local government until Michaelmas, when the elections fell due, was pretty well suspended. And on 28 September, instead of the new Council being elected by the retiring Council in accordance with 'the auld sett' of the town, the election was left to the burgesses of guild and the free craftsmen, who voted for Patrick Bannerman as Provost. From the hustings in Aberdeen at the 1832 election, his descendant, Alexander Bannerman, the subject of this notice, declared, 'It is a singular circumstance, that the last *popular* election in this city was that of my great-grandfather, who was chosen the Chief Magistrate of Aberdeen upwards of a century ago. He was not chosen by the self-elected Corporation but by his fellow-citizens. For the honour which was then conferred upon him, he narrowly escaped losing his head. You may, therefore, suppose he was guilty of some heinous offence. I believe he was guilty of being a firm adherent of the House of Stuart, and he, as well as the electors, were anxious to fulfil the sacred obligation they had come under to that unfortunate but infatuated family, and were, of course, considered rebels.' This, it may be remarked in passing, is a typically oblique description, not by any means unusual in the electioneering speeches of those who, like Alexander Bannerman, have persuaded themselves and try to persuade others they are the forward-looking people. Actually in 1715 the electors were rabbled and had to do as they were told, with pistols in their backs.

And so Patrick Bannerman, when the Old Pretender reached this country, presented him at Dunnottar with an address of congratulation, which won him a 'knighthood' of no validity, although he continued to call himself Sir for the rest of his life and the title is retained on his tombstone in St. Nicholas Churchyard. Under Bannerman the town had to raise a substantial tax and a loan for the Jacobite army in Perth, along with its only printing-press, which with its case of types was sent south to a party who, it must be admitted, were better aware of the value of public relations than the legitimate authorities. When in a few brief weeks the rising was over Bannerman was carried to Carlisle and there tried for treason, but like most of the other prisoners was allowed to go free. He lived on unmolested in Aberdeen until his death in 1733. One of his daughters married Alexander Milne, an Aberdeen merchant who became proprietor of Crimonmogate. Margaret's son, Patrick Milne, willed it to his relative Sir Charles Bannerman, eighth baronet of Elsick, who was head of the cotton firm Gordon, Barron & Company, in the Bannermills (named after the Bannermans). Sir Charles's granddaughter, Ethel, her father's sole heir, married in 1891 the eldest son of the Earl of Southesk, and Crimonmogate is still in that family, whose name is of course Carnegie. The Duke of Fife, son of the present Earl of Southesk, has Elsick.

It has been a long and slightly tortuous road to the subject of our tale, the exceedingly political Alexander Bannerman; though it is perhaps natural seeing that in politics there are 'so many paths that wind and wind'. He was not in the direct line of the head of the family. His uncle, Sir Alexander the seventh baronet was Professor of Medicine at King's College. The Sir Charles who inherited Crimonmogate was another uncle. His cousin was Sir Alexander, the ninth baronet of Elsick and Crimonmogate and Kirkhill in the parish of Dyce. His father, Thomas Bannerman, who was a wine merchant in Aberdeen, married a daughter of George Simpson of Hazlehead and died in 1820. The subject of our sketch was born in 1788. For two years he attended Marischal College, of which in 1834 he was elected Lord Rector, and in which from 1835 to 1847 he was to be dean of the faculty of law, while such eminent men held the Rectorship as Lord Lyndhurst, Lord Brougham, Sir John Herschel the astronomer, and Archibald Alison the historian who on his mother's side belonged to the great Gregory family; in 1847 no Rector was elected, Thomas Babington Macaulay being one of the candidates. Bannerman all his life took a close interest in his college. In 1835 he brought in a Bill in Parliament for the union of King's and Marischal. Like many of his suggestions, it aroused bitter feelings, and it fell through. The following year, along with Provost James Blaikie, he helped to promote the building improvements at Marischal College, which met the college's needs until the whole place was overhauled at the beginning of this century. Before politics fully claimed him he was prominent in Aberdeen business life. He was a partner in the family firm at the Bannermill, in Milne, Cruden and Company, another textile firm; and in Duffus and Company, shipbuilders, which, though only a small concern, built Aberdeen's first steamboat, the *Queen of Scotland*, in 1829. But quite early in his career he began to take a part in the public life of the community, an interest which gradually led him on into the wider political arena.

Politics is the department in which Aberdeen has been least successful in the production of notabilities. This may, to the cynic, be due to an innate practical strain in the Aberdonian, or it may arise from their preference for other forms of power than that which springs from meddling with other people's business. Apart from the famous provost Alexander Jaffray, who has already figured in this series, there is really no one in political history with an Aberdeen origin who matters very much, Alexander Bannerman's two radical contemporaries, Joseph Hume and Sir James Mackintosh, both Aberdeen graduates, being natives the one of Angus and the other of the Black Isle. Bannerman, it must be confessed, added little to our sum of civic wisdom, and accomplished much more for his own social advancement than for the welfare of his constituents or compatriots. But he had to a degree that today, now we have no Irishmen at Westminster, would be considered extraordinary, though it was not all that unusual between Waterloo and the first Reform Act, the faculty of arousing the most acerbated controversy and the most lively polemics. He started off in local politics. The building of Union Street, and a habit in local government of reticence in financial affairs (which today is pretty general with administration everywhere) landed the Corporation of Aberdeen in Queer Street, and its finances had to be put in the hands of trustees. The crisis was greatly exaggerated, and did not, all things considered, last long. The City Fathers had allowed their enthusiasm for the essential and inevitable expansion of the city to outrun their native caution; they calculated too optimistically on the taking up of feus on the new thoroughfare, which would meet the cost of the improvements, and it was only when the canny Aberdonians saw beyond question the practical benefits of the scheme that the money came in at the necessary and prematurely expected rate. The town went into the receiver's hands in 1817 and was released in 1825, its finances once more shipshape. It was the time of the Hadden ascendency. James and Gavin Hadden, from 1801 to 1831, were one or the other of them in the Chair for fifteen years. Although it was Provost Thomas Leys of Glasgoforest who pioneered the Union Street development and although Charles Forbes of Auchmedden, ancestor of the Forbeses of Newe, was Provost when the blow fell, it was James Hadden who, on the early death of Leys, carried through the scheme, and it was on him principally that the odium for the breakdown fell.

Alexander Bannerman entered the Town Council in 1811 and immediately began to conduct himself with the reckless assertiveness so often associated with so-called reformers. He had the gift of lively invective, a command of wild and whirling words, conjoined with an almost complete absence of practical ability which during the next two dozen years or so was to throw him into bold contrast with his great local antagonist James Hadden. For instance, in 1826 Hadden proposed that the Harbour Board should consist of eleven town councillors and nine popularly elected members. This proportion Bannerman denounced as undemocratic and was responsible for having it rejected by Parliament, the lobbying costing the town £3,000. But in 1829 Bannerman petitioned Parliament, successfully, for a Board consisting of all the nineteen members of the Town Council (as it was then constituted) and only six popularly elected members. This remarkable disparity between liberal ideas in theory and in action is not unknown in our own day. Then there was the affair of the steam tugboat at Aberdeen which under Bannerman's direction came to financial grief, and which when James Hadden and the magistrates took it over prospered greatly. In our own day George Bernard Shaw remarked of a Prime Minister that he could not run a whelk stall successfully. That sort of thing, like the poor, is always with us.

But it was not until the passing of the Reform Act of 1832 that the antagonism of the two men came to a head. Bannerman of course was a member of the party of Reform—they were still mainly Whigs with radical tendencies who only after 1832 adopted the designation Liberal which had previously been applied as a depreciatory term. For the first Reform Parliament James Hadden stood as a Tory, with Bannerman as his opponent. Those were great days in British politics. The law of libel then was neither very stringent nor generally respected. Slanders and innuendos that today would land the originator in court were then countered by more emphatic slanders and suggestions. In such an atmosphere Bannerman's wit and eloquence throve. He wrote outrageous but usually funny squibs and pasquils, he made the most damaging allegations, all of which were replied to by champions of the Tory cause. Bannerman and John Davidson, a lawyer's clerk who displayed satirical gifts were the principal authors of the Reform literature, while Alexander Robb, deacon of the Tailor Incorporation, was the outstanding Tory publicist. Near the outset of this series of sketches some samples of that polemical literature were given in the article on the Haddens and no more need be illustrated here. But attention should be drawn to the wonderful store of such 'fringe' papers that have found a safe refuge from time to time in the muniment room of the Town House, a library that has no rival amongst the Scottish burghs for the variety and value of its contents. And the hope may be expressed that these documents may yet find an editor and be given to the public by the Town Council.

When Bannerman challenged James Hadden at the 1832 General Election he made all sorts of allegations about his opponent's conduct of the affairs of the town. These assertions were later impartially investigated and shown to be completely without foundation, but Hadden withdrew from the contest to give Bannerman a walk-over. But the Tories did not allow the victor to get away with it at the time, and their criticisms have stood the test of time rather better than his. Here is one of them: 'It must now be set down as a matter of history that you—a man "on terms of intimacy and friendship with many aristocrats both Whigs and Tories" (a phrase from Bannerman's electioneering papers)—were conducted to a meeting anxious to make you a member of Parliament *by your own nephew and your own barber*, in consequence of a motion made by a sporting *tailor*! O, that but one of the many aristocrats had been present to do the barber's office for one brief hour! O where, in the hour of need, were the many aristocrats loitering, unmindful of their intimate friend? . . . Where was your friend, your associate in borough-mongering, Lord Kintore? Where was his Waddling Fatness, the sylph-like Lord of Panmure?'

And here is part of a most sarcastic poster from a subsequent election:

Great Attraction!
Feats of
Legerdemain
Under the distinguished patronage of the
Non-intrusion Clergy

Signor Bannermanno,
From the Royal Hospital of Greenwich,
Has the honour to announce that he will
repeat this day, and on Monday, his
hitherto unparalleled
Slight-of-hand performances.
Among the extraordinary
Illusions,
Deceptions,
and
Tergiversations
the Signor will perform the following admirable tricks—
1.
The Signor will convert a pampered pensioner and a hireling place man
into a disinterested Patriot and an Independent Member of Parliament.

So on it goes, getting nearer and nearer the bone every time. Mr. Bannerman may have won elections, but he had to pay for them.

He sat for Aberdeen City until 1847, was knighted and on retirement he was appointed lieutenant-governor of Prince Edward Island. In 1854 he became governor of the Bahamas and in 1857 of Newfoundland, Britain's oldest Dominion, so that he must have made a good showing in these posts. Perhaps in some respects he has an even greater claim on our remembrance by having been the husband of Thomas Carlyle's first sweetheart, Margaret Gordon. From a practical joker and local humorist he won a wider contemporary reputation as a clever speaker and a companionable fellow. It is rather his misfortune that his mistakes and his methods evoked protests that, while savage, were well enough written to be worth re-reading even at this distance of time. He died in 1865, just a hundred years ago, as a result of falling on the stairs of his London residence.

Thomas Leys

and the city's expansion

The misguided mortal who seeks to collect personalities as others amass pictures and books and curios is doomed to encounter much frustration in his search for the particulars that are the materials of his hobby. The first personality collector of all, the celebrated Plutarch, comments with unwonted asperity upon the difficulty of acquiring the data necessary to build up a character sketch. The trouble is that most people, when they consider the affairs of men, tend to concentrate upon the affairs rather than the men. From that basic error many of the disabilities of society have arisen. For what matters in life is not events but men, not what is done but the brain and the will that were responsible for the doing.

In the history of our city there can be no better illustration of the frustration caused by this fundamental mistake than our knowledge of the career and personality of one of the greatest of Aberdeen's benefactors. Thomas Leys of Glasgoforest was twice Provost of the burgh. He was also, what no other Provost has been, at his death Convener of the County of Aberdeen. He was the driving force behind the scheme that enabled the burgh to burst through the bonds of its medieval tradition. He was head of the greatest industrial concern not merely in the Aberdeen of his day, but in the whole of Scotland in its particular line of business, a concern upon which patriotic Aberdonians may justifiably look back with pride as the example which all its best firms have followed since its time. It is clear too that Thomas Leys took an active and engaging part in the social life of his contemporaries. But apart from a phrase or a sentence here and there we have precious little in the way of record upon which to reconstruct his life.

It was a short life even by the standards of that time. He was only in his forty-fifth year. He was born in 1764, son of Francis Leys, a substantial burgess and baillie of Aberdeen, and Elizabeth Ingram, whose father was a merchant in Huntly. Before his birth, indeed before his parents were married, Francis Leys had been prominent in the founding, in 1749, of the firm of Leys, Still and Company, for the manufacture of linen thread and cloth. Their premises were at Gordon's Mills, Woodside, on the banks of the Don. We may pause, in passing, to remark on the date of the foundation of the firm. The years immediately succeeding the close of the Forty-Five were, in Aberdeen particularly, characterised by an amazing outburst of financial, commercial, intellectual and social activity. This was due partly to the delayed tonic action of the Legislative Union of 1709 with certain consequential payments to compensate for Scotland's losses in the Darien Scheme (Aberdeen may thus have got quite a few thousands of capital that had been written off as a dead loss), and partly through the removal of the fear of civil commotion by the defeat of the Jacobites.

Old Leys died in 1788. In a letter dated 7 November of that year we read: 'Mr. Leys died on Tuesday afternoon, at 4 o'clock; his corpse remains still unburied; his son being in a feaver for these two days, and Lairney (Alexander Brebner of Learney, his son-in-law) was not come to town, unless late last night.' Three weeks later the same correspondent reports: 'Its said Leys has left better than £20,000; what will not saving accumulate.' It is hardly necessary here to remark that a pound in 1778 was worth ten or twelve today. Thomas Leys therefore succeeded to a substantial fortune. At once he proceeded to use it wisely. The old man had, as the above extract implies, been cautious in his spending. Only three years after his death we find not only the name of his famous firm altered, but its whole policy remodelled. In 1791 Leys, Still and Company became Leys, Masson and Company. John Still, the father's partner, a merchant in Aberdeen and proprietor of the small estate of Millden, near Balmedie, had died in 1790. The partners of Leys, Masson and Company were Francis Leys, his brother-in-law Alexander Brebner of Learney, and James Hadden, all of them destined to occupy Aberdeen's civic chair, Leys and Brebner twice and Hadden four times. As partner there was joined with them a little later James Masson, who was a town councillor.

In 1792 the company arranged with the superior, John Paton of Grandholm to be allowed to open a canal or water-course to drive their spinning-mill machinery. Besides the mill, they had a bleachfield with elaborate cuts for watering; an iron foundry, and other equipment. The first spinning-mill was seven storeys high and had 386 windows. They spanned the Don with a 150-foot wooden bridge that cost £1,200, with an access road 40 feet wide and a bridge over the Aberdeenshire Canal when it was made later. Between 1805 and 1820 the firm spent £62,594 16s. 2½d. on machinery, and up to 1828 their total expenditure on the place was over £100,000. In the great mill there were 240 spinning-frames, 15,000 spindles, and 100 power looms. They paid out nearly £40,000 a year in wages, more or less carrying the community of Woodside on their back. They even ran a canteen for their employees, supplying breakfast and dinner at three half-pence a meal per head. Dundee's mills were as nothing to them. Leys, Masson and Company towered in majestic grandeur over all their competitors.

Much of that is looking forward a little, beyond Thomas Leys's death. And while our sights are thus aligned, it would seem to be silly to omit the tale of an exploit which could be read today as an industrial parable. The firm, having acquired some adjacent industrial equipment, which involved the use of additional water-power, secured from Gordon, Barron and Company, the cotton manufacturers, who had a mill on the other bank of the Don, permission to apply this water to their own purposes. In 1816 the linen firm of Milne, Cruden and Company at Upper Persley closed down and Leys, Masson and Company bought the remainder of their lease. That was on 20 August. On 21 August James Hadden, now the senior partner, and his son Alexander had collected seventy or eighty labourers, taken them out to the mills with all the barrows, pickaxes, shovels and other gear that belonged to the Corporation and the Harbour Trustees, and set them at 2 a.m. to the task of deepening the channel of the lade that served Milne, Cruden's works. They toiled to such effect, under the eye and with the oral encouragement of the redoubtable James himself, that before the day was out they had so deepened not merely the lade but the Don itself at the point of outfall that the volume of water capable of being carried was increased sixfold. It is hardly necessary to remark that the proceedings were a complete abuse of Gordon, Barron's permit, and the latter firm applied for and got an interdict. But before their application could be made the job was done and could not be undone. For nearly twenty years to come actions for damages by Gordon, Barron and by the riparian proprietors upstream against Leys, Masson and Company constituted a rich dreepin' roast to the legal profession, and in the end were settled out of court. But the episode illustrates how our forefathers could get a job done when they sought to increase productivity. Today, what with local authority and Home Department sanction, sanitary and planning conditions, even at a time when it is recognised at the seats of the mighty that unless we step up production the national economy is sunk, it would take years to get done what James Hadden and his scratch squad of dargers and his borrowed tools accomplished overnight.

Until his death Thomas Leys was very much the inspiration behind the development of this great firm between 1791 and 1809. During the same period he performed a like service for the community of Aberdeen. In the final third of the eighteenth century the population of the burgh pretty well doubled. The town was intolerably congested. Expanding business, new ideas of health and sanitation, and improved transport—although all of them would no doubt seem rather trivial in scope and extent to us —were putting a terrific pressure upon public life. In the eighties there was considerable talk of finding a speedier and more commodious exit from the town than the line of the Green, the Bow Brig over the Denburn (its arch is still preserved in Union Terrace Gardens), Windmill Brae, the Crabstane, and the Hardgate. The Castlegate may have been the finest square in Scotland but its western end was a jumble of mean alleys and a clutter of old houses, and it was only through these that the traveller could set out, from the New Inn next the Tolbooth, on journeys south, west or north. The Castlegate's main western exit was a lane upon the fairway of which there was little more than sufficient room to swing the proverbial cat, called accurately the Narrow Wynd, running along the line of what is now the southern face of the Townhouse and the northern side of Union Street. It connected deviously with the Netherkirkgate, via another narrow alley called Rotten Row, which ran from the top of the Shiprow to the southern end of the Guestrow. Covering the present terrain of the eastern end of Union Street were the northern slopes, with their houses and gardens, of St. Katherine's Hill. It may be added that there has been much speculation as to the derivation of Rotten Row, but no one hitherto has suggested Rottan Row, the street of the rats, which would have come up from the boats in the harbour by way of the Shiprow to the cosier parts of the town.

While Thomas Leys was still busily engaged in developing the family firm, he may as proprietor of the small estate of Glasgoforest, on the boundary of the parishes of Kintore and Kinellar, have been interested in the county road-making which was in progress under the direction of Charles Abercrombie, a well-known surveyor. It is significant that the main road to the North was laid out to run within a hundred yards of the Leys country house instead of half a mile to the east along the old Wine (or Wain, meaning waggon) Causeway that had borne the public traffic since the days of Robert the Bruce. No doubt his interest was drawn in a practical way to the subject of transport communications, and although he was not, apparently, present at the meetings in Aberdeen at which Aberdeen's access problems were discussed, he very quickly, once he did appear on the scene, played a leading part. From the point of view of Aberdeen Town Council which round about the year 1801 (the Year One as our forefathers used to call it) had irons in the fire to the tune of half a million pounds, this question of a way out and in for the Town's travellers and trade had come at a rather inconvenient juncture. There was the Aberdeenshire Canal project; there was the improvement of the harbour, upon which the two most distinguished engineers of the day, Rennie and Telford, had been consulted, and which was to cost a mint of money; there was the Bridewell, the female prison, halfway along what is now Rose Street; and there was the burgh's participation in the road to the south beyond the Bridge of Dee.

As regards the way out of the Castlegate to the west, the first plan apparently was to drive a road at the south-west corner right over the crown of St. Katherine's Hill, and then along the old line of the Green and Windmill Brae improving the existing way as the works progressed. But eventually, after the Town Council had deliberated and hesitated and deliberated again, and after a meeting of the ratepayers had set up a committee under Provost Leys's chairmanship, the decision was reached to clear away the Narrow Wynd and Rotten Row and the whole accumulation of hovels there and to make for the Denburn on what is now the line of Union Street. This involved slicing a huge chunk off the northern slope of St. Katherine's Hill, but as it was equally necessary, in order to achieve sufficient elevation to throw a bridge over the Denburn, to build up the line of route as we now know it, the soil could be used to form the embankment. Besides the bridge over the Denburn, subsidiary bridges were required to span Carnegie's Brae and Correction Wynd. The whole cost of the works from Union Street to the Denburn, and including Union Bridge, was put at £6,493 6s. 8d. and of the making of the south end of King Street at £625 3s. 4d. To meet the cost it was first estimated that to buy up the property between the Castlegate and the Denburn would require £20,000; but that figure soon rose to £30,000, towards which the reckoning was that new feus along the street would be given off to the value of £27,000, leaving the town to find £3,000. But the owners of the property concerned dug in their toes, there were then no compulsory powers of purchase for local authorities, and between inflated compensation and Union Bridge swallowing up £13,000, the expense was soon at the level of £73,000. And as was mentioned in the previous article of this series, the accumulated burden finally landed the Corporation in bankruptcy.

Leys was Provost for the two years to Michaelmas 1799, and upon him fell the burden of resolving the doubts and demurrings of his colleagues on the Town Council, and of acting first as their liaison officer with the general public and later as leader of the public towards the goal which the public had chosen. It was his successor in the civic chair, John Dingwall of Ardo and Rannieston, about the last of the great Aberdeen stocking manufacturers, to whom there fell the satisfaction of sending up and in due course of announcing the passing of the bill embodying the proposals that led to the making of Union Street and King Street and through that, of the modern Aberdeen. And it was John Dingwall who, when he laid the foundation-stone of Union Bridge in July 1801, said in reference to a remark by Alexander Allardyce, M.P. for Aberdeen, 'I cannot omit this opportunity of joining you, as I am sure all present will, in the just eulogium you have bestowed upon the exertions of my worthy predecessor, Mr. Leys, who has, by his perseverance and zeal, contributed so essentially to bring this work to its present advanced stage'. That was all the thanks Provost Leys got for putting through an improvement in Aberdeen's civic and economic situation equal to the clearing of the harbour channel by Davie do A'thing 200 years before and the enterprises of Alexander Anderson a generation afterwards. When in 1803 Union Street was completed to the western end of the bridge the then Provost, James Hadden, was called 'the father of the city'. But Leys was the father, Hadden the step-father.

The story of Provost Leys has so far been about his interests, both private and public, rather than himself. There is regrettably little more to say. He was a captain in the Royal Aberdeen Volunteer Corps, raised in 1801 for home defence in case of invasion by Napoleon. The Corps was disbanded on the signing of the Peace of Amiens that autumn but when war was resumed in 1803 and new bodies were raised, the Lieutenant-Colonel Commandant of the Aberdeen Volunteers was Thomas Leys, with his partners James Hadden as Lieutenant-Colonel and Alexander Brebner as

Major. At Michaelmas 1803 he became Provost for a second term of two years and in that capacity and as chairman of Leys, Masson and Company he would have been present at the opening of the Canal in 1806 between Aberdeen and Port Elphinstone. He died on 24 October 1809. We could gladly have known much more of him. There is a social glimpse of him in a letter of December 1790 by an Aberdeen baillie. 'I am dress'd, so far as an old fellow ought to be—to dine with young Leys; what would his father have said to Tom giving dinners, the hour four o'clock.' In those days one or two o'clock was the accepted dining hour. And in that store-house of Aberdeen lore, *A Short Memoir of James Young*, we are informed that James Hadden as Provost 'carried out with energetic decision' the ideas of his deceased friend Thomas Leys. 'The new streets . . . were not—as by many at the present day they are believed to have been—projected by Mr. Hadden, but owed their origin principally to the taste and discriminating foresight of Provost Thomas Leys of Glasgoforest.' It's a good epitaph.

Epilogue: The mighty firm of Leys, Masson and Company crashed in the economic blizzard of 1848, which caused the allied Hadden firm also to close temporarily. Under James Hadden's son Alexander and another, Leys, Masson restarted in 1850, a shadow of its former self, and in 1854 it shut down for ever. Like a certain Clyde shipyard of our own day, it had been too progressive. Unlike that firm, it existed in an age when Governments knew enough of their own shortcomings to deter them from engaging in business.

Alexander Bain

weaver's son who popularised psychology

Whether those who acquire a national or international reputation are on that account greater or more useful men than those whose fame and achievement are confined to a local habitation is perhaps hardly a subject for discussion here. But it does irresistibly obtrude itself in any such series a this. No Aberdonian was better known in the world in the nineteenth century, few Aberdonians of the past are so often mentioned today, as Alexander Bain. Yet, was his advancement of the study of psychology more to the benefit of mankind than the inspired work of such contemporaries as Alexander Anderson in local government, as William McCombie in agricultural improvement, as J. F. White or Alexander Macdonald or James Melvin in the diffusion of cultural equipment to their own and subsequent generations? Perhaps the judgment will depend upon what the judge thinks of psychology!

Alexander Bain, quite apart from his academic eminence, gives the impression of being a queer mixture of contradictions. His face was that of a poet or artist, with clear-cut features and kindly but what Carlyle would have called 'seeing eyes'. Few portraits deserve more the epithet 'high-souled' than his, yet he himself denied the existence of a soul. To judge by his looks, his writings should be stylish, exciting, even glamorous; instead, they are if anything dull and far from inspiring. Yet he was within limits a great teacher, and he was over a wide field an independent and a creative thinker, regarded in the second half of last century as worthy to be mentioned in the same sentence as John Stuart Mill and Herbert Spencer and Thomas Henry Huxley—which was pretty good going for a poor Gilcomston laddie. His grandfather had had a small farm in Leochel-Cushnie, his father served in the reserve battalion of the 92nd, the Gordon Highlanders, from 1803 to 1814, when he returned to Aberdeen, took to the trade of handloom weaving, and raised a family of eight, of whom only the second, Alexander, lived to see forty. No representative of the family now remains. Alexander was born on 11 June 1818, in Skene Square.

Anyone raised and permanently residing in a given locality makes contact in some way with most of the outstanding personalities in it. My mother was brought up on Bain's English grammar and composition textbooks, which she used as a groundwork for my education before ever I went to school. My old friend William Walker's father worked in the same 'shop' as Bain's father and used to recall the boy running messages and bringing tobacco for the weavers. Many years later when Bain was famous and comparatively well-to-do, he always gave a sixpence or a shilling for a halfpenny or penny paper to a certain newsboy with a Union Street stance, who had been employed in that now forgotten weaving shop. This liberality I have heard described as not in Bain's character, but it is most certainly in keeping with the expression of benevolence in his portraits. Even Sir George Reid's profile of him, which conveys a slightly cynical smugness—and Reid was probably the only artist with the discernment to see the scepticism in Bain's face—nevertheless suggests a well-informed philanthropy in repose. He could, it should be added, be pretty caustic when he liked.

His father, then an old dame, then a couple of students who ran a kind of school, then the school attached to Gilcomston Church—such was his education, which came to a close when he was eleven. He had by then some Latin, a good deal of mathematics, some knowledge of English, a little history and geography and quite a lot of Biblical instruction. His father could not afford, as he would have liked, to send him to the Grammar School. Today there would of course be no difficulty, yet how many of those modern 'assisted passengers' reach the University, as Bain by his own efforts did, and how few are likely to reach the eminence to which he attained! Until 1836, when mainly through the help of another great Aberdeen teacher, Dr. Cruickshank, he entered Marischal College, Bain's classrooms were an auctioneer's office, a smithy, and the Mechanics Institution, and he made a living first as an auctioneer's messenger, then at the loom, while at the same time he was secretary and a mathematics teacher in the Mechanics Institution, which he and some friends had helped to revive. He put himself through College, graduating in 1840 equal first as the best Arts student of his year.

Among his college friends at Aberdeen was David Masson, who like many an eminent Aberdonian of the Victorian era spent part of his life as a journalist, and who eventually settled in Edinburgh where he became Professor of English and was responsible for an edition of John Milton which still is the standard work on the poet. Bain had for another close friend Andrew Findlater, a native of New Aberdour, who was for a time headmaster of Gordon's College, and became the first editor of *Chambers's Encyclopedia.* But for ten years after completing his university course, Bain's ways and work lay outside Aberdeen. He did some duty as an assistant or deputy professor at Marischal College, then he was elected to what was called a professorship in Mathematics and Natural Philosophy in the Andersonian University of Glasgow, from which he soon resigned as it 'did not reward the trouble'. He had for years been doing a great deal of work in the shape of articles in various learned journals and reviews in London, and at the close of 1847 he was invited 'to examine and digest a number of returns connected with the work of the Metropolitan Sanitary Commission then recently appointed'. The report he presented led to his being appointed to the Commission on Sewers under the Board of Health which coincided with a serious outbreak of cholera in London and elsewhere that eventually overwhelmed the Commission with a load of work for which it was not fitted or intended. So in 1850 Bain left the Board, being to a considerable extent influenced by the fact that he had acquired the habit of doing literary work during office hours when official business did not engross the whole time; and that literary work was more congenial if not more remunerative.

By this time Bain's contributions to the philosophical and scientific journals were beginning to attract attention in the circles where recognition was most likely to be valuable to him professionally. He owed his introduction to London's learned society first of all to John Robertson, the Aberdonian who migrated thither and became not only a leading art critic but the father of Sir Johnston Forbes Robertson the great Shakespearean actor, and so grandfather of the delightful lady whom we all associate with Peter Pan. Bain's earliest extant experiment in literature was a speech a few weeks after he entered Marischal College in 1836 at a dinner in honour of James

Adam, the extremely competent and combative editor of the *Aberdeen Herald*. Next came an essay, entered unsuccessfully for the Blackwell Prize, consisting of a comparison of the styles of the leading writers in the reigns of Elizabeth and Anne. Yet another unsuccessful attempt to win a prize was on the rather unexpected subject of 'the sin of cruelty to animals'. His first appearance in the metropolitan press was in the *Westminster Review* of July 1840, and the subject again was rather out of character with the writer's subsequent career. It dealt with two recent discoveries, the electrotype and the daguerreotype, and it is evident that Bain hit on these subjects much as a journalist finds a novel topic when he has been unable to exploit a chosen theme. This in Bain's case had been no less formidable than 'Induction', one of the great methods of reasoning employed by philosophers, and one which in his later years he himself practised while marshalling his examples on empirical lines. The editors of the *Westminster Review*, perhaps not surprisingly, hesitated to entrust the development of so intricate a subject to a young man of twenty-two. For those who may have secret ambitions for the pursuit of a literary career or even of writing as a hobby, Bain's description of his plan in his first London essay is not without value. 'The method of the exposition was to isolate all the steps of the process of the two portions (i.e. the electrotype and the daguerreotype), and to give a clear and emphatic expression to each in such language as would be generally intelligible.' The last eight words are crucial, but how few of the latter-day philosophers or scientists ever practise that style!

The *Westminster Review* had been started by John Stuart Mill in 1820 to further the beliefs of the Utilitarian school of philosophy. Just before Bain's first article appeared, Mill had sold the magazine but it was through his influence that the new owner-editors began to accept his contributions. Mill's father James was an Angus man, who changed the spelling of his name from Milne because the English habitually pronounced the silent 'n' in it, a custom which has deplorably crept into Scottish usage. John Stuart Mill was one of Bain's leading friends and helpers at the beginning of his career. Robertson brought the two together, and it was Robertson also who introduced Bain to Thomas Carlyle, from whose 'Heroes' he records that he 'derived from it a portion of the stimulation that it gave to the then young generation'. Mill introduced him to George Grote, the celebrated historian of ancient Greece, and during a visit to Paris in 1851 he met Auguste Comte, whom Mill and Grote had rescued from destitution and who has come down in history as the founder of the Positivist school of philosophy. In fact, Bain began to touch life at many points. In those days prospects for a young Aberdonian with any kind of brains in London could be very exciting, and although the subjects in which Bain had made up his mind to specialise may not today seem to many people to offer many opportunities for advancement, he was in fact a pretty good all-round scholar and he was developing along lines which were to be of the utmost importance in the development of the structure of our economy today.

Besides reviews of numerous scientific, philosophical and historical works, Bain at this time became the author of several educational treatises or articles upon such subjects as electricity, astronomy, language, logic and rhetoric—foreshadowing future developments in his career. In 1855 he published the first of his important books, *The Senses and the Intellect*, and in 1859 the second, *The Emotions and the Will*, in which he made a systematic survey of the make-up of man. A little later the first overt signs appeared of his steadily deepening interest in psychology, with which today his name is chiefly associated, although it had attracted him from the very beginning of his intellectual career. The foundations had been laid by John Locke and David Hume and the great French encyclopædists of the Age of Reason. In 1868 he collected and compressed his thoughts on the subject in *Mental and Moral Science*, sub-titling the book 'a compendium of psychology and ethics' and this ground plan, as it were, was built upon four years later in a series of sectional studies in mental and moral science. In 1876 he founded the magazine *Mind*, still in existence and printed in Aberdeen, whose first editor, George Croom Robertson, was one of Bain's old students. The importance of psychology in industrial and commercial relations, and the influence, for good or ill on our business economy today, of whatever theories happen for the time being to be fashionable in that field, do not require to be more than mentioned to intelligent observers such as read this journal. But it may safely be hazarded that Bain himself would have got a scare had he lived to see the consequences of his pioneering.

Bain's enterprise in philosophical exploration does not exhaust, nor is it the chief part of, his contribution to the civilisation and culture not merely of Aberdeen and the North-East but through Aberdonians abroad, of the world. In 1860 he was appointed, in the teeth of very strong opposition from the then Principal, from both the Established Church and the Free (with some notable exceptions in individual ministers), and from many of the Professors of both King's and Marischal, on the eve of the union that created the University of Aberdeen, to the Chair of Logic. It was a three or even four-legged chair for in addition to logic, rhetoric, English and psychology were included in the syllabus of his department. It is hardly an exaggeration to say that Bain was chiefly responsible for laying those sound foundations upon which Aberdeen's reputation for higher education was raised. Great teachers like James Melvin had paved the way, and educational benefactions like the Dick and Milne bequests had helped, but for eighty years after 1860 the chair that Bain won and made his own did more than any other, in itself and latterly in its progeny, the Chalmers Chair of English, to keep the Lamp of the North burning brightly. His textbooks upon English grammar and composition, on logic and on the science of education may be out of circulation today, but ere they were superseded their influence had ensured that they could be superseded with impunity. In the Logic and Psychology class, which engrossed the main work of the chair, Bain was of course in his element, and his influence was naturally direct and powerful. Only sixty half-hours were allowed to English, yet curiously it was here, although he discarded all attempts to discuss literature, that he taught most truly. 'His clean, polished elocution, that modulated itself so perfectly to fit all shades of emphasis, completed the charm and the general effect was magical and immediate.' The same student summed up Bain's English teaching as laying 'great stress on the homely and prosaic virtues of clearness and precision, on the merits of brevity, on the arts of transition and connection, and on the building of paragraphs'. Alexander, thou shouldst be living at this hour; Aberdeen hath need of thee!

When he retired in 1880 he was almost immediately elected Rector of the University, after a good deal of opposition, but in 1884 he was re-elected, defeating no less redoubtable a rival than Lord Randolph Churchill. He was succeeded in the Logic Chair by another of his old students, William Minto, who in turn was followed—in the newly formed Chair of English—by Herbert John Clifford Grierson, and he in 1915 by Adolphus Alfred Jack. The quartet accomplished something in academic achievement that has not been excelled by any similar succession in Scotland, not even by that notable foursome in the corresponding chair at Edinburgh, William Edmondstoune Aytoun, David Masson, George Saintsbury and H. J. C. Grierson. Bit by bit and facet by facet a magnificent cultured edifice was built up which has reacted not merely upon the corporate and business life in the hinterland of the university, but also wherever the post-union graduates have spent their lives, not least in India and the Dominions. The extent to which that academic tradition inspired first-class administrative and managerial, as well as purely cultural, intelligence is probably appreciated by only the few who have taken the trouble to follow the careers of its product.

Bain died in 1903. His *Autobiography*, published in 1904 with a supplement by W. L. Davidson ('Bourtie'), his assistant and successor in the Logic Chair, is a remarkable record of great achievement recorded in plain prose with an occasional twinkle of slightly caustic humour.

The Rev James Robertson

founder of the fertiliser industry

The contribution, outside their strictly professional activities, that ministers of the Church of Scotland have made to the administrative, cultural, commercial and industrial life of the North-East of Scotland has never been properly appraised. Beginning with Dr. William Guild, first patron of the Incorporated Trades, who has already figured in this series these services extend in almost unbroken sequence to the present day. Quite recently we had ministers of the Kirk filling the offices of Lord Provost of Aberdeen and Convener of the County, while in education it is perhaps natural that a profession which has always been associated with the training of youth should still be in the forefront—so far as modern bureaucracy allows—of educational administration. When Aberdeen's first School Board was formed, the phalanx in it of divines of all denominations was formidable both in numbers and in the impetus they gave to the encouragement of Aberdeen's scholastic ambitions.

While there are few spheres of human endeavour into which clergymen have not ventured, perhaps that in which their presence is most unexpected is what we may term the market place. Invention, industry, commerce, practical science, have all claimed the attention of Aberdonian luminaries of Auld Zion. In the spacious days of the eighteenth century the Principal of King's College, the Rev. John Chalmers, was tenant of the farm of Cairntradlin, in Kinellar, and through the Gordon's Mill Farming Club helped to spread progressive ideas throughout the agricultural population. Towards the end of the century two of the most illustrious of Scottish scientists—they were 'amateurs' in that, like Principal Chalmers, they drove their profession and their hobby as a tandem—were the incumbents of Aberdeenshire parishes. The Rev. George Skene Keith was minister of Montkeggie, now called Keith-hall. The author of the Agricultural Survey of Aberdeenshire, he was a most versatile researcher in many branches of natural science. He was also a shrewd psychologist. At the back door of his manse there stood a barrel of ale and a pannikin, so that thirsty souls might weet their thrapples. No minister was so much sought after by his male parishioners. His son, who succeeded him, substituted water for ale, and the flow of visitors ceased.

The Rev. Alexander John Forsyth, minister of Belhelvie for more than half a century, invented the percussion lock which, with the alteration of the firing tube made by Major Patrick Ferguson of Pitfour, gave us substantially the modern rifle. Forsyth spent some years during the Napoleonic Wars in the Tower of London, perfecting his invention in a laboratory there, but the War Office of those days, like its successor with the tank a century later, was unimpressed, and both the German and French armies had the needle gun and the chassepot respectively before the Black Watch in 1840 were armed with the Forsyth invention. Like Skene Keith, an excellent natural scientist, Forsyth divined the presence of a peat moss under the sea opposite the coast of his parish, a surmise substantiated by the present writer when the digging of a drainage course through the links uncovered a deep bed of peat at a depth of about 8 feet. No doubt Forsyth, had he lived today, would have shown his usual perception in associating the presence of the peat with the proximity of deposits of natural gas, which may well prove to be greater off the Aberdeenshire coast than anywhere in the North Sea. But being 'Scotland' they no doubt will be the last to be exploited.

But of all the Kirk ministers who have influenced the community on lines not strictly ecclesiastical, the Rev. Dr. James Robertson, at one time minister of Ellon, must surely bear the palm. His name will not be mentioned in the encyclopaedias. The credit for his most enduring achievement is denied to him by a silence which probably is more likely to cover ignorance or national prejudice than any argument against his having done what he actually did do, and when. Robertson has in fact never got full credit for a life full of good and constructive work in several spheres. He was a prominent educationist, a first-rate scientist, a progressive farmer, and to him more than to any other man the Church of Scotland is indebted for its remarkable recovery from the deep wounds inflicted upon it by the Disruption and the consequent loss of more than a third of its ministers and its members. Even at this distance of time we still hear much of the genius and eloquence and character of Thomas Chalmers, which were undoubtedly very great. But of the man who stood over against him, accomplishing the much more difficult task of shoring up a crumbling building and supporting a cause that, whether good or bad, was sufficiently open to criticism to have alienated such a massive section of the quondam faithful, we get nothing. The Scottish biographical dictionaries compiled by Anderson and by Thomson, like the *Encyclopaedia Britannica* and *Chambers's Encyclopaedia*, although the one shortly before then was edited by an Aberdonian and the other was started by a native of the parish next to that where Robertson was born, never allude to him. He gets a short notice in the *Dictionary of National Biography* which records the salient points in his career without punching them out as their importance deserves.

This illustrious member of Clan Donachy, which is credited with having been the mob of camp followers whose appearance on the rising ground behind Bruce's army is said to have struck panic into the hearts of the English at Bannockburn, was born the first of ten children to the farmer of Ardlaw, in the parish of Pitsligo. His mother was an Anderson and although her lineage is not established, readers of these articles will be inclined to wag sapient heads and remark that James Robertson with that blood in him could not fail to be pretty good. His birthday was the second day of the year 1803. At the age of six he appeared at the neighbouring school of Tyrie with the Proverbs of Solomon under his arm; he plunged into the Classics the following year, and when he was 12, after a couple of months with the rector of Aberdeen Grammar School he entered Marischal College. Ill health held him up for a bit, but in 1818 he was being professionally hailed as the second best mathematician, and the best student in moral philosophy and logic in living memory. For a term or two James Outram, later the Bayard of India, was a classmate. From Arts he went into Divinity, and in accordance with the custom then for poor young fellows aiming at the pulpit he was appointed schoolmaster at Pitsligo in 1825, a few months before he was licensed to preach. Within a year or so, in consequence of a pamphlet he wrote upon the effect of Free Trade upon the cultivation of corn, the Duke of Gordon made him tutor and librarian at Gordon Castle.

Thence in 1829 he entered public life on his appointment as Headmaster of Robert Gordon's College. That famous seminary had then got rather out of hand as regards the conduct of its inmates—it was still a boarding-school—and the quality of its teaching. In his three years as head Robertson improved the one temporarily and the other permanently. He for long took the maths classes in addition to his duties as headmaster, and there is emphatic testimony to the excellence of his mode of instruction. He appears, however, to have had his heart in the ministry and in 1832 Lord Aberdeen, the principal heritor in Ellon, presented him on the advice of the Duke of Gordon to the Ythanside parish. There for a dozen years he reigned supreme not so much as 'pope of the parish', but rather as guide, philosopher and friend to all and sundry, and not least as preceptor in their own business to such of the farmers as paid attention to his advice. His brother Alexander was one of the leading farmers in the county, extending the family farm and leaving it in the condition it still enjoys, that of one of the best and earliest in the North-East. James had worked like the rest of the family on the farm during the very lengthy college vacations of those days, and in fact only a few days before his death he challenged and beat at the shearing-hook a younger man considered proficient in that art. Given a parish with a glebe and such an upbringing, it was inevitable that Ellon's minister should turn farmer, and being a keen mathematician with a fair grounding in the natural sciences it was almost impossible that he should fail to experiment.

Outwith his outstanding services to his church, Robertson's chief claim on our remembrance, and especially on the remembrance of the industrial and farming community, is his work on chemical fertilisers. On the authority probably of his biographer, Professor Charteris (himself son-in-law, by the way, of Sir Alexander Anderson), the *Dictionary of National Biography* credits Robertson with having been the first in Great Britain to apply what was called dissolved bones as manure. It is rather an involved and in some ways a somewhat obscure story which the present writer has never had the leisure or opportunity thoroughly to sort out. But something like this was what happened. In the thirties of last century, when Robertson entered into enjoyment of his glebe, it had become fairly common for progressive farmers to apply what was called bone dust to their turnip ground. Only recently had turnips ceased to be sown broadcast. With the spread of the drill method of sowing the crop had been considerably increased and its handling simplified, and the gradual substitution of the selling of fat cattle to the south (whither they were consigned by boat from Aberdeen harbour) for the raising of stores to be sold at Falkirk Tryst, the aim was naturally to make the most of a vegetable which, whatever the pundits may say, is still supreme for the production of quality beef.

In his long and masterly contribution on the parish of Ellon to the *New Statistical Account of Scotland*, Robertson, dating his essay as in May 1841 alludes to the use of bone-dust for the manuring of turnips, which he says is 'beyond belief' in the area, 60,000 bushels being imported by sea into Newburgh alone. He also makes a plea for the establishment of an experimental farm to further the principles enunciated in 1840 in an epoch making work on agricultural chemistry by Baron Justus von Liebig. For several years Robertson had been experimenting on the glebe with turnips and bone meal. About the same time Sir John Bennett Lawes, the farming baronet of Rothamsted, began to make similar trials in pots, which he eventually extended to the field scale. In the course of his investigations, and influenced by the Liebig publication already alluded to, Robertson developed his researches by applying sulphuric acid to the bone dust, and thus producing the equivalent of what we now know as super-phosphates. Lawes in 1842 began to treat rock phosphates (not bones) with sulphuric acid, and most English authorities accordingly credit him with having invented super-phosphates and with having started the artificial fertiliser industry. One of the obscure aspects of the story, however, is a statement (which the present writer has not tried to substantiate) that a patent for this new fertiliser was refused on the strength of articles in the *Mark Lane Express* and the *Farmers' Magazine*. These articles were written by William Hay, the schoolmaster of Tillydesk, near Arnage, who was a close friend of Robertson and was associated with him in the experiments. The truth of the matter seems to be that Liebig the professional chemist, Robertson the clerical farmer, and Lawes the inquiring lord of the manor had all the same idea about the same time, that Robertson on a field scale and Lawes in pots were seeking the vital clue to the viability of their experiments, that Liebig hit on the clue, which Robertson, being further advanced in his researches, was the first to be able to exploit on a practical scale. The Scottish Agricultural Industries' chemical fertiliser factories at Sandilands and Dyce both owe their origin to James Robertson, and at Sandilands his inspiring lead has always been recognised.

No doubt Robertson, while proud of his agricultural pioneering, would have regarded it as much less important than the great campaign which became the aim and object of his life after he left Ellon in 1843. His promotion of super-phosphates was in some degree an accident, the work of an enthusiastic amateur. But in saying that we must observe that we are drawing attention to the cardinal weakness of specialisation, whether in education or in life. Specialisation may provide greater efficiency on a narrow front, but it is the man with disseminated interests who becomes the true leader and who, in himself, leads the fullest and the happiest existence. Professionally, Robertson could be described by the old eighteenth century term of Moderate, to which section of the Church of Scotland belonged the great historian, Principal Robertson, 'Jupiter' Carlyle of Inveresk (which parish in the early twenties of this century was occupied by a native of Methlick), and John Horne the author of the Scottish play 'Douglas' which evoked from an excited Edinburgh patriot the triumphant ejaculation, 'Whaur's your Willie Shakespeare noo?' Robertson was not so far to the religious Right as that. Indeed, such words of his as have come down to us are, like those of Thomas Chalmers and William Robertson Smith, vibrant with a passionate belief which is not nowadays quite so obvious in the ecumenical debates that are in the contemporary fashion. Robertson had no difficulty like many another 'hameowre' minister of his own and the next generation or two, in bringing the farm servants to church—which few of them enter now. Thorough was his ascendancy in Ellon. When, before the Disruption, the party in the Church who wanted the abolition of that patronage which eventually was one of the main causes of the split, held a meeting in the village woodyard, an Aberdeenshire baronet who made a remark that was taken to be an aspersion on the minister was summarily dropped into a sawpit in the yard.

Up to the Disruption James Robertson and the destined leader of the seceders, Thomas Chalmers, were friends, united in their approach to one of the Church's great problems. Population was expanding—there was quite a lot of emigration even then, but proportionally it was hardly noticeable—and there weren't churches, or for that matter parishes, to meet the need. When the battle was over, Chalmers had a big enough assignment in the amazing campaign which led to the building of a church, a manse, and often a hall in practically every parish in Scotland. Robertson, on his appointment to the Chair of Divinity and Church History in the Divinity Hall in Edinburgh, became convener of the Auld Kirk Committee which was variously known as Church Extension and Endowment. By the time of his death on 2 December 1860, he had pretty well filled up the blanks, and by the end of the century the scheme that he had directed had made sixty-five new parishes, many more churches, and had disbursed half a million pounds.

At the Disruption Robertson, nominally the second man in the Church of Scotland hierarchy, was in reality its leader. Here he is, as described by Hugh Miller, the scribe of the Free Church in those days. After a reference to Dr. Cook, of Haddington, the nominal leader, Miller proceeds: 'Now mark, beside the Doctor, a man of a very different appearance, in stature not exceeding the middle size, but otherwise of such large proportions that they might serve a robust man of six feet. He speaks, and the voice seems as uncommon as the appearance of the man, and the effect is heightened by a strong northern accent, which rings powerfully on the ear, and in the remote galleries—not a single tone is lost. That man might address in the open air some eight or ten thousand people. He is the very beau ideal of a vigorous democrat, that uncouth, powerful-looking man, so fitted apparently for leading the masses is the great friend and confidant to the Tory Earls of Dalhousie, Haddington and Aberdeen.' Miller meant the last phrases as disparagement, but many a cottared man and wife could have testified to Robertson's being as much their friend and confidant as he could ever be to any belted earl. (To prevent misconception, it had better be stated that had the writer been alive at the Disruption, he would have 'come out' with Chalmers and the eight ministers of Aberdeen!)

James Robertson became Moderator of the General Assembly of the Church of Scotland in 1857. He did not live to see the passage of the Act that abolished the patronage that was so obnoxious to the seceders, and which actually was a breach of the Treaty of Union. What he would have thought of Reunion and the amalgamation of parishes and discarding of churches that have come as consequences is not difficult to divine, granted his robust and practical common sense.

Some acclimatised strangers

Bishop Elphinstone

Hitherto in this series the subjects have been, if not all native-born Aberdonians, at least sons of the North-East from Elgin to the North-water of Esk. But Aberdeen has always been prepared to welcome the stranger within its gates. For that matter, the rise and prosperity of the burgh as a commercial and industrial community were originally due to Saxons and Flemings who, in migrations and plantations during Scotland's formative centuries, settled in the town and by their efforts and enterprise made themselves and it prosperous. These pioneers, however, were men without a name and being thus anonymous are unfitted for inclusion in a series such as this. But the roll of those whose identities we know is formidable and varied.

First in point of time—and perhaps also in the enduring value of his service to the good town—is William Elphinstone, Bishop of Aberdeen from 1484 to 1514. Born in 1431, son of the rector of Kirkmichael, he was a graduate of Glasgow University, took up canon law, and after four years as rector in his father's old parish, proceeded to Paris where he lectured for some years on canon law. After a further spell of teaching at Orleans, he came home, got an appointment in Edinburgh, and for several years spent a great deal of his time on embassies to England, France and Germany. Eventually he was appointed Bishop of Aberdeen, combining that post in the last few months of King James III's life with the highly important duties of Chancellor of Scotland. On the King's murder he retired to Aberdeen and devoted himself to diocesan enterprises.

He continued the architectural work of his predecessors in the see by building the great central tower of the Cathedral of St. Machar (which fell in Cromwellian times owing to the Protector's troops having abstracted the buttresses to help build a barracks). He also planned the building of the choir. He restored the services in the church to their original dignity and reformed the Gregorian chant. In 1490 he came into closer contact with King James IV and began to develop his scheme for the erection of a university. Through the King and probably in conjunction with him, he petitioned the Pope who on 10 February 1494-95, issued a Bull sanctioning the foundation of a university in Old Aberdeen. The Pope was the notorious Alexander Borgia, but he by this order performed at least one good deed. In 1500 Elphinstone became Keeper of the Privy Seal and the trusted counsellor of the glamorous but not very level-headed king. He failed to persuade him to drop the project of invading England which culminated in the catastrophe of Flodden, and he died a few months later after a hasty journey to Edinburgh to try to reconcile the contending factions that, then as so often in Scottish history were threatening the safety of the Kingdom. Before his death he had projected the Bridge of Dee, for which he made provision, as well as leaving a substantial sum to the University. The Bridge of Dee was as powerful an influence in developing the commercial prospects of Aberdeen as had been the building of the Brig of Balgownie at Robert the Bruce's orders in 1319 and as the removal of the Maitland Rock by Davie do A'thing from the fairway of Aberdeen harbour was to be at the beginning of the seventeenth century. It was at his instigation, and in order to print the Aberdeen Breviary which is today one of the chief treasures of King's College, that James IV gave authority for the establishment of Scotland's first printing-house.

It is hardly necessary in an Aberdeen publication to mention the tremendous part Elphinstone's foundation has played in keeping Aberdeen and the North-East in the van not merely of academic and cultural, but also of all civilised achievement. The university's first Principal, Hector Boece (1465-1536), was a Dundonian, a most erudite scholar of Paris University, and a historian whose Latin *History of Scotland* and *Lives of the Bishops* have perhaps been more savagely criticised than they deserve.

If you should bid me count the lies
Of Hector's history,
I might as well essay to sum
The stars, or waves of sea.

It was his *History*, translated by Holinshed, that provided Shakespeare with the raw material for his *Macbeth*, surely an adequate passport to immortality. John Bellenden translated the *History* into Scots, which was printed in 1537 by the second of the Edinburgh printers, an Aberdonian named Thomas Davidson. Boece had a salary as Principal of £2 4s. 6d. sterling, a substantial sum in those days, and besides there were 'pickings'. In 1528 Aberdeen Town Council, then very liberal towards well-doing indwellers, offered him a tun of wine or if he preferred it, £20 Scots 'to help to buy him bonnets'. He had also a pension from what would today be called the Civil List.

Although the Pynours, now known as the Shore Porters Society, trace their history back to 1498, if not earlier, there was not much sign of any industrial complexes, such as we understand them today, for a full century thereafter. But at the opening of the seventeenth century we find a Fleming named Michael Wandel turning up in Aberdeen, where he was permitted to give instruction in the making of worsteds and the weaving of the wool which Aberdeen's hinterland had produced in abundance from time immemorial. Unfortunately his name and his trade are all we know of this precursor of the big fellows in what was to be, and still is, one of Aberdeen's principal industries. Nor have we much about the town's first recorded shipbuilder, Alexander Davidson, a St. Andrews man, despite his Aberdonian name, who got the Town Council's permit in 1606 to use the old churchyard of the Trinity friars as a shipyard, and who bought timber from Drum to make his first ship.

We are much better off for information regarding a real 'character', pioneer of another craft in which Aberdeen in the intervening 350 years has continued to excel—

Edward Raban, the town's first printer. A German, born in England, and who had served as a soldier in Europe, he had practised his craft in Edinburgh and St. Andrews before he came to Aberdeen in 1622 under the patronage of the provost and the bishop, Raban was a character if ever there was one. He arrived in a small ship which decanted him, his wife and a child, and some printing plant at the foot of the Shiprow. He set up in business on the North side of the Castlegate, in a new house above the meal market. His productions were many and good, but none was so famous as the *Aberdeen Almanack,* first published in 1623, a four leaf sheet and until its demise a few years ago the oldest publication of its kind in Europe. When his friend David Melville, Aberdeen's first bookseller, died, Raban moved into his shop at the end of the Broadgate and displayed the sign, 'Laird of Letters' on the frontage. Nearly 250 of his productions have been traced. He was quite a good printer and sometimes could be more than merely good.

As a man he makes a rather complicated study. He himself, besides printing the work of others, wrote both prose and verse. One of his own compositions, published in 1638, was entitled *The Glorie of Man consisting in the Excellence and Perfection of Woman.* This he said he wrote 'to vindicate and deliver myself from the imputation of Sarcastick, bitter, too loose and liberall speeches against the most noble, worthie, and transcendent sexe of Women'. We may set this excuse against Raban's conviction for breach of the peace in what was apparently a stairhead row with his second wife, whose maiden name was rather significantly Ailhous, his first having died in 1627. During 'the troubles' of the Bishops' and Civil Wars, Raban published the effusions of the Aberdeen Doctors, and he got into trouble from the General Assembly for omitting in one religious point some references to 'Papists', which he explained away as 'being done for want of paper', a transparent excuse apparently opaque enough to satisfy the parsons, who admonished him and he 'gott license to be gone'. He died in 1658.

There is a long gap before we come to the next on our list of 'invaders'. He is John Ewen, the author of *The Boatie Rows,* but in his day and generation celebrated in other and very different ways. Born somewhere about Montrose, he was said to be the son of a tinker, but the tinker was more likely to be a 'chapman billie', because when he settled in Aberdeen he was himself a packman 'selling buckles, sleeve-buttons, penknives, etc.' In the town he set up as a jeweller and in due course had a kenspeckle bow-windowed shop looking up Castle Street from where the Athenaeum now is. Will Walker in *The Bards of Bon-Accord,* describes him as 'for half a century a prominent figure in Aberdeen society, whose gentlemanly manners, benevolent disposition, staunch liberalism and diligence on civic affairs are yet (1887) remembered amongst us'. In 1783 Aberdeen ratepayers—if at that time they could be so described—set up a committee to promote the reform of burghal elections, then a strictly closed shop with more or less the old council electing the new. John Ewen was secretary of the committee and wrote a letter to the young Prime Minister William Pitt setting forth the aims and contentions of the movement. Pitt is said to have been contemplating a measure on the lines suggested when the French Revolution knocked such plans on the head. John, however, was more successful with the Aberdeen Police Act of 1795, mostly his conception, which set up the Police Commissioners to have responsibility for the streets, water supply and other social amenities of the burgh. Of the Commissioners during his lifetime Ewen was the life and soul. When he died in 1821 at the age of 80 he left the then not inconsiderable fortune of £14,000.

Rather senior to John Ewen was another worthy man whose surname is still commemorated in Peacock's Close, off Castle Street. Francis Peacock (1723-1807) was Aberdeen's most celebrated dancing master. Up to about 1700 dancing was frowned upon by the authorities, the Town Council in 1698 having prohibited one of the profession 'from having any public halls of dancing in this place'. But soon after that the magistrates licensed a master with a salary of 100 marks 'for the purpose of teaching the young citizens manners and good breeding'. By 1742, however, there was a public demand for 'a right dancing master to educate their children'. The request was granted but the first appointment did not prove satisfactory and in 1747 Francis Peacock, a native of Edinburgh, was selected with permission 'to take seven shillings sterling monthly for each scholar, besides payment for the music'. He started off his school in the Earl Marischal's old house, where Marischal Street now debouches from the Castlegate, but after it was cleared away he took up his quarters at the back of the inn known as Skipper Scott's tavern, in the close that still bears his name. He taught for sixty years, wrote a treatise on the art, painted miniatures, composed music, published *Fifty Favourite Scottish Airs for the Violin*, and built the Villa Franca, a country house on the site of what is now 156 Hamilton Place. He left quite a lot of money to be distributed amongst local charities. In fact, a thoroughly respectable citizen was Mr. Francis Peacock, whatever—and it was not much—our grandparents thought of his close.

One of the great industrial concerns of modern Aberdeen was founded by a cockney, John Maberly, who is commemorated, like Peacock, by a street bearing his name, and who in his way was just as much of a wonder. He was a linen-draper in London with a flair for public life and became M.P. for Abingdon in Berkshire. In 1810 he bought a factory at Broadford that had been established for a number of years in the manufacture of linen, and he and his brother carried it on along with a bleachfield at Rubislaw, a drysaltery also in Aberdeen, and a mill at Montrose. He took a leading part in the institution in 1815 of the Education Society, based upon a scheme of education by mutual instruction—however that could work. In 1818 the Town Council gave him the freedom of the burgh, in recognition of his services to the community 'in introducing several branches of useful manufactures, which have not failed to produce increased industry and prosperity among the manufacturing classes'. In that year he started a bank on the principles of expediting the process of exchange and encouraging small depositors. For reasons not altogether within his control it failed in 1832, and many small depositors were ruined. In 1820 he survived a famous lawsuit when James Skene of Rubislaw sought to have him interdicted from discharging effluent from his bleachfield into the Den burn at Rubislaw. Skene, whose counsel was the great Henry Cockburn, would not have had to raise the issue today—Maberly would have been dealt with by the local authority. But in 1820 he won his case, with Francis Jeffrey defending him. In 1835 Broadford Works were sold to Richards & Co., but by that time poor Maberly, adjudged bankrupt, had lost his Parliamentary seat and retired to the Continent.

An incomer to Aberdeen and a citizen of it for only four years was James Clerk Maxwell, son of a Lothians laird who from 1856 to 1860 held the chair of Natural Philosophy in Marischal College. On the fusion of Marischal with King's in 1860 he was passed over for one who in physics was (or at least now is) a nonentity. This was one of Aberdeen's mistakes for Maxwell is today regarded as the key figure in the scientific understanding of electricity, the basis of practically all modern scientific thought and indirectly of industrial development. In a newspaper of those days an obscure paragraph recorded that an Aberdeen professor was experimenting on a farm near Dyce in the use of magnetism for the production of crops. Could the professor have been Maxwell?

Another immigrant professor whose contributions to the welfare of Aberdeen were very substantial, and to whom industry and commerce in the town and area are deeply indebted was Dr. Matthew Hay. In 1883, at the age of twenty-seven he was appointed to succeed Dr. Francis Ogston in the Chair of Forensic Medicine (which, incidentally, was abolished when he retired in 1926). Five years later he became Medical Officer for the city. He retired in 1923 and died in 1932. While he was M.O.H. Oldmill Hospital, now Woodend, was opened in 1907, the City 'Fever' Hospital was extended and modernised. Kingseat Mental Hospital got its first patients in 1904, a Public Health Laboratory was started in 1920, and many other advances were promoted. The greatest of these was the joint hospital scheme at Foresterhill, which Matthew Hay submitted to historic meetings of the Aberdeen Medico-Chirurgical Society in 1920. It involved the building of a new general Royal Infirmary, Sick Children's Hospital and Maternity Hospital, and the eventual transference of the Medical School from Marischal College to Foresterhill.

This magnificent concept, which has enabled Aberdeen to remain in the forefront of medical and hospital progress, was opened by the then Duke of York in 1936. The new Infirmary buildings at that date had cost £535,000, a sum which makes an interesting comparison with the building cost of £16,700 for the Infirmary in the Schoolhill which Archibald Simpson designed in 1840. Amongst those who performed essential services in the realisation of Hay's idea was the then President of the Medico-Chirurgical Society and Professor of Medicine in Aberdeen University, Sir Ashley W. Mackintosh, a native of Morayshire, a First Bursar, an M.A. with First Class honours in Classics and Mathematics and an M.B. and M.D. with similar distinction. On the severely practical or money raising side was Lord Provost Sir Andrew Lewis, himself the grandson of an immigrant from south of the border and, like so many others whose forebears have cast in their lot with the city, a most patriotic and progressive son of Bon-Accord.

The rise of the trawling industry in the 1880s and 1890s brought a swarm of Englishmen from the East Coast fishing ports to Aberdeen where many of them stayed and made very good. But there were so many of them that it would be invidious to single out any one of them for special mention. Accordingly, we may end as we began with a Principal of the University—Sir George Adam Smith. For about half a century as Free Church minister and professor (in the chair of the heretic Aberdonian, William Robertson Smith) and as head of the University George Adam Smith was a familiar figure in the city and an inspiration to its citizens, whether academic or otherwise. His tremendous scholarship, his magnificent voice, his powerful oratory, his fine head and virile figure combined with his humour and kindliness to make a personality of singular distinction. As a student in Germany he had reported the Congress of Berlin in 1878 for that vivacious periodical, *Vanity Fair,* and he heard and saw Wagner conduct his massive composition, 'The Ring'. In the First World War his great work, *The Historical Geography of the Holy Land* was used by Allenby to help plan the remarkable campaigns that from Gaza to Megiddo cleared the Turks out of Palestine; while his advocacy of Britain's cause in North America was said to have excelled the efficacy of Arthur Balfour's oratory in persuading the United States to forget the war of 1812. As Sir Herbert Grierson once said, 'to know George Adam Smith was an event in one's life'. He was Principal from 1910 to 1936, and died in 1942.

With this article the series on Eminent Aberdonians, which has run for ten years, comes to a close. The writer, in drawing the curtain, touches his forelock to his readers (he can't afford a cap this winter!) and thanks them for their forbearance.

Honour for A.K.

[*Reprinted from* Aberdeen Chamber of Commerce Journal, *March 1967. Mr Andrew Lewis was at that time President of the Chamber.*]

The University's decision to honour Alex. Keith has been widely approved in the community of the North-East. The University will be recognising Mr. Keith's services to his own University; his literary work as journalist, authority in the field of the song and poetry of the North-East, and as local historian; his contribution to the agriculture and economy of the area; and his character as a man native to the area, whose whole life and work have admirably expressed some of its best and most characteristic features.

Nowhere has the news of the University's intention given greater pleasure than among the members of the Aberdeen Chamber of Commerce. His record of service to the Chamber is considerable. He was appointed to the Council in 1954, became Senior Vice-President in 1956, and, in 1957, started a memorable three-year period of office as President. Subsequently he has continued to serve on the Council and as Chairman of the Aberdeen and District Post Office Advisory Committee. He can be justifiably proud of recording 'perfect attendance' at Council and Committee meetings.

There is much more to be said, as his many friends in the Chamber know. I don't propose to say it all here, but we remember with gratitude the following respects in which the Chamber has benefited from A.K.'s association with it :

> his forging of new links between the business interests of town and country;
> his popularity as an ambassador for the Chamber at home and abroad;
> his charm and tact in receiving both official and unofficial business visitors from overseas;
> his continuing assistance to his successors in office who have benefited from his wisdom and guidance;
> the distilled common-sense and worldly wisdom which has gone into his *Journal* editorials for twelve years or so;
> the sheer readability and sense of fun that has characterised his series of forty articles on the lives of Eminent Aberdonians of the past.

Town shares Gown's view that Alexander Keith himself is an Aberdonian of eminence at least equal to that of those he himself has chronicled so skilfully.

ANDREW H. S. LEWIS

Complimentary Luncheon for A.K.

[*Reprinted from* Aberdeen Chamber of Commerce Journal, *September 1967. Mr A. R. Robertson had succeeded Mr Andrew Lewis as President of the Chamber in April 1967.*]

A large and representative gathering of members attended the Complimentary Luncheon given by the Chamber on 28 June to recognise the honour of Doctor of Laws (LL.D.) conferred upon Alexander Keith by the University of Aberdeen. The President, Mr. A. R. Robertson, was in the chair and Lord Provost Lennox was also present. On this very special occasion and to give some support to Mrs. Keith who accompanied her husband, a number of ladies graced the top table and added a touch of colour and charm to the informal proceedings.

The President in his opening remarks said the Council had felt that they should recognise in a tangible way the quite exceptional services rendered to the Aberdeen Chamber, and particularly to its *Journal*, by Alex. Keith. During the luncheon he presented Mr. Keith with a mechanical davenport which had been subscribed to by members of the Chamber. Mrs. Keith was presented with a hand-bag in recognition of the assistance which she had given over a number of years in the preparation of the *Journal*.

The President invited Mr. H. M. R. Watt, the Vice-President of the Chamber, to pay a tribute to A.K. on behalf of the members and at the request of many of those present Mr. Watt's address is reproduced below *verbatim* for the benefit of those who were unable to attend.

Mr. Keith, in his reply to Mr. Watt, thanked his audience in his usual reminiscent and delightful style. What he had done for the Chamber, he said, he had always enjoyed doing as he enjoyed doing most things: writing, meeting people and working. Although he had never aspired to any distinctions, as an Aberdonian he was tremendously proud of the honour conferred on him by the University and equally the honour which had been paid to him by the Chamber.

The luncheon terminated with a short tribute by the Lord Provost who also proposed the toast of *Bon-Accord*.

Tribute to A. K. by Mr. H. M. R. Watt, Vice-President of the Chamber

I am indeed privileged to be allowed to speak on behalf of everybody here, and on behalf of all A.K.'s many well-wishers within the membership of the Chamber.

I don't suppose that anybody, least of all Alex. himself, would feel that, on a family occasion, an encomium was appropriate—that made the man out to be perfect. . . . Anything approaching a full-scale evaluation or appraisal is 'out' on grounds of time. . . . We must, in any event, not follow the example of the Packman in the poem of A.K.'s friend Charles Murray—who 'Never spoiled a story by consid'rin' gin 'twas true'. That is to say we must first of all submit to the discipline of the facts.

So let's have a look at the facts about A.K.

Born at Kintore 72 years ago or thereby. Schooled there and at Strichen. An honours graduate of Aberdeen University of 1916. Thereafter journalism for 27 years. From 1943, farmer at Balmedie, but devoting the first eleven of the years after 1944 concurrently and most energetically to the secretaryship of the Aberdeen-Angus Cattle Society, and subsequently becoming increasingly involved in the affairs of the Chamber of Commerce. Within the Chamber, appointed to the Council in 1954; Senior Vice-President in 1956; then his two-year stint as President, extended by popular acclaim by a further year. He has continued on Council ever since—and has failed completely to be dislodged from the chairmanship of the Aberdeen and District Post Office Advisory Committee.

You will have discerned, ladies and gentlemen, no grand design so far about the facts of A.K.'s career, nor does his bare Chamber record tell us much. We might as well have been imagining that we were getting the measure of the man by recording his chest measurements or his size in collars (not that either of these is insignificant, certainly).

But let's seek a little further. In his day, he has written a great deal. First there was his journalism, and it was no ordinary journalism. It was literary journalism of the highest order, and anyone who lived in Aberdeen through the 1920s and 1930s knows that the vast number of contributions which A.K. made to the local paper, most memorably as the writer of the weekly causerie on literary and local historical subjects, had much more than ephemeral value.

Other writing activities of his were even less ephemeral, taking the more solid shape of books. *Burns and Folk Song* for example; the histories of businesses, like Glenlivet, the North Bank, the University Press; and the chronicling of the Aberdeen-Angus Breed (a quite monumental feat, as those of you who have seen that *magnum opus* will know).

Perhaps his greatest book, so far, entitled *Last Leaves of Traditional Ballads and Ballad Airs,* because it was published in 1925 and quickly went out of print, may not be well-known to a 1967 audience. Someone very well qualified to judge its merit says that the volume 'is a classic of the North-East and an indispensable source for any further study of its theme, or related themes'.

The *Sunday Times* of 13 December 1925 agreed: 'every library of real literature', it said, 'must get this splendid anthology'.

All of his writing, although damnably discursive at times, has been the opposite of slip-shod: it is invariably based on thorough study—he is a stickler for accuracy—and it has a natural vitality, often lit up by the couthy humour which we all know.

In brief, don't let's underestimate A.K.'s literary achievement.

What about his work as Secretary of the Aberdeen-Angus Cattle Society? Well, I can only again report to you the facts, as authoritatively recorded at the time of his retirement from the Society in the *Aberdeen-Angus Review* (which, incidentally, he had edited with the greatest gusto during his eleven years of office—and I think that Mrs. Keith had a very great deal to do with it as well). We are told that his work as Secretary had resulted in striking increases in membership of the Society (from 800 to 1,800), in annual income (from £5,000 to £20,000), and in the number of animals registered in the Herd Book. The Society recorded during his period of office conspicuous commercial success among both home and overseas breeders. Not bad for someone who only came to farming and the stockrearing world when he was almost 50 years of age!

Could it be then that everything that Alex. touches turns to gold? Perhaps not, but, to come back to what has greatest relevance to this gathering, there is no doubt that this Chamber has been greatly enriched by A.K.'s connection with it. He has been quite tireless in everything he has tackled on its behalf. Andrew Lewis reminded us in the *Journal* of the Chamber's good fortune:

> his forging of new links between the business interests of town and country;
> his popularity as an ambassador for the Chamber at home and abroad;
> his acceptability as receiver of business visitors from overseas;
> the distilled common-sense and wisdom which continue to go into his *Journal* editorials;
> the sheer readability and sense of fun that characterised his series of forty articles on the lives of *Eminent Aberdonians* of the past.

Browse again through that series which (in A.K.'s prefatory words) set out 'to illustrate and explain from the labours and ability of Aberdonians of past generations the background against which the modern Aberdonian must play his part'. Be introduced again by A.K. to these giants of Aberdeen men. With some of them (like William Walker, William Tawse and Charles Murray) he had been on terms of close personal friendship. Others, though dead before his day, he seemed to know almost as intimately, and, if their life-times had happened to coincide with Alex.'s—I am thinking of men like Alexander Anderson (founder of the North Bank and the Northern Assurance Company), William Alexander (of *Johnny Gibb*) and perhaps Sir Thomas Urquhart (translator of Rabelais)—they would, one feels quite sure, have recognised A.K. as a kindred spirit, and as a giant of men, like themselves. He will undoubtedly meet up with the more rascally of them in due course—although I am not sure under what aegis the reunion will be: perhaps the Sit Siccar Club, perhaps the Life Preservers.

I think we are getting warmer now in our search for the real A.K.—now that we have got him into the giant class (where he belongs). But we've got a little further to go, because he is certainly no ordinary giant.

*Presentation to A.K. by the President.
Mrs. Keith and the Vice-President Mr. Watt look on*

At the Graduation Ceremony later

Aberdeen Journals Ltd.

The whole, in his case, is quite obviously more than the sum of the parts. And, when the whole man is here himself, supremely articulate as he is, and able and ready to speak for himself, it is silly for me to be standing between him and you. But, if I've attempted an impossible task, and the real A.K. is in fact too elusive for words of mine to comprehend, let me nevertheless try to finish this poor portrait with a few very random brush strokes.

Yes, first of all, his articulacy (as none of us can quite bring ourselves to be)—articulate for the Chamber, articulate for the North-East, and articulate in the best North-East kind of way.

Then, his avoidance of solemnity. His ability to pursue serious objectives without being solemn about it. His knack of knocking solemnity out of others.

No one, of course, seriously doubts that the devil is in A.K.—and the drawing which was reproduced in the *Journal* in the spring proved it. But you know, there are other people inside him too: Puck—Peter Pan—Ariel. They must all be there, to explain the secret of the essential (the quintessential) spirit-quality (ethereal quality) of the man.

Now what have I forgotten?

Cats! He adores cats and understands cats, and is adored by them and is understood by them.

Paintings! He knows what he likes and what he likes makes up a most impressive collection at Eigie.

Gardening! His garden—one of the few alleviations of the Ellon road—is testimony to his skill in this direction—and Lewella helps him here, as, I am sure, in very many ways.

Books! His large, well-ordered private collection shows that he knows them, he loves them, cares for them—every one of them, as individual things.

Stories! Heracleitus had nothing on him as a conversationalist, in 'tiring the sun with talking and sending him down the sky'. Alex. would no doubt prefer the Charles Murray version. Unfortunately, it doesn't quite fit. But let Charles Murray have the last word:

An', faith, the ferlies I hae seen,
The ploys I've shared and daurna tell
Cheer mony a lanely winter's e'en,
Just kecklin' owre them to mysel'.

Then ca' me fey or ca' me feel
Clean daft or doitit, deil may care,
Aye faur there's fun, at Pase or Yeel,
Gin I be livin', I'll be there.

Aye faur there's fun, A.K. will be there.